ICONS 2019

The Fourteenth International Conference on Systems

March 24 - 28, 2019

Valencia, Spain

ICONS 2019 Editors

Sandra Sendra Compte, University of Granada, Spain

Printed from e-media with permission by:

Curran Associates, Inc.
57 Morehouse Lane
Red Hook, NY 12571

Some format issues inherent in the e-media version may also appear in this print version.

Printed by Curran Associates, Inc. (2019)

International Academy, Research, and Industry Association (IARIA)
412 Derby Way
Wilmington, DE 19810

Phone: (408) 893-6407
Fax: (408) 527-6351

petre@iaria.org

Additional copies of this publication are available from:

Curran Associates, Inc.
57 Morehouse Lane
Red Hook, NY 12571 USA
Phone: 845-758-0400
Fax: 845-758-2633
Email: curran@proceedings.com
Web: www.proceedings.com

Table of Contents

Algorithm for Dealing with Complaints Data from the Use Phase 1
Marius Heinrichsmeyer, Nadine Schluter, and Amirbabak Ansari

Resonance Thinking and Inductive Machine Learning 7
Yves Kodratoff and Marta Franova

Automated Irrigation System 14
Maryam Al kaabi, Ali Al-Humairi, Nafaa Jabeur, Aydin Azizi, Poorya Ghafoorpoor, Ali Fakhrulddin, and Hayat El Asri

papagenoPCB: An Automated Printed Circuit Board Generation Approach for Embedded Systems Prototyping 20
Tobias Scheipel and Marcel Baunach

A Security Aware Design Space Exploration Framework 26
Lukas Gressl, Christian Steger, and Ulrich Neffe

Cellular Automata-based Wear Leveling in Resistive Memory 32
Sutapa Sarkar

Development of Extended-STIL Pattern Compiler for Test Programming Environment 39
Seong-Jin Kim and Kwang-Man Ko

Method for Classification of Textures Based on Histogram and Random Events Analysis 45
Vladimir Iliev, Tzanko Georgiev, Alexander Tzokev, and Anton Mihaylov

The Use of Image Processing Techniques for Detection of Weed in Lawns 50
Lorena Parra, Virginia Torices, Jose Marin, Pedro Vicente Mauri, and Jaime Lloret

Automatic Ship Detection on Inland Waters: Problems and a Preliminary Solution 56
Tomasz Hyla and Natalia Wawrzyniak

Monte Carlo Tree Search for Optimizing Hyperparameters of Neural Network Training 61
Karolina Polanska, Wiktoria Dywan, Piotr Labuda, Leszek Koszalka, Iwona Pozniak-Koszalka, and Andrzej Kasprzak

Automatic Ship Identification Approach for Video Survelience Systems 65
Natalia Wawrzyniak and Tomasz Hyla

Investigating the Feasibility to Estimate System Performance Based Upon Limited Data of the Taipei Metro System 69
Snow Tseng and Tzu-Chia Kao

Low-Cost Virtual Coach for Diagnosis and Guidance in Baseball/Softball Batting Training 73
Hou-Chin Liu and Chung-Ta King

Octopus Algorithm as a New Support in Solving TSP 81
Marek Sosnicki, Iwona Pozniak-Koszalka, Leszek Koszalka, and Andrzej Kasprzak

ICONS 2019

Forward

The Fourteenth International Conference on Systems (ICONS 2019), held between March 24, 2019 and March 28, 2019 in Valencia, Spain, continued a series of events covering a broad spectrum of topics, including fundamentals on designing, implementing, testing, validating and maintaining various kinds of software and hardware systems.

In the last years, new system concepts have been promoted and partially embedded in new deployments. Anticipative systems, autonomic and autonomous systems, self-adapting systems, or on-demand systems are systems exposing advanced features. These features demand special requirements specification mechanisms, advanced behavioral design patterns, special interaction protocols, and flexible implementation platforms. Additionally, they require new monitoring and management paradigms, as self-protection, self-diagnosing, self-maintenance become core design features.

The design of application-oriented systems is driven by application-specific requirements that have a very large spectrum. Despite the adoption of uniform frameworks and system design methodologies supported by appropriate models and system specification languages, the deployment of application-oriented systems raises critical problems. Specific requirements in terms of scalability, real-time, security, performance, accuracy, distribution, and user interaction drive the design decisions and implementations.

This leads to the need for gathering application-specific knowledge and develop particular design and implementation skills that can be reused in developing similar systems.
Validation and verification of safety requirements for complex systems containing hardware, software and human subsystems must be considered from early design phases. There is a need for rigorous analysis on the role of people and process causing hazards within safety-related systems; however, these claims are often made without a rigorous analysis of the human factors involved. Accurate identification and implementation of safety requirements for all elements of a system, including people and procedures become crucial in complex and critical systems, especially in safety-related projects from the civil aviation, defense health, and transport sectors.

Fundamentals on safety-related systems concern both positive (desired properties) and negative (undesired properties) aspects. Safety requirements are expressed at the individual equipment level and at the operational-environment level. However, ambiguity in safety requirements may lead to reliable unsafe systems. Additionally, the distribution of safety requirements between people and machines makes difficult automated proofs of system safety. This is somehow obscured by the difficulty of applying formal techniques (usually used for equipment-related safety requirements) to derivation and satisfaction of human-related safety requirements (usually, human factors techniques are used).

We welcomed academic, research and industry contributions. The conference had the following tracks:

- Complex and specialized systems
- Embedded systems and applications/services
- Computer vision and computer graphics
- Application-oriented systems

We take here the opportunity to warmly thank all the members of the ICONS 2019 technical program committee, as well as all the reviewers. The creation of such a high quality conference program would not have been possible without their involvement. We also kindly thank all the authors who dedicated much of their time and effort to contribute to ICONS 2019. We truly believe that, thanks to all these efforts, the final conference program consisted of top quality contributions.

We also thank the members of the ICONS 2019 organizing committee for their help in handling the logistics and for their work that made this professional meeting a success.

We hope that ICONS 2019 was a successful international forum for the exchange of ideas and results between academia and industry and to promote further progress in the area of systems. We also hope that Valencia, Spain provided a pleasant environment during the conference and everyone saved some time to enjoy the historic charm of the city.

ICONS 2019 Chairs

ICONS Steering Committee
Marko Jäntti, University of Eastern Finland, Finland
Leszek Koszalka, Wroclaw University of Technology, Poland
Mark Austin, University of Maryland at College Park, USA
Zoubir Mammeri, IRIT - Paul Sabatier University, France
Raimund Ege, Northern Illinois University, USA
Andrew Snow, Ohio University, USA

ICONS Industry/Research Advisory Committee
Gary Weckman, Ohio University, USA
Tzung-Pei Hong [洪宗貝], National University of Kaohsiung, Taiwan

ICONS 2019 Special Tracks Chair
Sandra Sendra, University of Granada, Spain

ICONS 2019
Committee

ICONS Steering Committee

Marko Jäntti, University of Eastern Finland, Finland
Leszek Koszalka, Wroclaw University of Technology, Poland
Mark Austin, University of Maryland at College Park, USA
Zoubir Mammeri, IRIT - Paul Sabatier University, France
Raimund Ege, Northern Illinois University, USA
Andrew Snow, Ohio University, USA

ICONS Industry/Research Advisory Committee

Gary Weckman, Ohio University, USA
Tzung-Pei Hong [洪宗貝], National University of Kaohsiung, Taiwan

ICONS 2019 Special Tracks Chair

Sandra Sendra, University of Granada, Spain

ICONS 2019 Technical Program Committee

Mehmud Abliz, Google Inc., USA
Witold Abramowicz, Poznan University of Economics, Poland
Mehmet Aksit, University of Twente, Netherlands
Mark Austin, University of Maryland at College Park, USA
Lubomir Bakule, Institute of Information Theory and Automation of the CAS, Czech Republic
Zbigniew Banaszak, Technical University of Koszalin, Poland
Ateet Bhalla, Independent Consultant, India
Francesco Bianconi, University of Perugia, Italy
Isabelle Borne, University of South Brittany | IRISA Laboratory, France
Valérie Botta-Genoulaz, INSA - Lyon, France
Frédéric Bousefsaf, LCOMS - Université de Lorraine, France
Albert M. K. Cheng, University of Houston, USA
David Cordeau, University of Poitiers, France
Fabio M. Costa, Federal University of Goias, Brazil
Peter De Bruyn, University of Antwerp, Belgium
Bayram Deviren, Nevsehir Hacı Bektas Veli University, Turkey
Mario Di Castro, CERN, Genève, Switzerland
Yezyd Donoso, Universidad de los Andes - Bogotá, Colombia
L. Canan Dülger, İzmir University of Economics, Turkey
Raimund Ege, Northern Illinois University, USA
Hans-Dieter Ehrich, Technische Universität Braunschweig, Germany
Andras Farago, University of Texas at Dallas, USA
Francesco Fontanella, Università di Cassino e del Lazio meridionale, Italy

Miguel Franklin de Castro, Federal University of Ceará, Brazil
Marta Franova, CNRS, LRI & INRIA, Orsay, France
Matthias Galster, University of Canterbury, Christchurch, New Zealand
Christos Gatzidis, Bournemouth University, UK
Patrick Girard, LIRMM / CNRS, France
Frederic Guinand, Normandy University (Le Havre), France / Cardinal Stefan Wyszynski University in Warsaw, Poland
Said Hanafi, University of Valenciennces, France
Tzung-Pei Hong, National University of Kaohsiung, Taiwan
Matin Hosseini, University of Louisiana at Lafayette, USA
Michael Hübner, Ruhr-University of Bochum, Germany
William Hurst, Liverpool John Moores University, UK
Wen-Jyi Hwang, National Taiwan Normal University, Taiwan
Tomasz Hyla, West Pomeranian University of Technology, Szczecin, Poland
Fehmi Jaafar, Concordia University of Edmonton, Canada
Marko Jäntti, University of Eastern Finland, Finland
Omar Jaradat, Mälardalen University, Sweden
Imed Kacem, Université de Lorraine, France
Fu-Chien Kao, Da-Yeh University, Taiwan
Andrzej Kasprzak, Wroclaw University of Technology, Poland
Georgios Keramidas, Think Silicon S.A., Greece
Thomas Kessel, Baden-Wuerttemberg Cooperative State University Stuttgart | Center of Competence Open Source Stuttgart, Germany
Alexander Knapp, Institute for Software and Systems Engineering - University of Augsburg, Germany
Leszek Koszalka, Wroclaw University of Science and Technology, Poland
Karthik Kumaravelu, Duke University, USA
Wim Laurier, Université Saint-Louis / Ghent University, Belgium
Suzanne Lesecq, Commissariat à l'énergie atomique et aux énergies alternatives (CEA), France
Ivan Lukovic, University of Novi Sad, Serbia
Jia-Ning Luo, Ming Chuan University, Taiwan
Stephane Maag, Institut Mines-Telecom / Telecom SudParis, France
Avinash Malik, University of Auckland, New Zealand
Amel Mammar, IMT/Telecom SudParis, France
Zoubir Mammeri, IRIT - Paul Sabatier University, France
D. Manivannan, University of Kentucky, USA
Atif Mashkoor, Software Competence Center Hagenberg (SCCH) GmbH, Austria
Michele Melchiori, Università degli Studi di Brescia, Italy
Nacim Meslem, University Grenoble Alpes | CNRS, France
Daniel Moore, Valencell Inc., Raleigh, USA
Fernando Moreira, Universidade Portucalense, Portugal
Fabrice Mourlin, UPEC University, France
Anass Nagih, University of Lorraine, France
Jesús Emeterio Navarro-Barrientos, MBition GmbH, Germany

Copyright Information

Algorithm for Dealing with Complaints Data from the Use Phase

Is the application of the 8D report still contemporary and sufficient to deal with the predominant complexity in present time?

Nadine Schlüter
University of Wuppertal
Product Safety and Quality Engineering
Wuppertal, Germany
email: schluete@uni-wuppertal.de

Marius Heinrichsmeyer
University of Wuppertal
Product Safety and Quality Engineering
Wuppertal, Germany
email: heinrichsmeyer@uni-wuppertal.de

Amirbabak Ansari
University of Wuppertal
Product Safety and Quality Engineering
Wuppertal, Germany
email: Amirbabak.Ansari-hk@uni-wuppertal.de

Abstract — **The increasing complexity of products, services, and organizations, as well as the resulting surge in failures, demonstrate an increasing need for complaint management in organizations. Nevertheless, this raises the question of whether the possibilities of complaint management can even master the prevailing complexity. In order to investigate this, the method of the 8D report, which is highly regarded in the automotive industry, was questioned concerning its limits. First, the advantages and disadvantages of the 8D report were researched and analyzed related to the current problem. It turns out that the 8D report is no longer able to deal with the extensive flow of information. For this reason, an approach in form of an algorithm, which should make it possible to use complaint information for failure cause search and solution finding, is proposed in this article. It is a prototype that needs to be systematically validated and evaluated in the industry. With a total of four different phases, the algorithm should help to make the complaint management up-to-date and, above all, to improve the search for failure causes and the solution finding. The evaluation of the approach based on specific requirements for the algorithm showed that it is perfectly capable of making the enormous flow of information in the field of complaint management more usable. Nevertheless, further elaborations are needed on how a practical implementation of the algorithm can be realized.**

Keywords- Complexity; Systems; Failure; Algorithm; Complaint; Solution.

I. INTRODUCTION

Whether it is to increase the creation of new ideas for the innovation process [7] or to prevent customer churn [10], complaint management seems to be necessary, especially today. One aspect of this, among other things, is the sensible handling of complaints data from the use phase in order to estimate the customer's opinion, for example [12]. However, not only the measurement of customer satisfaction but also the detection of weaknesses and potentials to improve the company or the products can be realized with complaint data. Above all, the focus is on the identification of failures and the effective search for causes, since some failures and their causes can only be identified through complaints in the use phase [13]. It is important to use the data as an opportunity to improve continually the consumer protection and the image of the company. Despite the opportunity to profitably use complaint data from the use phase, companies often underestimate the relevance and importance of generated information [6]. One of its reasons is, that complaints are often seen as a nuisance of extra work, especially in medium-sized companies [2]. In addition there is a lack of complaints management in such companies [2]. A study from 2018 on data usage shows that data is often collected, however despite its potential, remain unused and "hoarded" [9]. Although this study refers to service companies, the problem can still be assigned to manufacturing companies. In order to counteract this kind of problem, some companies are focusing on methods such as the 8D report, which through their structured procedure should help to process complaints purposive and organize the search for causes of failures more efficient. Nevertheless, is this always the case? Kiem [4] rightly points out that the use of the 8D report also requires a great effort in order to be able to successfully handle complaints. Especially today, where product and production systems are becoming increasingly complex, the goal should be to minimize the effort so that the resource "time" can be used as efficient as possible. Accordingly, within the context of the problem, it must be questioned whether current methods, in this case explicitly the 8D report, can still meet this requirement or if it makes sense to develop new approaches that reduce the challenges for companies.

To find this out, Section 2 first gives an overview of the method of the 8D report. Therefore, the procedure and the advantages and disadvantages will be presented. In addition, requirements for the algorithm are derived based on the advantages and disadvantages. After that, Section 3 presents all four phases of the failure cause searching and the solution finding algorithm. For that, the theoretical concept will be clarified and then explained on the basis of a practical example. In Section 4, the algorithm will be evaluated in terms of derived requirements in order to obtain a summary of how the development of the algorithm should be progressed in the future. We conclude the paper in Section 5.

II. METHOD OF THE 8D REPORT

The method of the 8D report describes a problem-solving method, which is divided into a total of eight disciplines

(8D) and used by companies for complaint processing. It serves, as already mentioned, as a method of communication between supplier and customer. A targeted problem-solving can be achieved by the realization of a structured procedure in eight steps and the use of tools such as Ishikawa diagram, Failure Mode and Effects Analysis (FMEA) or Pareto Analysis [1] and [5].

A. Procedure

Beginning with the "Team Building" (S1), people, who should coordinate the problem-solving process, have to be defined. This might be persons such as the production section manager or the quality engineer, for example. This team will then initiate the second step, the "Problem Description" (S2). In this step, the relevant information has to be collected to ensure a clear and understandable acquisition of the problem. Available tools that can be used for the description are, among other things, Failure-Collecting Cards, Histograms or Pareto Analysis. Just after the description of the problem, the next step takes place, "Immediate Measures" (S3). This step minimizes the consequence of the problem, initially. Nevertheless, it should be noted at this point that these immediate measures are usually not sufficient to eliminate problems since the causes of the failures are often still unknown. Tools in step three are the Inspection Plan, for example. Since, as already mentioned, the cause of the failure is often still unknown, it is necessary to carry out a "Cause Analysis" (S4) in the fourth step. In the problem-solving team, causes of the problem and their interactions can be identified using tools such as Cause-and-Effect Analysis or the Correlation/Scatter Plot. If the causes of the failure are known, it is necessary to act. The "Definition of remedial Measures" (S5) should eliminate them. Nevertheless, it should be noted that the measures are only successful if tools such as the FMEA or Process Capability Tests could also prove their effectiveness. In addition, it should be noted that the measures would only serve their purpose if they are "Anchored in the Organization" (S6). For this purpose, the measures can be incorporated in Training Plans, for example. Building on the anchoring, the knowledge gained should be reflected. For this reason, "Prevention Measures are taken" (S7) in the seventh step. These measures are documented in Design Guidelines, for example. Finally, with the 8D report, the problem-solving process is completed (S8) [1] and [5].

B. Advantages and disadvantages

Based on the procedure, the first advantages and disadvantages of the method can already be deduced. Above all, the recording of the advantages and disadvantages should help to derive requirements for the handling of complaint data with the algorithm. Starting with the advantages of the method, it can be stated that the 8D report contributes to the problem-solving process through a structured and goal-oriented approach. Above all, the high level of acceptance, for example, in the automotive industry, highlights the importance of the method in practice. By identifying causes, deriving countermeasures, as well as documenting and anchoring, the method aims to continually improve the organization. The findings of problems that have already occurred are translated into improvement measures and often allow an increase in customer satisfaction through compliance with the measures. Nevertheless, the method also has weak points. A major disadvantage is, as already mentioned, the high time and personnel implementation effort. This can cause employees to consider the method as a burden and to use it only sporadically. However, especially nowadays it may also lead the employee to invest too much time and resources to use the method and therefor, postpone processing other tasks, such as performing process audits. Another disadvantage of this method is that although it provides a structured approach over eight-step sequence, it has a lack of a standardized survey of the required complaint data. This means that the method does not specify which parameters are necessary in order to promote efficient and goal-oriented problem solving. Companies often have their own company-specific approach. For example, the second step "Problem Description" (S2) is carried out very differently in different companies. This should be avoided in order to simplify cross-company communication as well as to facilitate efficient problem solving by setting uniform parameters. This should save time, which can be used for execution of other activities. In addition to the standardization, there is also a lack of automation of the processing of complaint data from the use phase. Again, the aspect of time is a crucial factor. The more automated the processing of data, the fewer resources are needed. This should also save time and above all costs. By way of example, the automation could be realized with the aid of an algorithm, which processes the complaint data. It turns out, therefore, that the method of the 8D report holds above all a potential for the time factor, which should be used [1] and [5]. The advantages and disadvantages are summarized in Table I.

TABLE I. PROS AND CONS OF THE 8D REPORT METHOD [3] AND [14]

Pros	• The method is widely accepted in the automotive industry and has been tried and tested in practice. • Detected problems will be avoided in the future by means of documentation. • Insights gained flow into improvement measures. • The method is based on a structured approach. • Cross process and departmental thinking are promoted. • It is an effective way to increase customer satisfaction.
Cons	• The method causes a high implementation effort, in terms of both time and personnel. • Hasty emergency measures could be problematic. • The method does not foresee the use or coupling of a model to master the currently prevalent complexity. • Standardized collection of complaint data from the usage phase is not specified. • Automated processing (eg. by means of an algorithm) of the collected complaint data from the usage data is not given.

C. Derivation of requirements

It was already mentioned at the beginning that based on the advantages and disadvantages of the 8D-Report, requirements on the method for the handling of the complaint data from the use phase are derived. On the one hand, it has the purpose that based on the requirements, a possibility for an algorithm can be developed, which takes the not fulfilled aspects by the 8D report into account. On the other hand, it offers a possibility of evaluating the proposed algorithm. By evaluating the algorithm concerning the fulfillment of the requirements, conclusions can be derived regarding improvement potentials and weaknesses of the algorithm. This points out, in turn, new research projects. By deriving the requirements it is especially important that the requirements for the algorithm are even more extensive than the requirements for the method of the 8D report. Therefore, all benefits of the 8D report are translated one-to-one as "must-have requirements" for the algorithm. Furthermore, "should requirements" are worked out by means of the disadvantages. To summarize, the requirements for the algorithm about dealing with complaint data are shown in Table II.

TABLE II. REQUIREMENTS FOR THE ALGORITHM

Must-have (MhRe)	1. High acceptance and validation in practice 2. Documentation of already detected problems 3. Derivation of improvement measures based on knowledge 4. Structured approach 5. Promotion of process and departmental thinking 6. Increase customer satisfaction
Should (SRe)	1. Time and personnel expenses should be as low as possible 2. Prevention of hasty emergency measures 3. Use of a model approach 4. Standardized collection of complaint data 5. Automated processing of the collected complaint data

The table illustrates that, among other things, the algorithm must be a structured approach, which document already recognized problems. In addition, the algorithm should use a model approach and make the automated processing of complaint information possible.

III. ALGORITHM FOR HANDLING COMPLAINT DATA

Based on the above-mentioned must-have and should requirements, it is now possible to develop a prototype for an algorithm. It is first necessary to determine which steps the algorithm should have to deal with complaint data. In considering of SRe 4 "standardized collection of complaint data", the algorithm must first be able to collect complaint data from the usage in such a way that they can be used for further processing. Furthermore, it must be able to extract relevant information from the complaint data, because further processing of all complaint data would not be expedient. In the second and third step of the algorithm, it should be possible to prioritize complaints and use the relevant information from the first step in order to locate the cause of the failure in the production system. Only by such a step, a clear system limitation can be made, which should reduce the additional expenses of solution finding. The final step is to find a solution to the located cause of the failure. Therefor, case-related solutions, depending on the cause of the failure, are used to illustrate ways to deal with the failure cause. In order to present the individual steps of the process in a more transparent way, a prototype of the algorithm was developed and tested on an application example from the industry (Complaint of Shaft W0943). This prototype will be explained in the following sections, first from a theoretical point of view and then based on the industrial example.

A. *Probing of complaint data*

The first step is called probing of complaint data. It should serve to filter relevant information from the amount of complaint data. This is necessary to make the unstructured volume of complaint data manageable for failure cause and solution finding and thereby making complaint management more attractive to employees.

To achieve this kind of probing process, the algorithm must be able to distinguish between relevant and irrelevant information. In order to put this process into practice, it was programmed using Visual Basic for Applications (VBA). Since the representation of the entire programming code would be too extensive, the process is shown schematically in Figure 1.

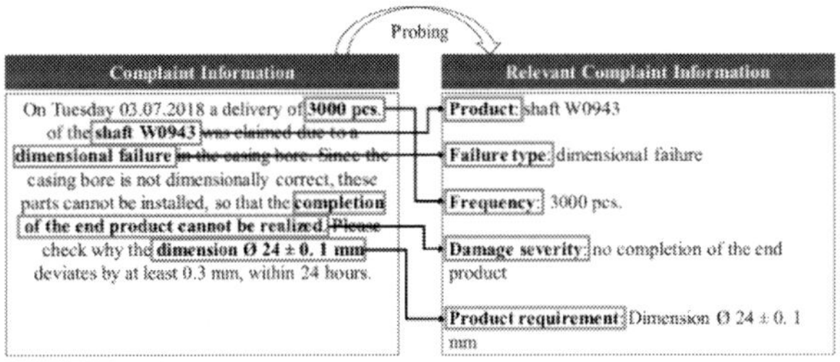

Figure 1. Schematic representation for probing complaint data.

From Figure 1, it can be seen that the algorithm is able to probe relevant complaint information for the application example of the "Shaft W0943". This is made possible by comparing the contents of the complaint text, for example, the product name "Shaft W0943" or the information on product requirements "Dimension Ø 24 ± 0.1 mm", with the information from systems of the company, including, for example, Enterprise-Resource-Planning (ERP) or Computer-Aided Quality (CAQ). If the algorithm detects relevant information within the complaint text, it probes them for further processing. Since this process can be automated and work on a wide variety of systems, a saving of personal and time resources is already realized in the first step. However, as there is still a lot of information to work with, it is important to investigate which complaint has the highest priority.

B. *Prioritization of failure causes*

In order to realize this, the previously probed relevant complaint information is being used for prioritization, thereby enabling the company to focus on the most relevant complaints. Only in this way the resources of the company can be used as effectively as possible for a targeted failure cause searching and solution finding.

To apply the prioritization of complaints successfully in practice, this step has also been programmed in VBA. Once again, a representation of the entire programming code is too extensive so that only a schematic representation of the prioritization step is shown in Figure 2.

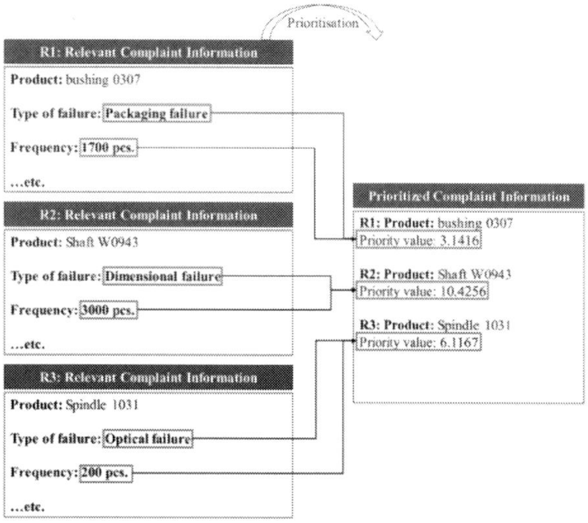

Figure 2. Schematic representation of the prioritization of complaints.

As shown in Figure 2, prioritization is based on different dimensions. The total of nine prioritization dimensions, including, for example, the type of failure or the frequency of the failure, are first calculated by the algorithm and subsequently evaluated. For example, in the case of the "Shaft W0943", the algorithm uses the failure type "dimensional failure" or the frequency "3000 pcs." and bundles all this information into a priority value. In this way it can be deduced which complaint is to be classified as very critical and which as less critical. Based on the most critical complaint, the algorithm initiates the third step, the localization of the cause of the failure.

C. Localization of failure causes

So that localization of causes of failure within a production system is even possible, it is necessary to connect the unfulfilled requirement (the failure) of the complaint with the production system. For the example of "Shaft W0943" this means that the algorithm has to find out at which point of the production system the requirement "dimension Ø 24 ± 0.1 mm" was not fulfilled. To make the complexity of the product system more manageable, it is recommended to use a model. This example uses the approach of enhanced Demand Compliant Design (eDeCoDe) by [8] and [15]. The background to the choice of eDeCoDe is that it can map socio-technical systems through a minimal number of views (requirements, persons, components, processes, and functions). On the other hand, it is able to record correlations and thus make the traceability of responsibilities possible. This is exemplified in Figure 3.

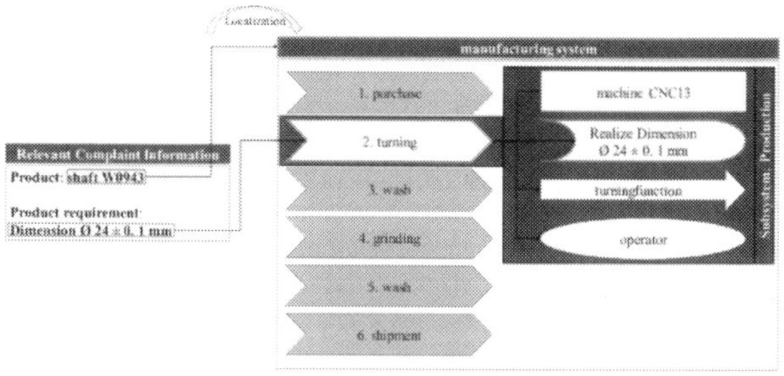

Figure 3. Schematic representation of the localization of failure causes.

Figure 3 shows the schematic process of locating the cause of the fault. This was also programmed with the help of VBA and checked based on the "Shaft W0943" example. The figure shows that the "Shaft W0943" is assigned to the corresponding manufacturing system. This is possible because the algorithm checks in which process step the requirement "Dimension Ø 24 ± 0.1 mm" theoretically should have been implemented. In this example, the algorithm explicitly recognized the „turning process“, which should realize the requirement "Dimension Ø 24 ± 0.1 mm". Because the requirement has not been fulfilled, the algorithm concludes that a cause of the failure is to be suspected within the "turning process". This achieves a decisive system limitation and leads to the fact that the cause of the fault is not searched within the systems in which it cannot occur. Thus, with the help of the third step, resource saving by focusing can be realized.

Although the algorithm is able to locate the cause of the failure, it cannot yet determine which exact cause led to the complaint.

D. Solution finding for failure causes

To determine the exact cause, it must be able to evaluate the system in which the cause of the fault was located. In the case of the example "Shaft W0943" this was the "turning process" which was recognized in the "manufacturing system" (Figure 4).

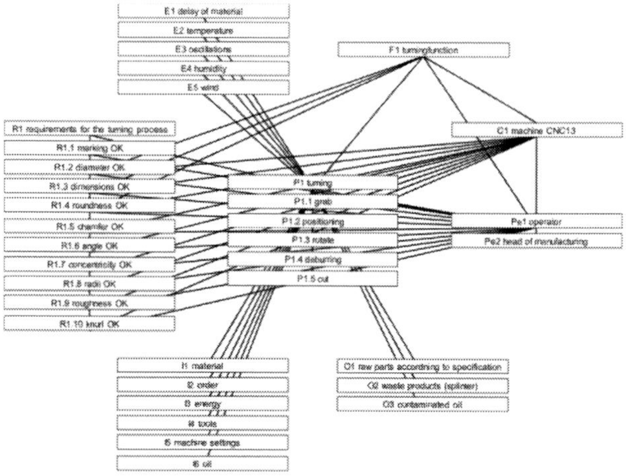

Figure 4. Schematic representation of complex visualization of the manufacturing subsystem

In order to be able to clearly assign a cause to the occurrence of the failure, it is necessary to analyze the interrelations of the unfulfilled requirement from the complaint, in this case, the imperfect dimensional compliance of the "diameter Ø 24 ± 0.1 mm". Since a manual evaluation would result in an extra effort, it is recommended to resort to a software solution, which makes the evaluation of causal chain relationships transparent and can be coupled with the eDeCoDe model. For example, the software LOOMEO from the company REDPOINT.TESION can be used for this purpose [11]. It allows systems to map over self-defined domains as well as the creation of elements and their interrelationships using matrices. In particular, the so-called "focus function" of the software is a decisive advantage if the limited subsystems are to be examined regarding isolated elements. Using the "focus function" for the requirement "diameter i.O", which was declared unfulfilled in the context of the complaint, the interrelations to other elements and thus pòssible causes of failures are clearly highlighted.

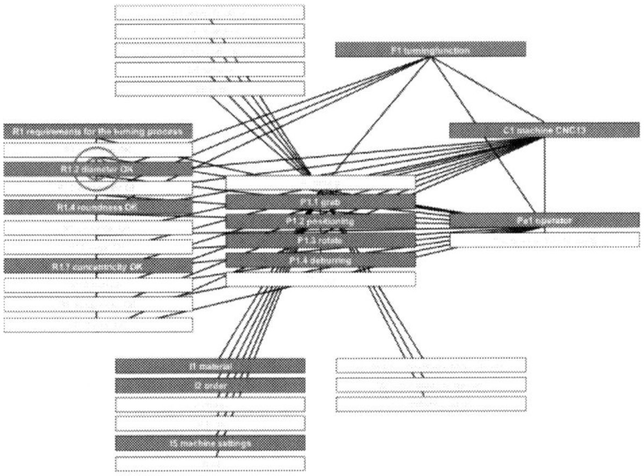

Figure 5. Schematic representation of the application of the "Focus Function" to the complex representation of the Subsystem Manufacturing

Figure 5 illustrates that by focusing on the unfulfilled requirement, it is possible to achieve a clear assignment of causes of failures through the relations. Thus, for example, the "operator" or the "machine CNC13" is a possible cause of failure, which resulted in the non-fulfillment of the diameter and thus the complaint. This presentation provides a basis for the desired solution finding. If the machine is actually the reason for the failure, constructive measures, such as the conversion or adaptation of the device, are necessary. If the operator is identified as the cause of the failure, organizational measures, such as training, are likely to be the solution. However, these approaches must be defined case-related and more specifically depending on the cause of the failure. The knowledge that results from the solution-finding must then be returned to the production system and the company to avoid consequential failure. All these steps should be bundled in course of the algorithm. In order to investigate the meaningfulness of the algorithm, it is now evaluated based on the previously defined requirements.

IV. Validation of the Algorithm

With the presentation of the algorithm, an evaluation can now be carried out based on the previously stated requirements. These will be subsequently evaluated regarding to their degree of fulfillment and the resulting conclusions used for further research projects in the outlook.

In order to be able to assess the fulfillment of the requirements, it is first necessary to define an assessment scheme. For this purpose, three classifications are considered. The symbol "●" describes requirements that have been fully met, "◑" requirements that were met only to a certain percentage and "○" requirements that could not be met. Once again, it should be noted that the both must-have requirements "MhRe 1: High acceptance and valid in practice" and "MhRe 6: Increase customer satisfaction" can only be validated by validation in practice, thus evaluating this is now not possible. Based on this rating, the requirements could be evaluated as follows:

A. Must-have requirements (MhRe):

◑ = MhRe 2: Documentation of already detected problems. As the knowledge gained through the feedback from production leads to continuous improvement, problems are "documented" by the already derived and implemented improvement measures. However, a separate recording by means of a document is not considered, as a result of which the requirements can only be met in part.

● = MhRe 3: Derivation of improvement measures based on knowledge. Based on the effective failure cause search, targeted improvement measures can be carried out. This means that the findings of the model evaluation are included in the derivation.

● = MhRe 4: Structured procedure. The structure specification by the eDeCoDe approach and the application of an automated four-step processing method by means of an algorithm contribute to a structured procedure. The identification of the cause of the failure using LOOMEO also follows a given structure.

● = MhRe 5: Promotion of process and departmental thinking. The cross process and departmental thinking are sharpened in the presentation and evaluation of individual subsystems of the production system.

B. Should requirements (SRe):

● = SRe 1: Time and personnel expenses should be as low as possible. Automated data sounding, troubleshooting and solution finding using algorithms help to reduce the time and effort required. Instead of a team from different disciplines, which typically performs the problem-solving process, it is only an employee required, who processes the complaint, and a person, who is responsible for the limited subsystem.

◑ = SRe 2: Prevention of hasty emergency measures. Due to the effectiveness of the algorithm, the causes of failure can be assigned much more specifically and also faster to a subsystem. According to that, the need of performing of hasty emergency measures should be greatly minimized.

Nevertheless, it cannot be completely proved, so that this requirement can only be partly met.

- = SRe 3: Use of a model approach. Using eDeCoDe, both the product system and the production system can be represented with a minimal number of system views.
- = SRe 4: Standardized collection of complaint data. By using a data-screening filter, information about the product is collected in a standardized manner. Thus, relevant information is filtered and provided uniformly.
- = SRe 5: Automated processing of the complaint data collected. Based on the presented four steps, which together shall form the automated algorithm, this requirement can be fulfilled completely.

Based on the symbols, it can be seen that all requirements, with the exception of "Documentation of already detected problems" and "Avoiding hasty emergency measures", could be assessed as completely fulfilled.

V. Conclusions

Based on the previous validation regarding the fulfillment of the requirements of the algorithm, the following conclusions can be made. On the one hand, it turned out that the method of the 8D report was able to establish itself very strongly in practice. Nevertheless, it could be shown that the disadvantages of the 8D report, especially in these days, should not be underestimated. This allows the statement that it makes sense to develop new approaches about dealing with complaint data from the usage phase. On the other hand, this should be more efficient in terms of personnel and time. In addition, a model approach should be used to minimize complexity. An automated evaluation should also have strived. Based on these requirements, the article developed an algorithm that incorporates the benefits of the 8D report while compensating for its disadvantages. The application of the eDeCoDe approach creates an efficient and, above all, goal-oriented process to localize causes of failure in the production process and to reduce or avoid them by carrying the solution out. By using the knowledge regarding the cause of the failure, potential for improvement can be identified and used.

It turns out in summary as an outlook that it makes sense to expand and further develop the presented algorithm within further research projects and carry out a systematic validation and evaluation in different companies in order to highlight the potential of the algorithm and to highlight weak points. In addition, it makes sense to investigate whether the algorithm can also be applied to complaints social networks and to measure the actual savings in terms of personnel and time-related implementation efforts and draw conclusions on how to save costs.

To achieve this, it applies to work out a uniform structure for the data screening filter from the survey and to prepare a procedure, which according to it, the prioritization of the complaints and finally the search for the causes of the failure are carried out. Furthermore, it makes sense to develop a method kit that provides solutions depending on the case-related cause of the failure.

Acknowledgment

The authors thank the German Research Foundation (DFG) for the support of the FusLa-Projekt [FKZ: SCHL 2225/1-1].

References

[1] M. A. Barsalou "The Quality Improvement Field Guide," vol. 1, CRC Press, Portland, 2015.

[2] M. Brückner "Complaint Management," vol. 2, Redline Wirtschaft, Heidelberg, 2011.

[3] P. Gorecki and P. Pautsch "Practical Book Lean Management," vol. 2, Hanser, München, 2014.

[4] R. Kiem "Quality 4.0," vol. 1, Hanser, München, 2016.

[5] V. Kumar "Total Quality Management," vol. 1, LuLu, Morrisville, North Carolina, 2013.

[6] V. Leiner "Complaint Management," vol. 1, Bachelor + Master Publishing, Hamburg, 2014.

[7] S. Nasir "Customer Retention Strategies and Customer Loyalty," in Advertising and Branding, vol. 3 Hershey, Pennsylvania IGI Global, 2017.

[8] J.-P. G. Nicklas "Approach to Model-Based Requirements Management for Business Networks," vol. 1, Shaker, Aachen, 2016.

[9] F. Optehostert "Data Collecting is no longer enough; Data Algorithm as a Success Factor for Service Companies," DGQ QZ the magazine for quality management and quality assurance, vol. 63, pp. 36–38, 2018.

[10] D. Peppers and M. Rogers "Managing Customer Relationships," vol. 1, John Wiley & Sons, Hoboken, N.J., 2004.

[11] REDPOINT.TESEON "LOOMEO," [Online]. Available from: https://redpoint.teseon.com/, 2019 [retrieved March, 2019].

[12] J. Rodríguez Pérez "Handbook of Investigation and effective CAPA Systems," vol. 2, ASQ, Milwaukee, WI, 2016.

[13] J. Stark "Product Lifecycle Management," vol. 3, Springer, Cham, 2016.

[14] G. Ullmann "Holistic Production Systems: IPH - Method Collection," [Online]. Available from: https://www.iph-hannover.de/_media/files/downloads/IPH_Lean_Methodensammlung.pdf, 2009 [retrieved January, 2019].

[15] P. Winzer "Generic Systems Engineering," vol. 2. Auflage, Springer Vieweg, Berlin, Heidelberg, 2016.

Resonance Thinking and Inductive Machine Learning

Yves Kodratoff, Marta Franova
LRI, UMR8623 du CNRS & INRIA Saclay
Bât. 660, Orsay, France
e-mail: yvekod@gmail.com, mf@lri.fr

***Abstract*—This paper presents one of the symbiotic parts deemed necessary to complete our theory of computer systems design devoted to incomplete domains, here called Cartesian Systemic Emergence (CSE). CSE is dealing with one version of the concept of (semi)-automated creativity. We call systems implementing this kind of creativity Symbiotic Recursive Pulsative Systems (SRPS). SRPS are intended to contribute to solving real-world problems in incomplete domains requiring control and prevention. CSE is concerned with strategic aspects of the conception of such SPRS. Each component of a SPRS has to be symbiotically linked to all the other components. This requirement is not very usual in Computer Science, hence we have to introduce notions that are not yet present in scientific vocabulary. This paper is devoted to the most important features of one particular way of thinking present in CSE. We call it 'Resonance Thinking' (RT). RT takes care of generating and handling experiments during CSE. We explain that RT causes the complexity of CSE to be analogous to Ackermann's function computation complexity.**

Keywords—Cartesian Systemic Emergence; Symbiotic Recursive Pulsative Systems; Resonance Thinking; Computer-based and Human-based creativity; Systems Design.

I. INTRODUCTION

The need for Symbiotic Recursive Pulsative Systems (SRPS) design raised during our search for a solution of a complex real-world application, namely automatic construction of recursive programs in incomplete domains [4] [7]. For simplicity, we refer to it as Program Synthesis (PS). Our aim in PS has been to tackle incompleteness and informal specifications that represent problems dealt with neither in classical PS nor in system design approaches [7] [13]. Incompleteness and informal specifications required the introduction of a new model and on-purpose methods in general system design. We call Cartesian Systemic Emergence (CSE) this new theory. CSE handles strategic aspects of the design and particular evolutive improvement of SRPS. The construction and desired improvements have to guarantee control and prevention in the system. Resonance Thinking (RT) introduced in this paper takes care of generating and handling experiments during CSE.

In [9], we describe several facets of CSE, namely tackling underspecified information, on-purpose invention instead of manipulating a specific search space, and formulating fruitful experiments. RT, as a symbiotic part of CSE, possesses also these facets and describes them in a more precise way, even though a formal description has still to be worked out. Since the illustrations of RT in PS are very complex, we shall re-use here the toy example presented in [9]. The purpose of this paper is four-fold: to

- describe particularities of RT taking place in CSE;
- illustrate this method on a toy example nevertheless dealing with a problem that many innovative researchers may have to face;
- explain that the complexity of RT is similar to a computation process of Ackermann's function;
- propose several new strategies relative to System Design.

The paper is organized as follows. Section II presents fundamental notions necessary for understanding CSE and RT. Section III recalls the notion of CSE. Section IV presents the RT problem formulation intertwined with an example. Finally, Section V describes several challenges that RT offers to implementation of a theory of creative thinking.

II. FUNDAMENTAL NOTIONS

The goal of CSE is to formalize strategic aspects of human creation of *informally* specified *symbiotic systems* in *incomplete domains* following our *pulsation* model. This formalization is performed in order to prepare fundamentals for designing automated tools that help to perform this complex task. In this section, we recall four terms by which this goal is expressed and that will be used also in our presentation of RT, namely

- informal specification,
- symbiosis,
- incompleteness, and
- pulsation.

Informal specification of a system that has to be constructed is a description of this system in terms that are not yet exactly defined and that, when considered out of a particular context, may even seem absurd. These terms, in which the specification is expressed, will evolve during the system construction. In other words, depending on some constraints and opportunities that will arise during the construction, the meaning of the terms used in the starting specification will evolve and will make a part of the solution. The initial ambiguity of terms is eliminated by the provided solution. We might say that notions used in an informal specification are of evolutive and flexible character. Their evolution will also bring an exact specification of the context to be considered.

In the context of CSE, the notion of informal specification needs to be completed by differentiating the notions of formalized and formal specification. *Formalized specification* is an intermediary state in the progress from informal to formal specification. It consists in a collection of basic working definitions and basic tools that seem plausibly pointing out a successful completion process, even though some inventive steps may still be needed to complete the tools so as giving their final form to the working definitions. *Formal specification* then consists in the complete solution represented by the working system, the methodology of the functioning as well as of the construction of the system. These all are needed in order to be used in further evolutive improvement.

As far as *incompleteness* is concerned, from a practical point of view, we know that full reality is unknown. What we may know at a given time can be formalized by an incomplete system. From a decision point of view, it is well-known that incompleteness constitutes a large drawback [12]. Incompleteness, however, is not at all a drawback for the practical purpose of solving real-world problems that are asking for some kind of innovation. This is due to the fact that, from a construction point of view, incompleteness brings a freedom for technological ingeniosity, resulting in possible new technological inventions. Since informal specification contains terms that are not exactly defined, a particular informal specification points out to a context that can be represented by an incomplete environment. CSE can then be seen not only as a construction process for a system in its informally specified initial environment but also as a fruitful strategy for a progressive completion of this environment.

By *symbiosis* we understand a composition of several parts which is vitally separation-sensitive. By vital separation-sensitivity we mean that eliminating one part leads to the destruction or to a non-recoverable mutilation of the other parts and of the whole composition. This means that the widely used divide and conquer strategy is not at all suitable when creating and extending symbiotic systems. We can also say that analysis and synthesis are inappropriate tools when creating and observing symbiotic systems. Symbiosis is therefore different from synergy that is a mutually profitable composition of the elements that are not destroyed nor mutilated by a separation.

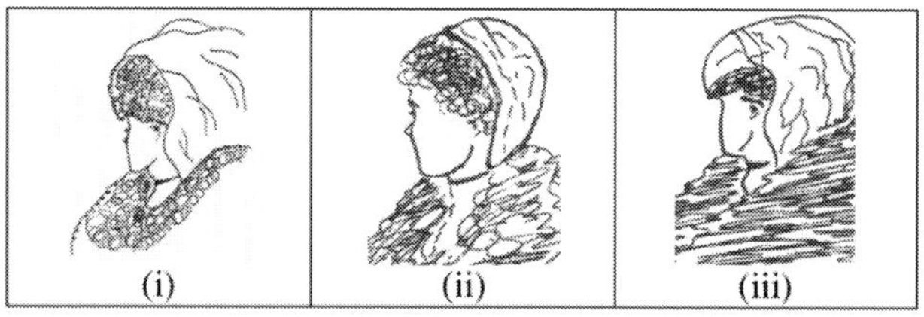

Figure 1. Example of pictorial symbiosis.

In Figure 1, (i) can be seen as a symbiosis of (ii) and (iii). Here, we need to point out that symbiotic parts do not necessarily need to overlap in the final symbiotic object. They may have a symbiotic, and maybe invisible, intersection that makes their whole symbiotic. From a pragmatic point of view, symbiosis of a system is embodied by the interdependence of all notions and parts of this system. We have illustrated this, in [6], on the example of Natural Numbers defined by Peano's axioms.

Pulsation is a model for construction and evolutive improvement of incomplete systems that are concerned with the factors of control and prevention. In other words, pulsation provides a rigorous framework for the completion process of incomplete systems. This model is described in [8]. It relies on our particular handling of Ackermann's function. We shall recall now the features of its handling that will be referred to, later in the paper.

Let 'ack' be Ackermann's function defined, as in [17], by its standard definition, i.e.,

$$ack(0,n) = n+1 \quad (1)$$

$$ack(m+1,0) = ack(m,1) \quad (2)$$

$$ack(m+1,n+1) = ack(m,ack(m+1,n)). \quad (3)$$

Since ack is a non-primitive recursive function, thus by definition of non-primitive recursion, it is a particular composition of an infinite sequence of primitive recursive functions. In similarity to the infinite sequence, which is used – in [11] – to construct Ackermann's function, the evolutive improvement (i.e., pulsation), relies on a construction of a potentially infinite sequence of systems that might, in an ideal world, be used to construct a global 'Ackermann's system' that contains all of these systems. In our work, by pulsation we thus understand a progressive construction of a potentially infinite sequence of incomplete theories T_0, T_1, …, T_n, T_{n+1}, … such that $T_i \subset T_{i+1}, T_i \neq T_{i+1}$ (for i = 0, 1, 2, …) and such that an infinite limit of this sequence represents an ideal, complete system. In addition, each T_i is practically complete in the sense that, from a practical point of view, it covers an exploitable formalization. (Think, for instance, of the incompleteness of natural numbers [12] but their practical completeness in our everyday use.) Pulsation does not reduce to one particular step in this sequence. This follows from that pulsative systems are formalized progressively and potentially indefinitely. Pulsation is a model that does not describes how the particular systems in this sequence are constructed. This is the role of Cartesian Systemic Emergence [9].

III. CARTESIAN SYSTEMIC EMERGENCE

As said above, CSE goal is formalizing strategic aspects of human creation of informally specified symbiotic systems in incomplete domains. In this section, we recall two paradigms that play a fundamental role in CSE and that will be referred to in Section IV. The first paradigm can be represented formally by the formula

$$\forall \text{ Problem } \exists \text{ System solves(System,Problem)}. \quad (4)$$

The second one can be represented by the formula

$$\exists \text{ System } \forall \text{ Problem solves(System,Problem)}. \quad (5)$$

There are two main differences between these two paradigms. The first difference is that, in (4), each problem or a class of problems related to a system can have its own solution while in (5) a unique, universal solution is looked for. The first paradigm leads to a library of particular heuristics, while the second paradigm results in a single universal method. CSE is concerned with the pulsative construction of a system that verifies (5).

As presented in [9], the main features of CSE are thus as follows:

- It works with an informally specified goal.
- It handles incompleteness.
- It takes into account symbiosis and pulsation.
- It generates experiences.
- It oscillates between the paradigms (4) and (5) in order to reach a solution described by (5).

To our best knowledge, there is no other work on simultaneously solving the problems addressed by these features of CSE. This explains why we need here so many new concepts and mechanisms. Moreover, because we deal with symbiosis, pulsation and informal specifications, CSE has to be considered in the framework of Cartesian Intuitionism and not in the framework of Newtonian Science. In [7], we explain in more details that the main keywords of Newtonian Science are

- exactness
- formal systems and tools justified in a logical way
- methods of demonstration reduced to some axioms and rules of inference
- decision and undecidability.

In contrast to this, as pointed out in the same paper, the main keywords of Cartesian Intuitionism are

- realization and ingeniosity
- systems and tools justified in an epistemological way
- methodology of construction taking into account also 'Cartesian Intuition' (i.e., a symbiotic composition)
- handling incompleteness in a constructive way.

This means that Cartesian Intuitionism has its own, we might say 'pragmatic', notion of rigor that enables, during the research and development stages, relying on methods and tools that do not verify the strict criteria of Newtonian Science. This non-conformity to logical criteria and a kind of 'rigorous freedom' will become clear in the next sections.

It happens that the process of construction of informally specified symbiotic systems is very difficult to describe exactly and in its full generality. Our CSE attempts to tackle the task of its description. In [9], we present a general, even though yet informal, scheme for CSE based on the method called Constructive Matching formula construction (*CM-formula construction*) which is used in PS (introduced in [3]). We shall refer here to it as CSE-scheme.

IV. Resonance Thinking

RT is a method for solving problems represented by paradigm (5). It takes care of generating and handling experiments in the process of CSE.

In order to take hold of RT complexity, it is necessary to keep in mind that CSE and RT are designed for the creation of systems that have to provide control and prevention. Therefore, the criterion of security is strongly involved already in the system's creation. Such a particular security follows from fulfilling four precepts of Descartes' method [2], p. 120:

a) "Carefully avoid precipitate conclusions and preconceptions.
b) Divide each of the difficulties into as many parts as possible and as may be required in order to resolve them better.
c) Suppose some order even among objects that have no natural order of precedence.
d) Make enumerations so complete and so comprehensive, so we can be sure of leaving nothing out."

Note that these four rules represent also four fundamental (symbiotic) facets of CSE in this order:

a') Pulsative Thinking, i.e., taking care of security, control and prevention [11].
b') Metamorphic Thinking, i.e., taking care of resulting epistemological equivalence between paradigm (5) and particular CSE-handling paradigm (4).
c') Symbiotic Thinking, i.e., taking care of construction of a symbiotic system.
d') RT, i.e., taking care of generating and handling experiments.

As one can realize while trying to give an *exact* description of old-young lady picture given in Figure 1.a, a description of a one part in a symbiotic composition (such as 'old lady' in Figure1.c) is not a simple task. Indeed, an exact description of the old lady part in Figure 1.a would imperatively require explicit references to young lady part of Figure 1.a. Therefore, in this paper, we do not intend yet to provide a complete description of RT, because we first need to describe in more details Metamorphic Thinking (MT) and Symbiotic Thinking (ST).

We shall present RT and its basic notions with the help of a toy example used in [9] for description of CSE. In comparison to examples provided by PS framework, this example is simpler and could illustrate many other scientific fields than PS-research does. The problem presented here concerns conveying a new original scientific knowledge in such a way that its essential content and creative potential are preserved by the next generations. This is not a trivial problem as already pointed out in the past [1] [2]. Our experience confirms that, for new knowledge relative to creation and extension of symbiotic recursive systems, this problem remains relevant today also.

Since CSE and RT handle incompleteness it is only natural that procedures and notions of CSE come out through a progressive evolution from informal specifications to formal specifications.

A. *Specification of a toy example*

In this section, we present our example illustrating CSE and RT. Let us suppose that René is a founder of a novel scientific theory with a high pulsative potential. Referring back to many unpleasant experiences of the past founders, he needs to ask himself how to build some 'works' able to convey the full complexity of his new theory while immediately preventing a degradation of its pulsative potential. In a more formal way, René must solve a problem informally specified as:

$$\exists \text{works} \ \forall \text{disciple conveys(René, works) \&} \\ \text{conveys(works,disciple)} \Rightarrow \\ \text{essential\_of(René)} = \text{essential\_of(disciple)} \quad (6)$$

Note that this problem has the same logical structure as the second paradigm presented in the form (5). Specification (6) is an informal specification. As said above, this means that the notions that appear in (6) are not defined in a rigorous way. They are only specified in an informal way in terms of some non-formal criteria (i.e., a kind of underspecified constraints). This means that a solution 'works' for (6) has to emerge simultaneously with suitable formalizations (thus, the final definitions) of notions that occur in (6). In the following, we shall denote by D_t the set of (initially underspecified) sentences specifying 'to convey' and by D_e the set of (initially underspecified) sentences specifying 'essential_of'. These two sets evolve in the process of CSE and RT towards a more rigorous final form. For simplicity of presentation, we do not involve such an evolution in our notation.

In [9], we mention that, in order to solve (6), there is a particular switch to a framework of experiences described by the formula

$$\forall \text{disciple} \ \exists \text{works conveys(René, works) \&} \\ \text{conveys(works,disciple)} \Rightarrow \\ \text{essential\_of(René)} = \text{essential\_of(disciple)} \quad (7)$$

This formula represents the paradigm (4). We have explained above that there is a difference between solving (4) and (5), and this obviously applies to their instances (6) and (7). In general, in order to be fruitful and justified, a switch from (5) to (4) has to rely on what we call Metamorphic Thinking (MT). Roughly speaking, MT takes care of a rigorous, epistemologically and pragmatically justified transformation of paradigm (5) into the context of paradigm (4). Our paper [9] gives its illustration in the field of program synthesis from specifications. A more detailed description of MT is presently under development. Note that we call *oscillation* the process of switching between these two paradigms.

In other words, MT provides a switch from (6) to (7) that is useful in order to generate experiences generating, within the framework of (7), some hints and inspiration for solving (6). These hints and inspirations represent temporary (see precept (a)) underspecified constraints that enlarge the already existing set of underspecified constraints. In order to generate such inspiring experiences, while considering (7), from the set of all disciples, we chose a finite number of disciples $d_0, d_1, \ldots, d_n$ that seem highly different so that each of them seems to need a different 'works'. Note that this step implicitly embodies the above precept (b). We shall call *representatives* these disciples. In other words, our experience shows us that challenging experiences are needed to obtain some inspirations contributing to a solution of (6) in the framework of paradigm (5). Note that we order these disciples in a numbered sequence just for the presentation purposes. This will be useful when describing recursive procedures that handle this finite set of disciples.

Very roughly speaking, in order to solve a problem represented by paradigm (5), it might seem possible to replace MT from paradigm (5) to (4) by a symbiotic composition of a set of solutions for carefully chosen representatives of universally quantified elements of this paradigm. A drawback of such a description lies in considering a lone symbiotic operation (i.e., one action), while RT, through precepts (a), (b), (c) and (d) requires performing a great number of interdependent symbiotic compositions, as will be described below.

Recall that the two operators 'conveys' and 'essential_of' are here specified informally only by some set of sentences that represent informal descriptions (i.e., underspecified constraints) relative to these notions. Thus, we shall replace these notions by their informal descriptions. Above, we have denoted by D_t the set of sentences specifying 'to convey' and by D_e the set of sentences specifying 'essence_of'. Therefore, (7) writes as

$$\forall \text{disciple} \ \exists \text{works} \ D_t(\text{René, works}) \ \& \\ D_t(\text{works,disciple}) \Rightarrow D_e(\text{René}) = D_e(\text{disciple}) \quad (8)$$

Let us consider (8) for each particular d_i, i.e.,

$$\exists \text{works} \ D_t(\text{René, works}) \\ \& \ D_t(\text{works}, d_i) \Rightarrow D_e(\text{René}) = D_e(d_i) \quad (9)$$

In [9], we show that a solution for (9) can be found for each d_i by following CSE-scheme and oscillating between paradigms (4) and (5). This solution consists of a concrete value w_i for 'works' and of less informal descriptors $D_{t,i}$ and $D_{e,i}$. We shall call this solution $Sol_i = \{w_i, D_{t,i}, D_{e,i}\}$. Due to a careful oscillation between paradigms (4) and (5), w_i and the descriptors $D_{t,i}$, $D_{e,i}$ refine 'works' and the operators 'to convey' and 'essential_of' in (6). These resulting refinements 'resonate' within paradigm (5) framework. By their resonating, we mean that during the experimentation process, we feel that they might, probably after some 'judicious adaptations', be applied also to other instances of 'disciple'.

B. Resonance Thinking

RT relies heavily on what Merriam-Webster Dictionary considers as resonance: a quality that makes something personally meaningful or important to someone. RT thus involves the ability to create and explore personally meaningful or important relations in the process of generating and handling experiences.

Procedurally, RT is based on two procedures of which we cannot here provide a detailed description, since it relies on other CSE symbiotic facets, not yet introduced ones (namely, MS and ST mentioned above). We shall therefore concentrate on explaining the role of these procedures. The first procedure will be called *topological symbiosis* (noted *ts*) and it is also a primitive operation for the second procedure. The second procedure is called *complementary topological symbiosis* (noted *cts*). Both these procedures require creativity in developing symbiotic systems. In this paper, we describe the way these procedures work: they are therefore to be handled, for the time being, by a creative human person. The following description of the role of *ts* and *cts* will illustrate some of the challenges that *ts* and *cts* have to tackle.

1) Topological Symbiosis and ILP

Our argumentation relies besides on some results recently obtained in the field of Inductive Machine Learning (see the relevant references in [15] and [16]) that proved a first instance of what a pioneer in ML, Donald Michie, thirty years ago called "Ultra-Strong Learning" (see [14]) that we dubbed as U-SL. The strategy of U-SL relies on four essential steps. Steps A. and B. are based on machine power, and steps C. and D. will be introduced later in the 'discussion' section of this paper. These two Muggelton et al. papers elaborate on a description of how Prolog programs might be understood or misunderstood by someone in the process of learning this programming language. A side remark may illustrate the depth of U-SL concept: in U-SL: this kind of learning 'unites' machine and human learning in a way that will become clear later.

Step A. Generating knowledge in the form of new predicates that have not been aforehand provided to the system. An efficient way to achieve this goal has been presented in [15] where the system makes use of a controlled pattern matching of the higher order knowledge, provided in the form of meta-knowledge handled by a meta-interpreter. New knowledge is obtained by proving that a meta-goal is valid on a selected set of true examples. Note that this procedure is not submitted to our constraints of symbiosis and pulsation.

In our presentation, Muggleton's Step A. can be seen as a partial instance of what we call here *ts*, the role of which is to create new relationships induced from the data. Since our examples deal with the field of inducing notions and programs from an incomplete specification (which imposes symbiosis and pulsation), we still need to define a *ts* adapted to this very complex task. This explains also why we have to provide a coherent description of *ts* before being able to implement it.

Step B. Once new rules a found during Step A., [16] makes use of these rules in order to select a set of significant examples. This creativity could work in a random way, generating a random mixture of examples illustrating both the old rules and the new generated one. In the context of U-SL, these examples are generated in such an order as to constitute the 'background knowledge' provided to a human learner. Thus, some selection among the possibly generated rules has to be done in order to be sure to obtain a 'significant' background knowledge.

In our presentation, Muggleton's step B. can be seen as a partial instance of what we call here *cts*. The goal of *cts*, similarly to step B., is to select a set of examples in order to complete or to enlarge the new knowledge initially generated by *ts*. However, in difference with step B., *cts* generates random examples because this provides a greater probability of generation of new (useful or missing) knowledge. This is coherent with our choice of a set of disciples for which solving (9) is rather difficult. We have mentioned above that this leads to a necessity of a greater creativity and thus leads more efficiently to practical completeness of resulting system, here 'works' as in (6). At this stage, we already can acknowledge that steps A. and B. may be used as an inspirational model for programming the main procedural features of *ts* and *cts*.

Now that we have provided more intuitive understanding to what are *ts* and *cts*, we can illustrate the strategy we will use in order to implement them through a description of our 'typically symbiotic' examples : 'two different women', 'Peano's axioms' and 'René's disciples'.

2) On symbiosis in RT

We need to point out here two particular features of *ts*. The first one concerns the character of possible "mutilations" performed by *ts* and the second one concerns its goal.

Let us recall first the above two different women given in Figure 1.b and Figure 1.c. The essential difference between these two figures can be expressed by the term 'age'. Indeed, the woman in Figure 1.c looks old and the woman in Figure 1.b looks young. We might say that the goal of topological symbiosis is here to 'merge' these two figures so that the descriptor 'age' has simultaneously two values, namely 'young' and 'old'. In the ML field, this operation is similar to now a classical one called Predicate Synthesis. Obviously, Figure 1.a is a solution for this task. We say that Figure 1.a is a symbiotic composition of Figure 1.b and Figure 1.c. We can however see that that the original figures Figure 1.b and Figure 1.c have been 'mutilated' to satisfy the requirement of this goal. For instance, the eye of old woman in Figure 1.c becomes an ear for young woman projection in Figure 1.a. This pictorial example, however, is too simple for illustrating an essential feature of symbiotic relations: the fact that we are starting with underspecified pieces of the puzzle (i.e., the axioms and constraints available at the start and which fail to solve our problem).

In [6], we used the example of Peano's axioms that are (also) symbiotic since, by deleting one of its axioms, the reduced set of axioms is either non sense or leads also to other interpretation structures (such as the set of Perfect Women in [5]). This example exhibits an explicit degradation due the presence of a set of notions and constraints that obviously became underspecified when one of Peano's axioms is deleted. This shows that symbiosis manifests itself not so much as 'merging' contradictory facets of the considered system, but as constructing an emergent vitally separation-sensitive interdependence (i.e., symbiosis) of parts of the system.

3) On generating experiments in RT

We are going to describe *ts* and *cts* in the framework of René's example. At this stage, we suppose that (9) for d_0 is already solved following the CSE-scheme providing the solution Sol_0 for d_0. Sol_0 represents a 'temporary' solution for d_0. By 'temporary' we mean that this solution will still have to be approved or modified by RT. We can now come to *ts* and *cts*. Similarly, for other disciples $d_1, \ldots, d_n$, we will obtain Sol_1, Sol_2 and so on. We assume here that the solutions are obtained in a particular 'linear' way, one after another. This 'linear' way looks as follows.

Once Sol_0 is constructed, a 'temporary' solution Sol_1 for d_1 is constructed ('temporary' in the same way as Sol_0 is a 'temporary' solution for d_0). Note that, in order to concentrate on the problem at hand, both these constructions may lead to new experiences and thus, *they modify the initial environment* by refining the informal notions of our definition (6) of our problem. For the sake of simplicity, we do not describe explicitly below this evolution of environment, though we take it into account by calling it a 'feedback' when we use it.

Now, suppose that we solved the problem for the first disciple. Before starting solving the problem for the next one, we try to take into account the informal specifications present in (6). This try amounts to an attempt to 'merge' the solutions Sol_0 and Sol_1 using topological symbiosis *ts*, i.e., we try to achieve their symbiotic composition that resonates (as explained in Section 4) with the informal specifications in (6). We shall denote this process by $ts(Sol_0,Sol_1)$.

If solving $ts(S_0,S_1)$ fails, i.e., we cannot find relevant refinements, we keep in mind the feedback obtained while constructing Sol_0 and Sol_1, as well as the failure reasons of $ts(S_0,S_1)$. This failed step will have to be redone later while relying on some inspirations that may rise while finding the solutions for the next disciples. If this process fails, or leads to an infinite number of repetitions, the problem will have to be considered as a challenge for one of the next pulsation steps.

If the process $ts(Sol_0,Sol_1)$ succeeds, both solutions are temporarily approved. Then, keeping in mind all the feedback obtained, a solution of (9) for d_2 is constructed. One might suppose that this process may continue linearly as suggested by its beginning, as we just have seen. However, recall that we work in an environment that requires control and prevention. Therefore, in this environment, we rely strongly on the above four precepts. This means that generating complementary experiments for topological symbiosis of solutions constructed is necessary. We call *complementary topological symbiosis* (noted *cts*) this procedure for generating new experiments.

Roughly speaking, *cts* is a particular generation process (defined with help of *ts*) for creating experiments. The goal of these complementary experiments is to provide inspirations for further refinement for underspecified notions and constraints. Similarly to computation of ack (see [10]), in the process of generating experiments (via *ts*) for Sol_m and Sol_n, i.e., while 'computing' $cts(Sol_m,Sol_n)$, the operation $ts(Sol_i,Sol_j)$ for other solutions Sol_i and Sol_j is performed several times.

Let us denote by $ts_1(Sol_i,Sol_j)$ the solution of the first computation, by $ts_2(Sol_i,Sol_j)$ the second computation, and so on. It is important to point out that $ts_p(Sol_i,Sol_j)$ and $ts_q(Sol_i,Sol_j)$ in this sequence of computations may carry two different feedbacks. Indeed, each inner step of *cts* (i.e., evaluating $cts(Sol_m,Sol_n)$), may bring new refinements, constraints as well as it may point out to missing knowledge or second-order notions and procedures. The procedures *ts* and *cts* have to insure that not only reasonable and achievable solutions are obtained but that a possibility of future evolutions are guaranteed while properly handling prevention and control.

The procedures *ts* and *cts* are, in our case, presently performed by a human mind. This means that human mind can rely on relevant creativity in order to decrease the number of repetitions. In consequence, even though *ts* and *cts* are not simple, CSE and RT are not overwhelming tasks for human performers. However, they may be overwhelming for a human observer even in this simplified form. For instance, an observation of the computation steps of ack(3,2) before its ending does suggest that the process leads nowhere because it seems to loop. The same holds for an external observer of CSE. This is why we believe that further research is necessary to give a reasonable formula for performing *cts* by machine.

V. DISCUSSION

It is interesting to check if steps C. and D. of Muggleton's approach to U-SL could serve as an Ariadne's golden thread for us to develop a similar computer-aided explanation of some features of our project.

In section IV.B, we already presented our possible interactions with U-SL Steps A and B. Its Steps C and D both try to measure how much students have been able to understand the way Prolog computes.

Step C. Remember that the students receive a set of rules during Step B. In Step C., the students are offered different programs at different levels of abstraction, i.e. more or less general clauses. They have to understand the relations between the clauses and the examples given.

Step D. The teachers create a questionnaire that checks if the students understood or not the information provided at Step B.

It has been observed that both success and failure provide information about the way the students manage their understanding of Prolog. Successful students provide information on some of their unexpected own way to handle Prolog (i.e., hints at handling it in a creative way), and the various failure cases provide hints to possible repair procedures within incorrectly structured Prolog knowledge. More than delivering a mark of value to the students' learning ability or to the teachers' teaching one, this U-SL approach rather provides clues about how to improve these abilities.

This successful trend of Machine Learning research opens us to some hope that human-based creation of programs from badly or incompletely specified may benefit of the U-SL attitude, as follows.

Example 1., relative to René's goal. Each solution of (9) will generate at least one improved 'works'. We could then, similarly to U-SL steps C. and D., organize a kind of consultation between René himself (the 'teacher') and each particular disciple (the 'student'). In this case, René would test whether his (so far) constructed partial 'works' brings to his potential disciples a correct comprehension of his fundamental notions.

Example 2., relative to Symbiosis among the components of a system. In section IV.B, we have shown that pictorial Symbiosis provides clues for handling symbiosis. As we have seen, symbiosis is better defined by its "vitally separation-sensitive interdependence" among the components, as symbiotic Peano's axioms illustrate. As far as we know, teaching the recognition and handling of separation-sensitive interdependent systems, a skill necessary to creative programmers, does not exist yet. The research presented here provides a few clues of how it could be formalized. A tight collaboration with specialists in Cognitive Sciences should enable us to provide a large enough battery of symbiotic and non symbiotic systems so that, mimicking US-L, we could unravel the deep features of systemic symbiosis, a necessary, if not sufficient, condition to safely handle creativity.

Example 3., relative to Oscillation. Oscillation has been introduced in section III where we underlined the difference between problems of the type (4): ∀ Problem ∃ System solves(System,Problem) and those of the type (5): ∃ System ∀ Problem solves(System,Problem). While exposing "René disciples" example, we used the switch between these two problems by replacing formula (6) by (7). Understanding the nature of a switch from a "∀ ∃" problem to a "∃ ∀" one is by itself not easy, and it is even more difficult to realize that the oscillation from one to the other may lead to a solution respecting the four basic requirements expressed at the beginning of section II. We think that a strategy *à la* U-SL may constitute a tool favoring the understanding of the importance of the shift proposed here.

VI. Conclusion

Cartesian Systemic Emergence is intended to become an implementable system design theory for Symbiotic Recursive Pulsative Systems. In this paper, we have introduced one of its symbiotic features, namely Resonance Thinking. RT takes care of generating and handling experiments during the creation process of symbiotic systems specified, at the start, by an informal specification. RT is very complex, since it has to deal with the requirements of control and prevention, as well as with the process of 'shrinking' the incompleteness in accordance with the pulsation model. We have described also a particular work in Inductive Machine Learning, namely U-SL, which seems to provide a fruitful inspiration for the final implementation of two main procedures of RT (topological symbiosis and complementary topological symbiosis).

RT is only one of four symbiotic features of CSE. We have already presented a basis for Pulsative Thinking, namely the Pulsation model [11]. We are currently working out on its last two features, Symbiotic Thinking and Metamorphic Thinking.

By its symbiotic character, the system design theory proposed by CSE differs from the contemporary approaches to system design (see [13]). However, it does not compete with those approaches. It completes their modular considerations by considerations that are suitable for handling symbiotic pulsative systems.

Acknowledments

We thank Michèle Sebag and Yannis Manoussakis for their moral support.

References

[1] F. Bacon, Novum Organum, P.U.F, 1986.

[2] R. Descartes, "Discourse on the Method," in. R. Descartes, translated by J. Cottingham, R.Stoothoff, D. Murdoch, Philosophical Writings of Descartes, vol. 1, Cambridge University Press, 2006, pp. 111-151.

[3] M. Franova, "CM-strategy: A Methodology for Inductive Theorem Proving or Constructive Well-Generalized Proofs," in A. K. Joshi ed., Proc. of the Ninth International Joint Conference on Artificial Intelligence, 1985, pp. 1214-1220.

[4] M. Franova, "An Implementation of Program Synthesis from Formal Specifications", in Y. Kodratoff, ed., Proceedings of the 8th European Conference on Artificial Intelligence, Pitman, 1988, pp. 559-564.

[5] M. Franova, "The Role of Recursion in and for Scientific Creativity," in R. Trappl ed., Cybernetics and Systems 2010, Proc. of the Twentieth European Meeting on Cybernetics and System research, Austrian Society for Cybernetic Studies, 2010, pp. 573-578.

[6] M. Franova, "A Cartesian Methodology for an Autonomous Program Synthesis System," in M.Jäntti, G. Weckman eds., proc. of ICONS 2014, The Ninth International Conference on Systems, ISBN, 978-1-61208-319-3, 2014, pp. 22-27.

[7] M. Franova, "Cartesian versus Newtonian Paradigms for Recursive Program Synthesis," International Journal on Advances in Systems and Measurements, vol. 7, no 3&4, 2014, pp. 209-222.

[8] M. Franova and Y. Kodratoff, "A Model of Pulsation for Evolutive Formalizing Incomplete Intelligent Systems," in L. van Moergestel, G. Goncalves, S. Kim, C. Leon eds., INTELLI 2017, The Sixth International Conference on Intelligent Systems and Applications, ISBN, 978-1-61208-576-0, 2017, pp. 1 - 6.

[9] M. Franova and Y. Kodratoff, "Cartesian Systemic Emergence - Tackling Underspecified Notions in Incomplete Domains," in O. Chernavskaya, K. Miwa eds., Proc. of COGNITIVE 2018, The Tenth International Conference on Advanced Cognitive Technologies and Applications, ISBN, 978-1-61208-609-5, 2018, pp. 1-6.

[10] M. Franova, "Trace of computation for ack(3,2)", https://sites.google.com/site/martafranovacnrs/trace-of-computation-for-ack-3-2, retrieved 2019.01.21.

[11] M. Franova and Y. Kodratoff, "Cartesian Systemic Pulsation – A Model for Evolutive Improvement of Incomplete Symbiotic Recursive Systems," International Journal On Advances in Intelligent Systems, vol 11, no 1&2, 2018, pp. 35-45.

[12] K. Gödel, "Some metamathematical results on completeness and consistency, On formally undecidable propositions of Principia Mathematica and related systems I, and On completeness and consistency," in J. van Heijenoort, From Frege to Godel, Harvard University Press, 1967, pp. 592-618.

[13] M. Levin, Modular system design and evaluation. Springer, 2015.

[14] D. Michie, "Machine learning in the next five years," Proceedings of the third European working session on learning, Pitman, 1988, pp. 107-122.

[15] S. Muggleton, D. Lin and A. Tamaddoni-Nezhad, "Meta-interpretive learning of higher-order dyadic datalog, predicate invention revisited," Machine Learning 100, 2015, pp. 49-73.

[16] S. Muggleton, U. Schmid, C. Zeller, A. Tamaddoni-Nezhad and T. Besold, "Ultra-Strong Machine Learning, comprehensibility of programs learned with ILP," Machine Learning 107, 2018, pp. 1119-1140.

[17] A. Yasuhara, Recursive Function Theory and Logic, Academic Press, New York, 1971.

Automated Irrigation System

Maryam Alkaabi[1], Ali Al-Humairi[12], Nafaa Jabeur[1]
[1]Department of Computer Science, German University of Technology in Oman, Oman
[2]Department of Communication Technologies, University of Duisburg-Essen, Duisburg, Germany
meamrashid@gmail.com
ali.alhumairi@gutech.edu.om
nafaa.jabeur@gutech.edu.om

Aydin Azizi, PooryaGhafoorpoor, Ali Fakhrulddin,
Department of Engineering, German University of Technology in Oman, Oman
aydin.azizi@gutech.edu.om, poorya.ghafoorpoor @gutech.edu.om, ali.fakhrulddin@gutech.edu.om

Hayat El Asri
Faculty of Engineering & Computing, Coventry University, United Kingdom
elasrih@uni.coventry.ac.uk

Abstract— This research paper tackles the issue of irrigation systems in the Gulf Cooperation Council (GCC), such as large consumption of water. It presents a contemporary model for an automated irrigation system controlled directly from a mobile application. The aim behind such a project is to minimize the use of resources (i.e., workers, water, and electricity) and manual intervention, maximize the operational speed and the agriculture production while preserving plants from fungi. All the above highly contribute to the sustainability of the proposed model and make it an exceptional option to be considered to improve the agriculture sector from an irrigation efficiency standpoint. The result of the analysis shows that the automated irrigation system is able to control and monitor three types of plants; we also found that the mint plant consumes the least resources when compared to the mango and lemon plants.

Keywords— Irrigation, Smart systems, Embedded System, Automated System, Agriculture.

I. INTRODUCTION

Over the past decades, quick advancements in smart agricultural systems were noted [1]. This showcases the great importance of the agriculture industry worldwide. In India, for instance, about 70% of the people rely on agriculture [1]. In the past, irrigation systems used to fully depend on the mills to irrigate farms by conventional methods without a thorough understanding of the appropriate quantities of these crops. Such systems contribute to the water waste problem, which, in turn, contributes to the destruction of crops as there is no understanding of adequate quantities of water. However, with the recent technological advancements, new innovative systems for irrigation without the farmer interfering in the irrigation process have seen light [2]. Furthermore, because of the geographical region where the Sultanate of Oman is located, it suffers from the lack of rain throughout the year and lack of groundwater, this modern irrigation system will reduce these two main issues. Indeed, smart systems have proven their capability to regulate the irrigation of crops while minimizing the water-waste and the number of resources, which, in turn, will reduce costs. This research paper intends to solve irrigation issues, such as the consumption of large quantities of water and the human-errors that affect trees and their fungi. The farmers experience is an important factor to be taken into account to achieve a high efficiency of modern irrigation systems. With the increase of the world population, the need for farming yields is increasing exponentially. Further, the farmers' potential and abilities in the agriculture filed are reduced due to different enterprises that attract workers away from the farming zone. For example, 28% of farmers in Japan are over 65 years old [3].The expected outcomes of this project are as follows: to facilitate the irrigation system by installing and designing an automatic system to increase crop performance, and to reduce overwatering a saturated soil. This system will also prevent irrigation happening at the wrong time by switching the engine ON or OFF by utilizing the irrigation system data. The system controller will be responsible for switching the engine ON or OFF depending on what is needed. This process is all automated and does not need any human interaction, which is the contribution of this project. This will help reduce human errors and preserve resources from waste. The rest of the paper is structured as follows. In Section 2, we present the literature review. In Section 3, we discuss the research objectives followed by design and implementation of the system. In the last section we present the results of implementing this system.

II. LITERATURE REVIEW

Several studies that address irrigation issues are found in literature, as follows:

1) Automated irrigation system using solar power in Bangladesh. This study was applied in the rice field in Bangladesh. The primary goal of this gadget is to balance out the level of water in agricultural fields to avoid losing the merchandise due to floods. The sensor sends a message from the field to an operator mentioning the level of water within the area and mentions whether it is expected to increase or decreases. The operator, then, controls the pump to regulate the water level accordingly [4].

2) Design and implementation of an Automatic irrigation system in Nigeria. The basic idea is to rely on the type of soil and the amount of water needed by each one. This process is carried out by measuring the level of moisture in each type and using the pump to supply water. The result indicates that sandy soil requires less water than clay soil [5].

3) Automated Irrigation System based on GSM for use of resource and crop planning in India. This device is placed on agricultural lands and works by using Bluetooth or GSM signal. The goal of this device is to monitor the humidity and temperature in the agricultural land in addition to monitoring the state of the climate through the weather temperature, humidity, and dew drops. It, then, sends a text message to the user's machine [6].

III. RESEARCH OBJECTIVES

The main objective of this project is to develop an automated system that solves problems related to irrigation and agriculture, such as controlling and saving resources (water mainly), increasing the agricultural production using small quantities of water, minimizing manual interventions in watering operations while increasing the watering speed, and preserving plants from fungi. All these features make the automated system a sustainable option to be considered to improve the agriculture and irrigation efficiency. The goal of this study is to discover the excellent automation technique for irrigation system automatically controlled through software in a way that allows the user to monitor all information and manage the device immediately from a mobile device. The objectives to consider are: Simplify the irrigation system by installing and designing the whole irrigation system, Optimize the water consumption, Fully automate the system, Decrease the cost of operation, and Make the system user-friendly. The system method includes the implementation of a prototype device that works robotically and is controlled through a mobile application. Reading the related works and drawing the timeline of the project constitutes step one of this project. After looking into the benefits and drawbacks of the previous studies on the matter, the implementation starts with the layout and the automation method for the executable. To implement this project, we start by describing the idea. Next, we identify the objects of this project, such as why this project is important, and what is the exact object of this project. The second step is to read related studies to know if there is such idea and how they implemented in different way. Then, comes the choice of materials; this step takes more time because the materials should be of certain specification. Following that, we started building a small version of the project to try the scenario and test materials. We write the code of each item and then combine all codes together. Next, we build the prototype and test the code, followed by the implementation of a mobile application for the system. The main idea of building a mobile application was to be able to control the system remotely. The last step is to review and test.

IV. DESIGN AND IMPLEMENTATION

To achieve the exact project objectives, using Arduino as the operating system seems to be the best choice as it contains a number of open supply hardware and software as well as it is cheap and available in our country. Choice of materials: The first step of this process of building the prototype of the automated irrigation system was the choice of materials. Field Control System: This step depends on the working of different sensors used in this project which are (moisture, temperature, light, and rain). First of all, we choose an open source operating system which is Arduino. Then, we programmed every sensor separately. We started with the moisture sensor, and so on, and then combined all nine sensors, including the rain, temperature, light and flow meter sensors. We included in our code pump and valve and tested. Project Preparation: For the purpose of building the structure of this project, two tables were used to make parts more stable. However, to create a perfect structure, the size was measured for each part that will be used in the project later on: the types of sensors based on the environment that they will work on, two 12 volt batteries, a small plastic tank, an LCD screen for monitoring, the different type of connecting wires, and controller (Arduino type AT mega 328V). Mechanical Design: In the beginning, a sketch design for the project was made, then the measurements were taken. Two wood tables (1.6-meter x 1.6 meter) have been chosen as a base and stand for this project. The first step of designing the system was to draw the sketch of the system to know the exact materials and measurements needed.

A. Design Process

As shown in Figures 1 and 2, three pieces of foam were used for the area below the grass mat and the area where all wires, flowmeter, and valves are located. The size of the grass mat was cut to make nine holes to set the plastic plates. A special cutter was used to cut the grass into nine equal squares. The plastic water tank was chosen in a way that it is large in size, but light in weight. Moreover, nine moisture sensors, one temperature sensor, four solenoid valves, one water pump, one breadboard, two (12 volts' batteries), wires and an LCD screen are the main parts that were used to implement this project. There were difficulties in choosing the type of pipes for this project since it should be easy to connect as well as easy in the cutting process. Thus, two types of connection joints (T-joint and L–joint) were needed to simplify the installation process. The Arduino controller has been chosen as the processor since it is an open source, simple program that combines three models at once, which are: a digital input, an analog input, and a processor. Every sensor and tool have been tested individually before being connected to a large-scale project, as shown in Figures 1 and 2. Tests were run for every part of the system to make sure it works as expected.

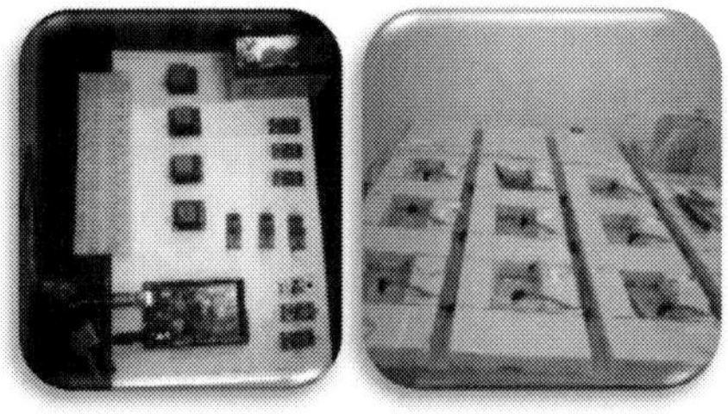

Figure 1. Control Tools and Wiring

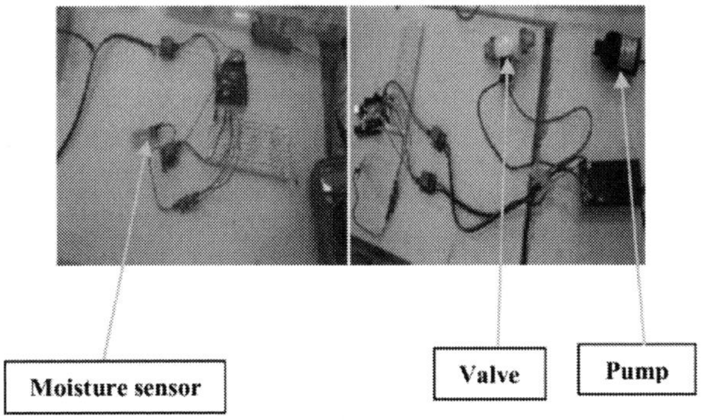

Figure 2. Valve Testing and Connection

Figure 3. Whole system

The last step was to assemble all parts together to finalize the project construction, as shown in Figure 3. The last step in the coding process was to gather all codes in one single program and run it in a large-scale project to make sure that everything is working perfectly. Figure 4 showcases the circuit design of the whole system with the wiring.

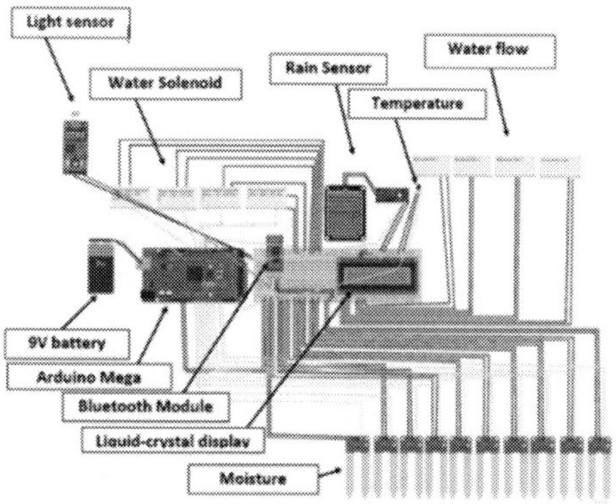

Figure 4. Circuit design

B. Sequence scenario of the system

As shown in Figure 3, the project was divided into 3 fields, namely: field A, field B, and field C. Each field will have one valve and one flow meter sensor in order to measure and monitor the amount of consumed water in each field. Field A has valve_1 and flow meter 1, field B has valve_2 and flow meter_2, field C has valve_3 and flow meter_3 in addition to valve_4 with flow meter that will be located near the tank in order to measure and monitor the total amount of consumed water. As it shows in the flow chart (Figure 5), if two or more moisture sensors are active, the system will automatically work. In addition, the temperature sensor and the light sensor work together. For example, when the temperature is more than 40°C and the light sensor is active, then the system will be switched OFF because the heat of the sun works to evaporate the water. This system was configured to stop the process and schedule it. Moreover, the purpose behind such a system is to work in a smart way; therefore, if it rains, the system will automatically be OFF. One should keep in mind that the main water tank will be monitored carefully so that it does not go below the level where the pump cannot suck the water. The system will not work if the water level is low.

C. Implementation

Figure 5 presents the start of the process where two or three moisture sensors of field B must be activated to move to the next step. Next, the rain sensor must be dry to continue the process and the weather temperature sensors should not exceed 40°C to enable the process to move to the next step. If the water tank level is not low, the pump will run, valve_2 and 4 will open and the flow meter_2 and 4 will have the same reading. If two or three moisture sensors of all fields (A, B, C) are active at the same time and the rain sensor is dry while the temperature sensor remains under 40°C and the light sensor is not active, then the system proceeds to the next step. Also, if the water level sensor is not below the threshold, then the pump will be ON and valves_1, 2, 3 and 4 will open and the flow meter (1,2,3, 4) will have the same readings.

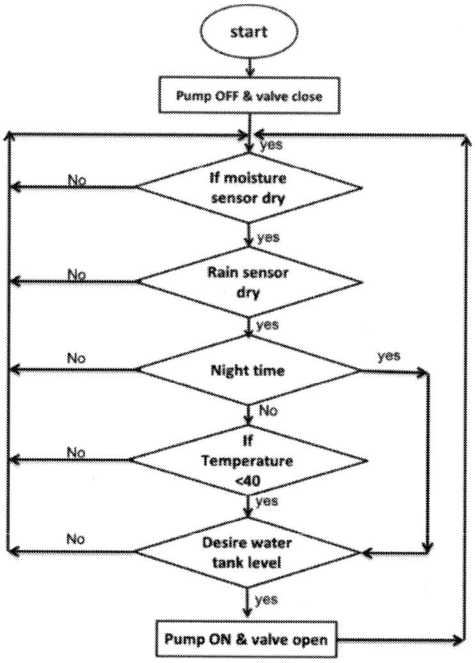

Figure 5. Flow chart of implementation process

D. Mobile Application

Figure 6 presents the application process of the mobile application. It starts with the app installation on a phone and opening it. First of all, the main screen (Figure 7) of the app will be loaded when the user will choose the device to be connected to Bluetooth. The system will check whether or not the device is connected and notify the user in either case. On the main screen, the user can directly switch ON /OFF the entire system. Moreover, if the "Details Button" is pressed, it will load the details screen (Figure 7). In this screen, the user will be able to see all details related to the whole system. For instance, if he pressed on the "plant 1 button", he will be able to see the amount of water, the soil moisture, and the temperature. Further, if a problem occurs in this line, the user has the option to switch it ON /OFF. The app inventor is an open source tool provided by Google. This program allows beginners to create programs that can run under Android. It uses a graphical user interface such as Scratch [8].

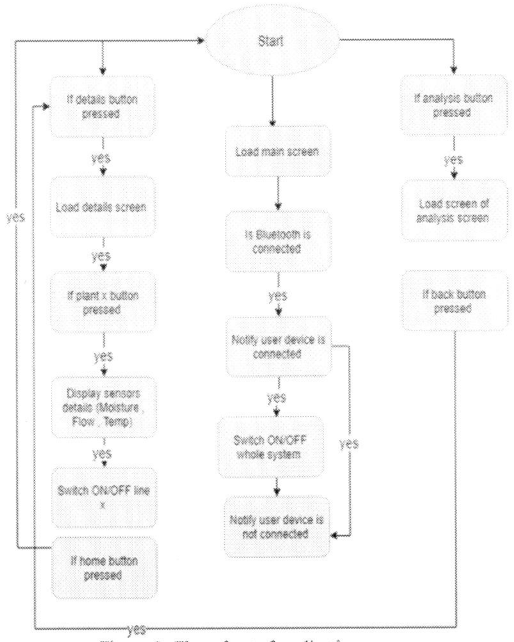

Figure 6. Flow chart of application process

In Figure 7:

1- If "Button 1"is pressed, it send the user to About Page, which provides app information.

2- If "Button 2" is pressed, the user gets directed to the Help Page.

3- When the List Picker is clicked, it shows a list of all connected Bluetooth devices When a Bluetooth device is clicked.

4- Regarding the connection, if the device is connected, the text colour changes to green for feedback and writes 'Connected'.

5- The "ON /OFF buttons" allow the user to switch on or off the system.

6- When the "Details button "is pressed, it takes the end user to a details page that shows all the information and let user control the system line by line.

7- When the "List Picker" is pressed, it shows a list of all connected Bluetooth devices.

8- The two labels show the temperature and amount of water going from tank flow 4 is the main one.

9- The "Plant" button shows the user a list of details about a plant, such as name of the plant, humidity and amount of water.

10- The three labels are not visible unless the user clicks on the plant button.

11- The "Responsive" button takes the user to the Home page.

12- The "ON/OFF" button in each line allows a user to switch on or off each line individually.

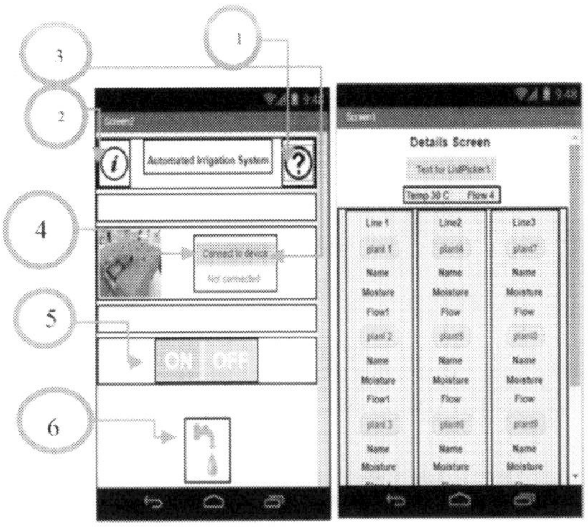

Figure 7. App Screenshot

V. RESULTS

The process of manual irrigation involving one user to control the irrigation process has been done in real world environment for three types of plants (lemon, mint, and mango) for one month and the results were recorded. The irrigation process takes place twice a week in the morning and the remaining days in the evening because the manual irrigation process is usually done at that time. For data analysis purposes, data of a chosen plant twice a day, once between 9 am - 5 pm and the second one between 6 pm-11pm, was taken. The line graph in Figure 8 depicts the humidity data of the mint. The y-axis represents the humidity rate while the x-axis represents the day and time. We notice that Sunday and Wednesday have the largest humidity rate, which is 900-800. When the humidity is more than 800, it means that the plant is dry and needs to be irrigated. The humidity rate decreases on Monday evening and Thursday morning and reaches 200-120. This means that the plant is not dry and does not need watering. From this data, we can say that the mint gradually dries up and it retains water more than other plants.

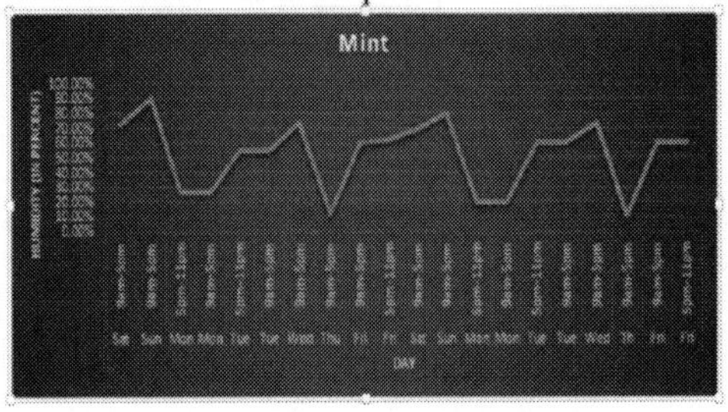

Figure 8. Humidity data of mint

The line graph in Figure 9 presents the humidity data of the lemon plant. The y-axis shows the humidity rate while the x-axis shows the day and time. Sunday and Wednesday have the largest humidity rate (1000); which means that the plant is very dry and needs to be irrigated as soon as possible. On Monday and Thursday, the humidity decreased; however, it is noticed from the graph and the data that the lemon needs to be irrigated more than twice a week because it loses water fast. Therefore, we conclude that lemon needs water more than mint.

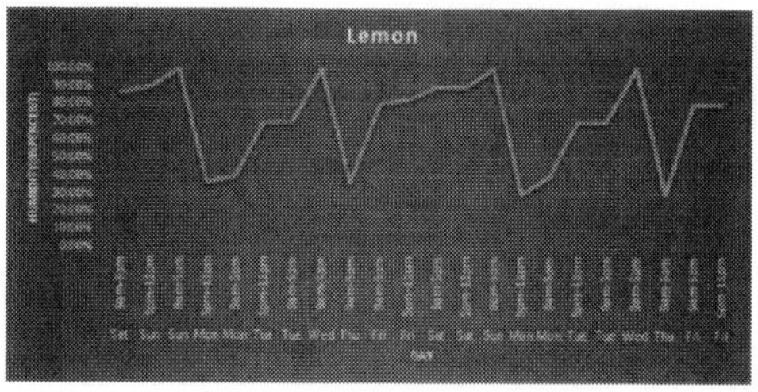

Figure 9. Humidity data of lemon

The line graph in Figure 10 shows the humidity data of the mango plant. Sunday, Thursday, and Saturday have the largest humidity rate; this means that the plant is very dry. We also notice a rapid decrease and a rapid increase in the amount of moisture; this means that mango loses water very fast and needs to be irrigated more than twice a week.

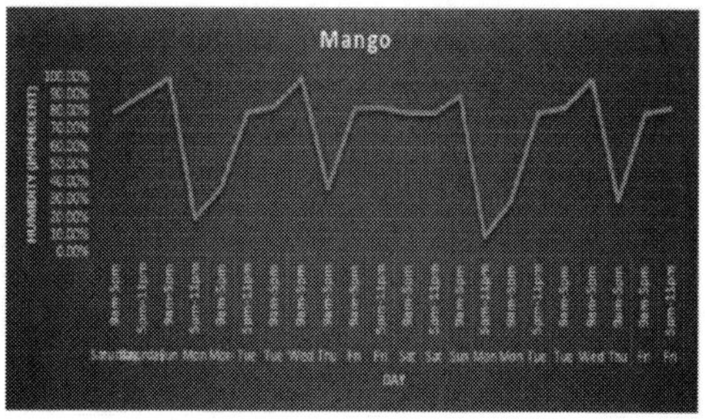

Figure 10. Humidity data of mango

Based on the data above, we observe the following in Figure 11. All the plants were watered at one time and in equal quantities almost twice a week, but after comparing the results, we found that the lemon and mango needed to be watered more than twice a week because the humidity ratio is significantly reduced (taking into account the temperature and the time of irrigation). When they are irrigated in the morning, the plants lose humidity quickly and very significantly because the irrigation is at the wrong time; the sun evaporates the water much faster. As for the mint plant, through the results, we found that this plant does not lose moisture quickly as it can withstand a longer period compared to the mango and the lemon. Hence, we conclude that using an automatic irrigation system is much more efficient because it solves almost all the problems of using a manual system. The automatic irrigation system works based on the needs of plants, so it solves the problem of irrigation at the wrong time by using light and temperature sensors together.

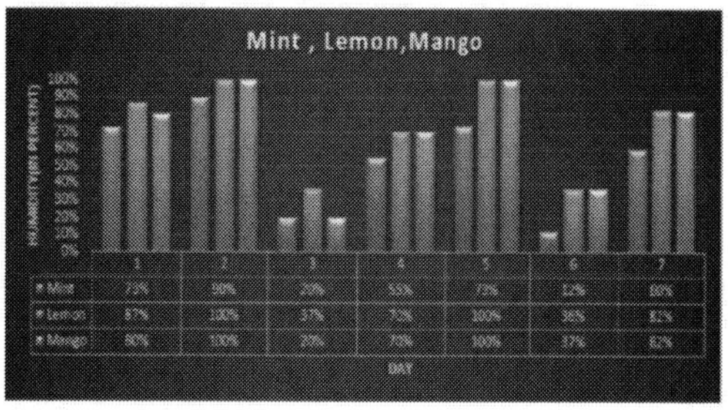

Figure 11. Humidity data of all plants

In Figure 12, the result of the flow meter sensor is presented. As shown in Figure 12, the amount of water using manual irrigation system is equal for all plants and administered at the same time. Because all plants do not need the same amount of water, using a moisture sensor connected to a flow meter gives better results.

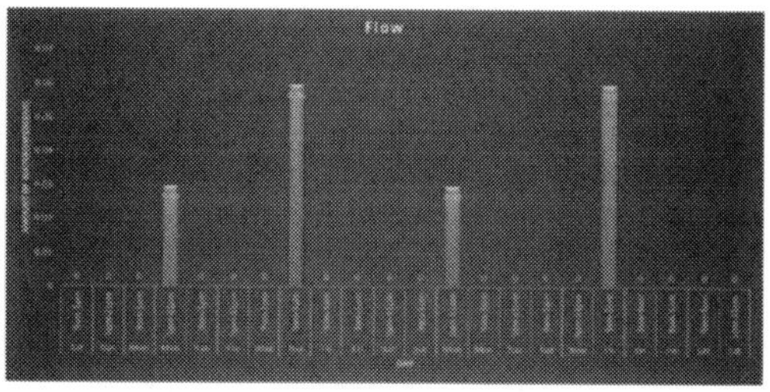

Figure 12. Flow meter data

VI. Discussion

After we completed the project and all the requirements were implemented, in order to finish this smart irrigation, system testing was the next step. In fact, the system will not work until two or three of the moisture sensors from any line of the 3 fields sends a signal to the Arduino that the soil is dry and the crop needs water. After the signal reaches the Arduino, it will send a command to the relay of that specific line field valve to be energized to open the valve and a command to the relay of the pump to exchange it directly to irrigate that field. Moreover, all 3 fields can be irrigated at the same time if a minimum of 2 of all 3 plants moisture sensors are activated. Thus, all solenoid valve relays may be energized to open all valves and the pump runs to irrigate all 3 plants. There has been a problem at the beginning to choose a suitable pump to irrigate all plants at the same time. The program of the system has been configured and the system will no longer operate unless two or three moisture sensors are activated. But, if one sensor is activated of any line, the system will no longer perform because that sensor can also be defective. If the water tank level is low, the system will not operate even if all plant sensors are activated to protect the water pump. Furthermore, this smart irrigation system has been configured in a way that, if it rains, it will not work. This is because the rain sensor will be activated and will send a signal to Arduino to stop the water pump and to close all valves as well. Further, during daytime, the system will no longer work due to the mild sensor that will be activated and that will close the plant's valve as well as switch OFF the pump. Concerning the system programming, it has been precisely chosen, as stated in the previous sections, to apply UNO Arduino. The wire connections from the controllers to the Arduino have been difficult to implement, as a single mistake can damage any electric element. It was not easy to program the smart irrigation system and upload it in Arduino to run the water pump and starting valves with eighteen sensors, but with the assistance of Arduino library, this system was completed. Connecting the wires can become complicated, but by using the plastic breadboard, it became easier to connect the wires. For designing the plant, special flexible pipes were used to facilitate the connection from the water tank to the plant. However, we faced the problem of connecting the pipes together. So, two types of pipe joints (T-joint and L-joint) were used to solve this issue.

VII. Conclusion

With this project, we achieved successful results. The purpose of the smart irrigation system for large or small scale is to make it the process more effective. Different sensors (soil moisture, light, temperature, level, rain, flow) together with other devices (water pump, battery, LCD screen, solenoid valve) have been used in this project. Using Arduino proved profitable, as it is able to serve a number of different sensors of various types and sizes. Arduino boards are other devices. Furthermore, two wood tables and three sheets of foam have been used in the project. Several design criteria have used in this system. The sensors used were suitable for detecting and sending signals to Arduino, to control the water pump and to open the solenoid valve. The system was tasted in indoor conditions similar to the ones on the farm. The purpose of the screen monitor is to show the flow for each line, which shows if there is any passing of water in pipes. Also, if it is raining, the system will not work in order to save the water. The mobile application is to control the system remotely. It allows a user to monitor the whole system and, if there is any problem or passing of water, the user can switch off the system through this application. Finally, results analysis proves that the proposed automated irrigation system is able to control and monitor three types of plants. We found that the mint plant consumes the least resources. Following what has been done for this project, in the future works, we intend to transfer the system to a larger scale. Furthermore, controlling the system via Zig Bee instead of using wire connections could be a great addition. Moreover, creating a more responsive mobile application would provide more controlled data. We can also think of developing this system by using renewable energy, which is solar power instead of batteries using solar energy, in an effort to help reduce future costs.

References

[1] FAO, "The Future of Food and Agriculture –Trends and Challenges" [online] Available at: http://www.fao.org/3/a-i6583e.pdf [Accessed: Sep. 2018].

[2] OECD, "Modern Irrigation Technologies." [online] Available at: https://www.oecd.org/env/outreach/KG_study_irrigation.pdf [Accessed: Sep. 2018].

[3] T. Clint, "Japan's Agriculture Dilemma", 2018 [online] Available at: https://thediplomat.com/2014/09/japans-agriculture-dilemma/ [Accesed Sep. 2018]

[4] J. Moller, "Computer Vision - A Versatile Technology in Automation of Agriculture Machinery", 2010. [online] https://pdfs.semanticscholar.org/2b94/d72a5088af674743caefe9fe04078db133ca.pdf [Accessed Sep., 208]

[5] Anon, International Journal of Science and Research (IJSR), 2017 [online] Available at: https://pdfs.semanticscholar.org/e560/202dd4acba3429bc64deb811e67f20d6abbc.

[6] Jee.ro, 2017 [online] Available at: http://www.jee.ro/covers/art.php?issue=WK1446219610W56338f5a49ec9

[7] Iosrjournals.org, 2017 [online] Available at: http://www.iosrjournals.org/iosr-jmce/papers/vol11-issue4/Version-1/I011414955.pdf

[8] Appinventor.mit.edu. About our new MIT App Inventor logo | Explore MIT App Inventor, 2018 [online] Available at: http://appinventor.mit.edu/explore/blogs/karen/2017/08/about.html [Accessed: May, 2018].

*papageno*PCB: An Automated Printed Circuit Board Generation Approach for Embedded Systems Prototyping

Tobias Scheipel and Marcel Baunach

Institute of Technical Informatics
Graz University of Technology
Graz, Austria
E-mail: {tobias.scheipel, baunach}@tugraz.at

Abstract—**Designing an embedded system from scratch is becoming increasingly challenging these days. In fact, the design process requires extensive manpower, comprising engineers with different fields of expertise. While most design principles for embedded systems start with a search for a suitable computing platform and the design of proper hardware to meet certain requirements, our novel vision involves using a completely different approach: The remainder of the embedded system can be automatically generated if the application software is available. In order to achieve automatic Printed Circuit Board (PCB) generation, we describe an approach, *papageno*PCB, in this paper, which is a part of a holistic approach called *papageno*X. *papageno*PCB provides a way to automatically generate schematics and layouts for printed circuit boards using an intermediate system description language. Therefore, the scope of the present work was to develop a concept, which could be used to analyze the embedded software and automatically generate the schematics and board layouts based on predefined hardware modules and connection interfaces. To be able to edit the plans once they have been generated, a file format for common electronic design automation applications, based on Extensible Markup Language (XML), was used to provide the final output.**

***Keywords*–embedded systems; printed circuit board; design automation; hardware/software codesign; systems engineering.**

I. INTRODUCTION

Embedded systems are relevant in almost every part of our society. From the simple electronics in dishwashers to the highly complex electronic control units in modern and autonomous cars – today, daily life is nearly inconceivable without those systems. As the technology improves, the complexity of embedded systems inevitably and steadily increases. A whole team of engineers usually plans, designs, and implements a novel system in several iteration steps. An example of such a process in the automotive industry is shown in Figure 1.

Designing an embedded system can be prone to errors due to a multitude of possible sources of such errors. This presents one major challenge when designing such a system: The challenge of how to eliminate error sources and make design processes more reliable and, therefore, cheaper. Nowadays, most design paradigms choose a bottom-up approach. This means that a suitable computing platform is chosen after defining all requirements with respect to these explicit requirements, prior experience, or educated guesses. Then, software development can either start based on an application kit of a computing platform, or some prototyping hardware must be built beforehand. If the requirements change during the development process, major problems could possibly arise,

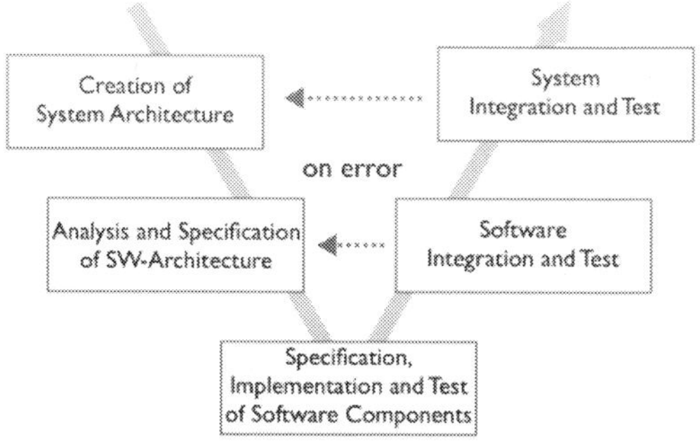

Figure 1. Automotive design process according to the V-Model [1].

e.g., new software features cannot be implemented due to computing power restrictions or additional devices cannot be interfaced because of hardware limitations. Another problem could arise if connection interfaces or buses become overloaded with too much communication traffic after the hardware has already been manufactured.

To tackle these problems, we propose a holistic approach, *papageno*X, and a sub-approach, *papageno*PCB, which are discussed in detail in the following sections. *papageno*X is a novel approach that has been developed for use while creating embedded systems with a top-down view. Therefore, it uses application source code to automatically generate the whole embedded system in hardware and software. One part of the concept behind this approach is *papageno*PCB. This concept handles the automatic generation of schematics and board layouts for printed circuit board design with standardized XML-based [2] output from intermediate system description models. To do so, a module-based description of the system hardware and software needs to be made. Furthermore, connections between the hardware modules on wire level are done automatically. The concept and its related challenges were the main topics of the work described in this paper, whereas software analysis and model generation is part of work that will be conducted in the future with *papageno*X.

The paper is organized as follows: Section II includes a summary of related work. The rough idea of the holistic vision of *papageno*X (this paper includes a detailed description of the first part of this concept) is illustrated in Section III, whereas Section IV starts with the system description format within *papageno*PCB. In Section V, an explanation is given of the necessary steps taken to create the final output, and Section VI includes a proof of concept example. The results of an analysis on the scalability and performance of the developed generator are presented in Section VII. The paper concludes with Section VIII, in which the steps that need to be taken to achieve a final version of *papageno*X are described.

II. Related Work

As this work dealt with the automatic generation of hardware and extensively utilized hardware definition models, it was influenced by existing solutions such as devicetree, which is used, e.g., within Linux [3]. The devicetree data structure is used by the target Operating System's (OS) kernel to handle hardware components. The handled components can comprise processors and memories, but also the internal or external buses and peripherals of the system. As the data structure is a description of the overall system, it must be created manually and cannot be generated in a modular way. It is mostly used with System-on-Chips (SoCs) and enables the usage of one compiled OS kernel with several hardware configurations. Different approaches have been taken to use annotated source code to extract information about the underlying system. Annotations can be used to analyze the worst-case execution times [4][5] of software in embedded systems. Other approaches that have been taken have used back-annotations to optimize the power consumption simulation [6]. These annotations have allowed researchers to gain a better idea of how the system works in a real-world application, meaning that the annotated information is based on estimations or measurements. As far as the automatic generation of schematics and board layouts is concerned, few solutions have been developed towards design automation. Some authors have dealt with the question of how to generate schematics using expert systems so their appearance is more pleasing to human readers [7]. Some work has even been carried out on the generation of circuit schematics by extracting connectivity data from net lists [8]. These approaches are all based on various kinds of network information and cannot be used to extract system data out of – or are even aware of – application source code or system descriptions.

All the approaches mentioned above have some advantages and inspired this work, as no solution has yet been proposed for how to automatically generate PCBs from source code.

III. Main Idea of *papageno*X

*papageno*X stands for **P**rototyping **AP**plication-based with **A**utomatic **GEN**eration **O**f **X**; it prospectively contains a toolchain that can be used to automatically generate the software, reconfigurable logic, and hardware of the final prototype of system X by simply using application software source code. In this context, system X could be an automotive Electronic Control Unit (ECU), a Cyber-Physical System (CPS), or an Internet-of-Things (IoT) device. After generating X, *papageno*X should also be able to check whether a new application version is still compatible with previously designed systems, or if it is not, which restrictions apply.

As depicted in Figure 2, *papageno*X uses Application Software (ASW) to generate software code that includes Basic Software (BSW) and an executable ASW, reconfigurable logic code in some hardware description language for Field Programmable Gate Arrays (FPGAs), as well as schematics

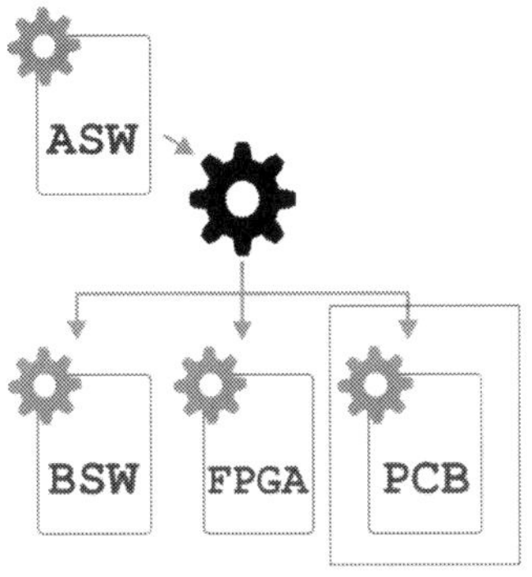

Figure 2. The main idea behind the *papageno*X approach.

and layouts for PCBs. In this context, the term BSW subsumes operating systems with, e.g., drivers, services. Even though the *papageno*X approach envisions generation of reconfigurable logic, it differs from, e.g., SystemC [9], because it also generates hardware on the PCB level.

In this paper, the very first step taken to generate a PCB from an intermediate system model (prospectively extracted from source code) is described.

IV. System Description Format

The system description format in *papageno*PCB is module-based. This means that every possible module, e.g., a Microcontroller Unit (MCU) board or different peripherals must be defined before they are connected with each other. The whole description and modeling approach taken is generic, which enables its easy adaptation to different use cases. The structure was defined according to a JavaScript Object Notation (JSON) [10] format, and three different kinds of definition files were established:

A. Module Definition: One single file that defines the hardware module, its interfaces and its pins, and a second file that contains the design block for creating schematics and board layouts concerning this module.
B. Interface Definition: Generic definition of several different interfaces between modules.
C. System Definition: Contains modules and connections between these; is abstractly wired with certain interface types.

All three types will be explained below. The example modules show footprints of a Texas Instruments (TI) LaunchPad™ [11] with a 16-bit, ultra-low-power MSP430F5529 MCU [12].

A. Module Definitions and Design Blocks

The module definition of a TI LaunchPad™ is shown in Figure 3. Apart from a name and a design block file property, this definition consists of an array of interfaces and pins. The design block file property refers to an EAGLE [13] design block file, comprising of a schematic placeholder (cf. Figure 4), and a board layout placeholder (cf. Figure 5). These placeholders will later be placed on the output schematics and board layouts. The array of interfaces may contain several different interface types of which the module is capable. The property *type* determines the corresponding interface type. In the case presented, two Serial Peripheral Interfaces (SPIs) are present. Both contain a name, the type *SPI*, and several pins.

```
1  {
2    name: "MSP430F5529_LaunchPad",
3    design: "MSP430F5529_LaunchPad.dbl",
4    interfaces: [{
5      name: "SPI0",
6      type: "SPI",
7      pins: { MISO: "P3.1", MOSI: "P3.0",
8        SCLK: "P3.2", CS: 'any@["P2.0", "P2.2"]' }
9    }, {
10     name: "SPI1",
11     type: "SPI",
12     pins: { MISO: "P4.5", MOSI: "P4.4",
13       SCLK: "P4.0", CS: any }
14   }
15   ],
16   pins: ["P6.5", "P3.4", "P3.3", "P1.6",
17   "P6.6", "P3.2", "P2.7", "P4.2", "P4.1",
18   "P6.0", "P6.1", "P6.2", "P6.3", "P6.4",
19   "P7.0", "P3.6", "P3.5", "P2.5", "P2.4",
20   "P1.5", "P1.4", "P1.3", "P1.2", "P4.3",
21   "P4.0", "P3.7", "P8.2", "P2.0", "P2.2",
22   "P7.4", "RST" , "P3.0", "P3.1", "P2.6",
23   "P2.3", "P8.1"]
24 }
```

Figure 3. Module definition of a TI LaunchPad™with two SPI interfaces.

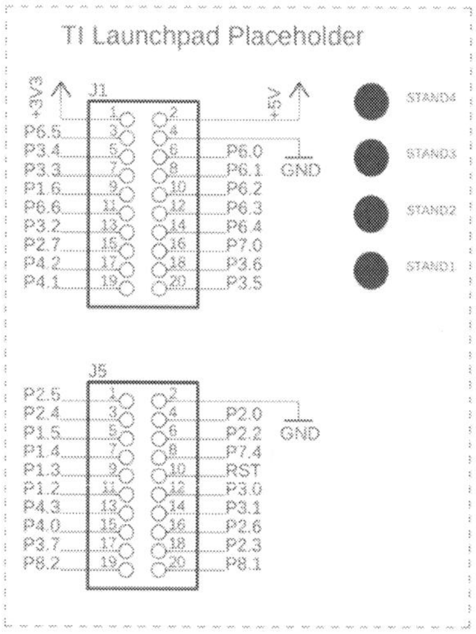

Figure 4. Schematics of a placeholder design block for a TI LaunchPad™ [11].

Pins within interfaces can either be directly assigned to hardware pins (e.g., `MISO: "P3.1"` in line 7) or left for automatic assignment (e.g., `CS: any` in line 13). It is also possible to automatically assign a wire from a dedicated pool by using `any@somearray` (cf. line 8) syntax. Each module definition file is associated with its corresponding design block. It is of utmost importance that pin names are coherent in both module representations, as coherence of naming later ensures that proper interconnections are made between modules. Furthermore, a standard format for power supply connections must be used to avoid creating discrepancies between modules. The bus speed of the SPI was not taken into account in this work and will be addressed in future developments. As depicted in Figure 5, the board layout of a module only consists of its pins. The main idea here was to create a motherboard upon which modules can be placed using their exterior connections (e.g., pin headers or similar connectors). Therefore, the placeholder serves as interface layout between fully assembled PCB modules, such as the LaunchPad™, and can then be connected to other modules through interfaces.

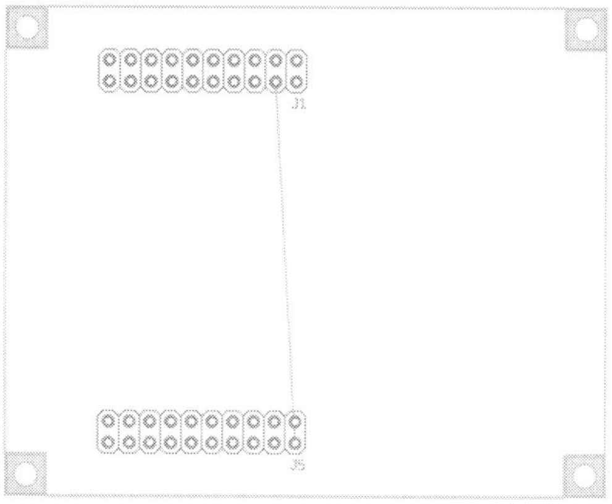

Figure 5. Board layout of a placeholder design block for a TI LaunchPad™ [11].

```
1  {
2    interfaces: [
3      {
4        type: "SPI",
5        connections: [
6          { "master.MOSI" : "bus.MOSI" },
7          { "master.MISO" : "bus.MISO" },
8          { "master.SCLK" : "bus.SCLK" },
9          { "slave.MOSI"  : "bus.MOSI" },
10         { "slave.MISO"  : "bus.MISO" },
11         { "slave.SCLK"  : "bus.SCLK" },
12         { "master.CS"   : "wiremultiple" },
13         { "slave.CS"    : "wiresingle" }
14       ]
15     }
16   ]
17 }
```

Figure 6. Interface definition containing SPI.

B. Interface Definitions

After defining the modules, the generic interfaces must be defined. The interface definition collection is centralized in a single file, and its structure is shown in Figure 6. In this example, only SPI [14] has been defined with its standard connections. As the format is generic, other interface types, e.g., Inter-Integrated Circuit (I^2C, [15]) or even a Controller Area Network (CAN, [16]), are also feasible. It also shows how masters and slaves within this communication protocol are connected to the bus wires. As the SPI also has so-called Chip Select (CS) wires for every slave selection, special treatment must be used here: A slave only has one CS wire, which is marked with *wiresingle* (cf. line 13), whereas a master has as many CS wires as it has slaves connected to it (marked with *wiremultiple*; cf. line 12).

C. System Definition

The final step taken was to define the system itself, which was built from modules and the connections between them. To do so, a single project file must be created, as illustrated in Figure 7. Initially, all necessary modules are imported and named accordingly within the *modules* array. Once defined, they can be interconnected using the previously defined interface definitions. In our example, LaunchPad™ *MSP1* was connected to a microSD board *SD1* of type "MicroSD Breakout Board" [17] via SPI. This particular SPI connection is called *SPI_Connection1* of type *SPI* and has two participants with different roles: *MSP1* as a master and *SD1* as a slave. This system definition will prospectively be generated and extracted

```
{
  modules: [
    { name: "MSP1",
      type: "MSP430F5529_LaunchPad"},
    { name: "SD1",
      type: "MicroSD_BreakoutBoard"}
  ],
  connections: [
    {
      name: "SPI_Connection1",
      type: "SPI",
      participants: [
        { name: "MSP1", role: "master" },
        { name: "SD1", role: "slave" }
      ]
    }
  ]
}
```

Figure 7. A system model containing two modules connected via SPI.

out of the ASW code by *papageno*X. The *papageno*PCB approach is taken to generate PCBs only.

V. Implementation of PCB Generation

After having defined the modules, interfaces, and implemented a system definition, PCB generation can start. The generation consists of two major steps: *(A.)* establishing connection wires based on predefined module and system definitions, and assigning dedicated pins and *(B.)* generating XML-based schematic files from its output. The final step *(C.)*, which is carried out to deal with the final layout of the schematics, must be done (in part manually) afterwards. The generator is developed as a Java command line application to maintain platform-independence and ensure that it can be integrated into standard tool chains and build management tools.

A. Connection Establishment and Pin Assignment

During this first step, JSON data structure analysis presents the main challenge. The whole system must be interconnected appropriately using the previously explained definition files. To do so, all connections within the system definition must be matched at the beginning of the process. This task subsumes the discovery of connections between modules, their mapping to certain interface types, and the final wire allocation required to interconnect all participants. Specifically, each connection has a type and a finite number of participants with different roles, interfaces, and pins. These pins must then be connected to the newly introduced wires, belonging to the communication. Several different types of wires can be used to connect the participants with each other:

The easiest wires to use are common wires, which can be assigned to a pool of free pins of the module. These wires are marked with *wiresingle* within the interface definition. Due to the fact that all unused General-Purpose Input/Output (GPIO) pins of a module can be used for this purpose, they need to be assigned last.

Furthermore, every participant can connect itself directly to bus wires via its dedicated pins, depending on, e.g., the type of MCU used. In the case of an MSP430 MCU, certain pins are electrically connected to an interface circuit, as defined in its module definition (cf. Figure 3). These pins must, therefore, be matched with the connection's wires (cf. Figure 6). The interface definition must match roles and pins accordingly to correctly interconnect the participants of each connection.

Another type of wires that can be used are multiple wires. If we take SPI as an example, the master needs to have as many chip-select wires as slaves with which it wants to communicate. Therefore, this type of wire – marked with *wiremultiple*, as previously defined – must clone itself to obtain the number of wires needed.

These different types of wires must be connected to the pins of the modules to establish a proper connection or *net* according to the interface definition. The interconnected modules with their nets form a holistic JSON-based description of the system.

B. Schematic and Board Layout Generation

Utilizing the interconnected system description, schematics and board layouts can be generated. In our case, EAGLE's XML data structure [2] was used to form a dedicated output file for schematics and board layouts. To generate those plans, (1) design blocks for each module must be loaded, (2) the previously found connections must be applied and (3) the connected design blocks must be placed on an empty schematic plan or board layout.

(1) In this step, each module has to be instantiated by loading the corresponding design block of its type.
(2) This step must carried out to form the whole system according to the JSON-based holistic description. Therefore, pins of each module must be assigned to the wires of a connection within the system. To do so, each connection again must be applied separately to each participant. As the system description already contains information, as to which pin of a module must be connected to which wire, this can be done quite easily.
(3) This step, which is the computationally most expensive step, must be carried out to merge the connected instances of each module into an empty plan, as a great deal of XML parsing is required here. To create consistent plans, the design blocks must be prepared well beforehand to avoid, e.g., inconsistencies within board layers or signal names. To keep the modules from overlapping, a two-dimensional translation of each module must be executed as part of each merge procedure as well. In total, two merging steps are required for each module – one for the schematic and one for the board layout. As this approach generates connection PCBs ("motherboards") where one can plug in modules, only placeholders are used.

Finally, the two generated XML structures are exported and saved into different files for further usage.

C. Routing Generated Schematics and Board Layouts

As layouting and routing of PCBs is a non-trivial task, and engineers need a great deal of experience when performing a task like this, *papageno*PCB cannot be used to produce final variants of a board. It is recommended to use EAGLE's auto-routing functionality or manual routing to finalize the already well-prepared layouts.

VI. Proof of Concept

The proof of concept comprises the generation of the system definition as shown in Figure 7. As mentioned before, the system created consists of two modules interconnected with

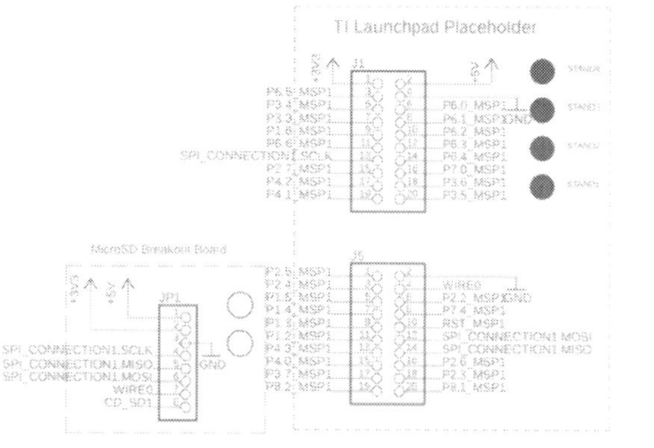

Figure 8. Raw output of the schematics generated as displayed in EAGLE.

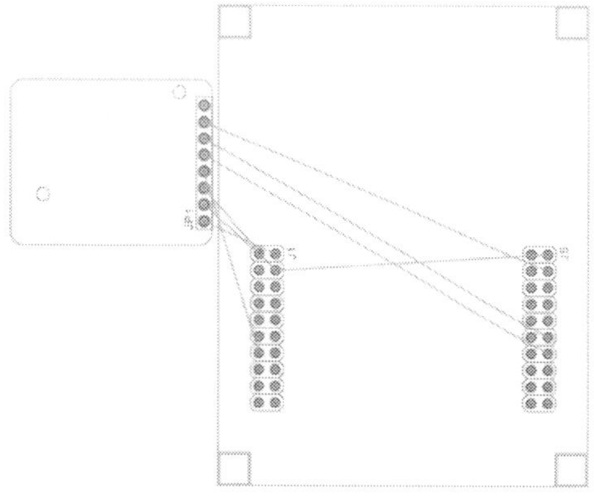

Figure 9. Raw output of the board layout generated as displayed in EAGLE.

one SPI bus, whereas the processor board serves as master. The schematics generation step yields in the drawing depicted in Figure 8.

Compared with the LaunchPad™'s design block shown in Figure 4, one can see the differences in the net names. As examples, *P2.0* has been replaced with *WIRE0*, and *P3.0* is now assigned to *SPI_CONNECTION1.MOSI*. These wires connect to pins 7 and 6 of the MicroSD Breakout Board on the left, respectively. Also, each unconnected pin gets a suffix describing its module (cf. *_MSP1*). These newly introduced net names are the results of the wire generation explained in Section V-A. As the reusability of schematic plans is an important aspect, the feature of non-overlapping module placement can be emphasized as well. The result of the board layout generation step is shown in Figure 9, as described in Section V-B. The fine lines show non-routed connections between the pins. As the plan will be manufactured as a real hardware PCB, no part can overlap. Routing of the board has to be either performed manually or by using a design tool's built-in auto router. A feasible layout variant is presented in Figure 10. EAGLE can also be used to check the correctness of the XML file format.

VII. Scalability and Performance

In this Section, we describe measurements and investigations that concern the performance of the PCB-generating process. All discussed evaluations use one setup as a reference. The application was executed with a Java 10 virtual machine on an Intel Core i7 7500U@2.7GHz with 16 gigabytes of RAM. Table I shows the mean execution time and the combined output XML file size of the generation process of different test case scenarios, which are explained below. All test cases featured a different number of participants (part.) which consisted of masters (M) and slaves (S) with different connection types.

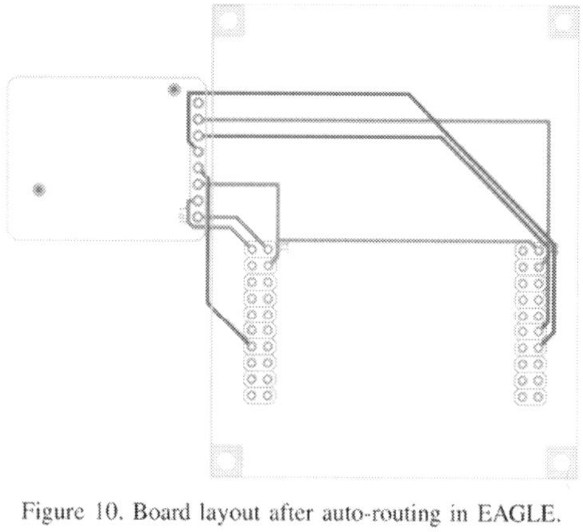

Figure 10. Board layout after auto-routing in EAGLE.

TABLE I. MEAN EXECUTION TIMES FOR DIFFERENT SCENARIOS.

#	*test scenario description*	*execution time*	*file size*
	1 SPI conn. (scenario 1)		
0	2 part. (1 M, 1 S)	678.98 ms	94 KiB
1	3 part. (1 M, 2 S)	793.56 ms	100 KiB
2	4 part. (1 M, 3 S)	893.89 ms	105 KiB
3	5 part. (1 M, 4 S)	983.56 ms	110 KiB
4	6 part. (1 M, 5 S)	1 060.70 ms	116 KiB
5	7 part. (1 M, 6 S)	1 151.37 ms	122 KiB
	2 SPI conn. (scenario 2)		
0	4 part. (1 M and 1 S each)	910.93 ms	115 KiB
1	6 part. (1 M and 2 S each)	1 079.78 ms	126 KiB
2	8 part. (1 M and 3 S each)	1 242.88 ms	137 KiB
3	10 part. (1 M and 4 S each)	1 388.39 ms	149 KiB
4	12 part. (1 M and 5 S each)	1 500.44 ms	160 KiB
5	14 part. (1 M and 6 S each)	1 613.93 ms	171 KiB
	1 I^2C conn. (scenario 3)		
0	2 part. (1 M, 1 S)	693.04 ms	105 KiB
1	3 part. (1 M, 2 S)	813.64 ms	111 KiB
2	4 part. (1 M, 3 S)	918.96 ms	117 KiB
3	5 part. (1 M, 4 S)	1 010.40 ms	123 KiB
4	6 part. (1 M, 5 S)	1 107.56 ms	129 KiB
5	7 part. (1 M, 6 S)	1 198.17 ms	135 KiB
	1 I^2C and 1 SPI conn. (scenario 4)		
0	3 part. (1 M, 1 S each)	828.13 ms	127 KiB
1	5 part. (1 M, 2 S each)	1 020.54 ms	138 KiB
2	7 part. (1 M, 3 S each)	1 195.82 ms	150 KiB
3	9 part. (1 M, 4 S each)	1 337.50 ms	162 KiB
4	11 part. (1 M, 5 S each)	1 493.75 ms	173 KiB
5	13 part. (1 M, 6 S each)	1 612.04 ms	185 KiB

Each test case is based on the example described in Section VI but with different constellations concerning the numbers and types of participants and connections. All test cases were executed 100 times. Four types of test scenarios with six test cases each were conducted: Within the first scenario, just one SPI connection was present, with a varying number of slaves each test case. The second scenario comprised two SPI connections with an increasing number of slaves. Test scenario three had one I^2C connection and was similar to scenario one, whereas scenario four included SPI and I^2C connections to a single master with an increasing number of slaves. The devolution of the mean execution time (in ms) in all test scenarios is shown in Figure 11. When comparing all scenarios, the trend observed is quite similar: All performance graphs show a linear devolution with an additive, logarithmic-

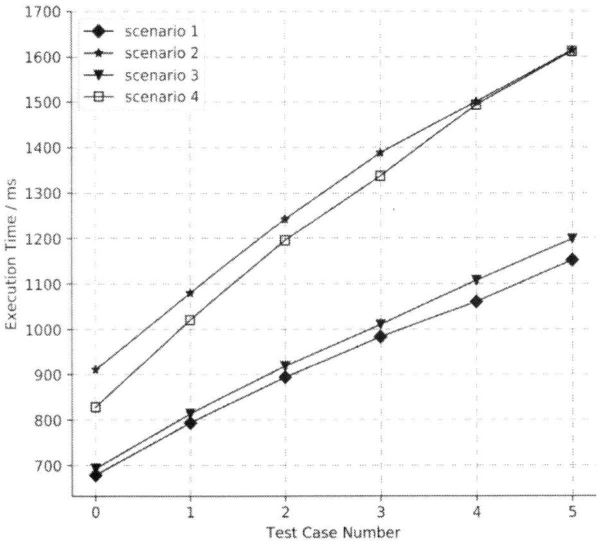

Figure 11. Performance graph for different test cases.

like component. The linear component is due to the linear increase in the complexity of the test cases. The logarithmic-like growth observed can be explained by the decreasing, additive overhead of the linear component when processing similar connection reasoning, as well as the XML schematic and layout data. This is also the reason why doubling the numbers in the first test case yielded in much higher values than in test case two. Test scenario four is the only one that displays a steeper curve. This is due to the combination of different connection types, yielding less-optimal algorithm executions. As XML processing is quite costly, some further optimizations are needed. As the overall file size displayed linear growth, no correlation was observed between file size and execution time.

VIII. Conclusion and Future Work

In conclusion, *papageno*PCB represents a novel, top-down approach that can be taken to develop an embedded system. With just having a model-based system description at hand, it is possible to use *papageno*PCB to generate hardware schematics and board layouts accordingly. This opens up a numerous new possibilities on higher abstraction levels. It is feasible to carry out automatic bus balancing or bandwidth engineering before building the hardware. The use of these concepts requires the availability of in-depth information about the electrical and mechanical characteristics of all parts of a PCB, so that the hardware can be optimized regarding non-functional metrics such as bandwidth or power consumption. Due to the generic design, new models can be integrated easily, and it will be even possible to take a non-module-based approach on the device level (if the proper definitions are available).

In the future, work must be carried out to extract system models from ASW source code. Therefore, we are working on introducing annotations into our operating system environment [18], which will enable us to automatically generate system definition files. These annotations can either be introduced into the code as compiler keywords (e.g., pragmas, defines) or as comments. As some work is already being conducted to improve the automatic portability of real-time operating systems [19], the proposed approach could be used to build a system for which only the application code must be programmed. The rest of the system can then be generated automatically. Even suitable and application-optimized processor architectures [20] could be created by taking this approach. The ultimate goal is to establish *papageno*X as a universal embedded systems generator using only annotated ASW code.

Acknowledgment

This research project was partially funded by AVL List GmbH, the Austrian Federal Ministry of Education, Science and Research (bmbwf), and Graz University of Technology.

References

[1] J. Schäuffele and T. Zurawka, *Automotive Software Engineering*, ser. ATZ/MTZ-Fachbuch. Springer Fachmedien Wiesbaden, 2016.

[2] Autodesk, Inc., *EAGLE XML Data Structure 9.1.0*, 2018.

[3] devicetree.org, *Devicetree Specification*, Dec. 2017, release v0.2.

[4] J. Schnerr, O. Bringmann, A. Viehl, and W. Rosenstiel, "High-performance Timing Simulation of Embedded Software," in *Proc. of the 45th Annual Design Automation Conference*, June 2008, pp. 290–295.

[5] B. Schommer, C. Cullmann, G. Gebhard, X. Leroy, M. Schmidt, and S. Wegener, "Embedded Program Annotations for WCET Analysis," in *WCET 2018: 18th Int'l Workshop on Worst-Case Execution Time Analysis*, Barcelona, Spain, Jul. 2018, pp. 8:1–8:13.

[6] S. Chakravarty, Z. Zhao, and A. Gerstlauer, "Automated, Retargetable Back-annotation for Host Compiled Performance and Power Modeling," in *Int'l Conference on Hardware/Software Codesign and System Synthesis*, Piscataway, NJ, USA, 2013, pp. 1–10.

[7] G. M. Swinkels and L. Hafer, "Schematic generation with an expert system," *IEEE Transactions on Computer-Aided Design of Integrated Circuits and Systems*, vol. 9, no. 12, pp. 1289–1306, Dec 1990.

[8] B. Singh *et al.*, "System and method for circuit schematic generation," US Patent US7917877B2, 2011.

[9] IEEE Standards Association, *IEEE 1666-2011 - IEEE Standard for Standard SystemC Language*, Sep. 2012.

[10] ECMA International, *ECMA-404: The JSON Data Interchange Syntax*, 2nd ed., Dec. 2017.

[11] Texas Instruments, *MSP430F5529 LaunchPad™ Development Kit (MSP--EXP430F5529LP)*, Apr. 2017.

[12] ——, *MSP430x5xx and MSP430x6xx Family User's Guide*, Mar. 2018, [retrieved: Jan, 2019]. [Online]. Available: http://www.ti.com/lit/ug/slau208q/slau208q.pdf

[13] Autodesk, Inc., "EAGLE," [retrieved: Jan, 2019]. [Online]. Available: https://www.autodesk.com/products/eagle/

[14] S. Hill *et al.*, "Queued serial peripheral interface for use in a data processing system," US Patent US4816996, 1989.

[15] NXP Semiconductors, Inc., *UM10204: I2C-bus specification and user manual*, Apr. 2014, rev. 6.

[16] International Organization for Standardization, *ISO 11898: Road vehicles – Controller area network (CAN)* , 2nd ed., Dec. 2015.

[17] Adafruit Industries, *Micro SD Card Breakout Board Tutorial*, Jan. 2019, [retrieved: Jan, 2019]. [Online]. Available: https://cdn-learn.adafruit.com/downloads/pdf/adafruit-micro-sd-breakout-board-card-tutorial.pdf

[18] R. Martins Gomes, M. Baunach, M. Malenko, L. Batista Ribeiro, and F. Mauroner, "A Co-Designed RTOS and MCU Concept for Dynamically Composed Embedded Systems," in *Proc. of the 13th Workshop on Operating Systems Platforms for Embedded Real-Time Applications*, 2017, pp. 41–46.

[19] R. Martins Gomes and M. Baunach, "A Model-Based Concept for RTOS Portability," in *Proc. of the 15th Int'l Conference on Computer Systems and Applications*, Oct. 2018, pp. 1–6.

[20] F. Mauroner and M. Baunach, "mosartMCU: Multi-Core Operating-System-Aware Real-Time Microcontroller," in *Proc. of the 7th Mediterranean Conference on Embedded Computing*, Jun. 2018, pp. 1–4.

A Security Aware Design Space Exploration Framework

Lukas Gressl
Institute of Technical Informatics
Graz University of Technology
Graz, Austria 8010
Email: gressl@tugraz.at

Christian Steger
Institute of Technical Informatics
Graz University of Technology
Graz, Austria 8010
Email: steger@tugraz.at

Ulrich Neffe
NXP Semiconductors Austria GmbH
Graz University of Technology
Email: ulrich.neffe@nxp.com

Abstract—**System designers are often faced with a huge variety of alternative hardware platforms and architectures, when designing new products. Especially the various options for allocating a set of tasks to processing units greatly influences the overall system performance and power consumption. As the possible design space is too complex for manual evaluation, automatic Design Space Exploration (DSE) tools are used for selecting first system designs. These tools assess the various mappings between tasks and processing units. They target the best allocation, optimizing the system's performance and power consumption, while considering other predefined design constraints. Traditionally, security requirements do not belong to the set of design constraints these tools deal with. Thus, security requirements must be introduced manually, which might induce additional costs to the overall project. To enable security-by-design using DSE, the Security Aware Design Space Exploration (SADSE) Framework was developed. This framework allows the integration of attack scenarios and security requirements, as well as platform security features into the DSE, at a level of detail not yet considered by other tools. SADSE allows an optimal allocation of tasks onto hardware platforms, while satisfying predefined security constraints. This paper shows how security requirements and attack vectors are modeled in SADSE, followed by the evaluation of a keyless entry system use case, where the tool finds a secure mapping of tasks to processing units.**

Keywords–Security; Design Space Exploration; Embedded Systems.

I. INTRODUCTION

Designing a new product means making a lot of decisions, ranging from which hardware components to take to what system functionality and on which component to place them on. This variety opens up a huge space of alternative designs which must be considered by designers, system architects and product owners. The resulting design influences the power and performance characteristic. This design choice is an issue, especially in the domain of embedded systems and stretches from selecting hardware components to mapping of system functionality. The optimal allocation of system functionality to dedicated hardware blocks, such as special hardware or general purpose processors, poses a complex problem. This allocation cannot be solved manually regarding more than one characteristic. To tackle this problem and to shorten the design process, automatic Design Space Exploration (DSE) tools are used. These tools scan a space of alternative designs and allocation options, and compute an optimized solution.

Especially for devices in the domain of the Internet of Things and Cyber Physical Systems (CPS), the information security plays a vital role. CPS sense data and handle confidential or even personal information, which imposes security requirements to these devices. The security requirements are usually defined by an expert, and depend on the project setup. These requirements are considered right at the beginning or integrated later. Later on integration of security requirements increases the project's costs significantly more than introducing security at the beginning of the design flow. Therefore, most companies, producing secure products, introduce security requirements initially at the design phase. In this phase, DSE tools can be used to support designers in their choices. As traditional DSE tools lack the ability of considering information security, their usability for designing secure products is limited.

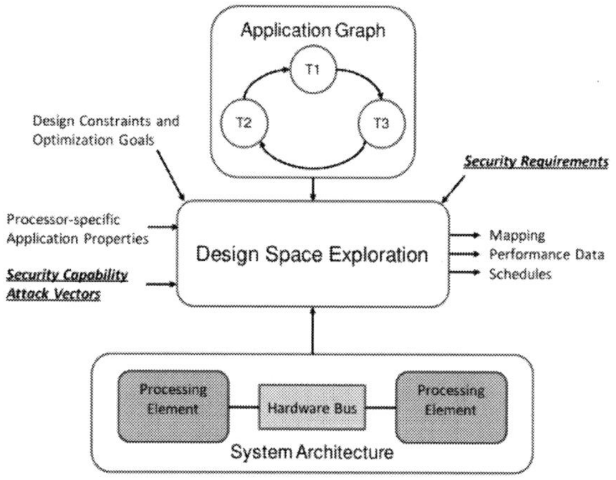

Figure 1. DSE process, based on [1] extended by security requirements, security capabilities, and attack vectors.

To bridge this gap in the design flow, we present a Security Aware Design Space Exploration framework (SADSE). The SADSE framework allows an automatic DSE under consideration of security requirements and threat scenarios. The framework offers the designer to define security requirements for single data entities the system tasks operate on, and attack scenarios for the individual function blocks. Given these security requirements and attack scenarios together with the defined hardware platform, the framework performs an optimized allocation of functionality to hardware blocks. Thereby, it considers the security requirements and the hardware components' security capabilities. Figure 1 shows an overview of the traditional DSE process extended with the additional security assets introduced in this paper.

The basis of the SADSE framework implementation is the

Constraint Programming (CP) based Design Space Exploration for System Design tool, as described in [2]. The extension of considering security constraints in the DSE is presented in this paper and the SADSE framework's functionality is evaluated using an embedded access control device as a use case. The rest of the paper is structured into the following sections: in Section II previous work considering DSE and security requirements is presented; in Section III the methodology introduced by this paper is explained in detail; in Section IV the SADSE framework is used to evaluate a secure task mapping of a keyless entry system and the framework's performance is evaluated; in Section V a conclusion is drawn and future work is discussed.

II. Related Work

The optimal allocation of tasks to hardware components considering the overall system execution time, power consumption, scheduling, etc. is a well described problem for embedded devices, multiprocessor- and multicore-systems.

Other works already proposed frameworks performing automatic DSE for embedded systems under consideration of hardware software codesign. The optimal allocation of streaming applications onto a heterogeneous multi-processor system is investigated in the works of Khalilzad et al. [3], and Rosvall et al. [1] [2]. In the framework proposed by these authors, streaming applications are represented as synchronous data flow graphs, and their tasks are mapped to distinct heterogeneous processors. The framework describes the problem of the optimal mapping of tasks to processors as a constraint satisfaction problem, which is solved by using CP. Finding the optimal hardware-software split for embedded devices using heuristic algorithms in DSE was investigated by Knerr [4]. In his work, Knerr considers the problem of finding the best partitioning of functionality implemented in software and hardware components, considering a predefined hardware platform. His approach considers various optimization criteria, such as chip area size, power consumption or performance.

Security requirements in DSE are described in a range of modeling and analysis techniques. In this area, the work of Kang [5], Stierand et al. [6], and Hasan et al. [7] are prominent. In their work, Hasan et al. consider an already existing task schedule of an real time operating system on a predefined multicore-system. The authors present a framework allowing to insert security tasks into this schedule without changing it and without breaking the system's real time constraints. Kang describes a tool which supports system designers in their decisions considering the correct use of security features.

Stierand et al. [6] present a framework in which security parameters are introduced into automatic DSE, putting it into the context of the automotive domain. They focus on the communication part between tasks, assessing the attack vulnerability of the channels connecting them. This vulnerability is determined by the capability of the attacker. Thus, they add security requirements to the exploration. To mitigate these attacks, Stierand et al. propose to map these vulnerable tasks onto architecture modules providing hardware security extensions, ensuring that such attacks cannot be performed. As the task model of their approach combines functionality and data as one, the correct mapping of the single tasks to hardware secured electronic control units depends on the definition of what operations a task executes on some piece of information.

From the described DSE tools, only Stierand's framework focuses on the correct allocation of security vulnerable tasks on dedicated hardware components during an automatic DSE. In comparison to their work, the framework presented in this paper regards data and control flow separately. With this separation, multiple interpretation variants of a task functionality are overcome. This allows a more detailed attribution of security requirements to the respective information blocks. Furthermore, we do not regard these security requirements exclusive to the communication channels between tasks. Our approach pursues a more holistic way of introducing security into automatic DSE. We consider the attack scenarios not only on the communication but also on the tasks, and the architectural blocks and assign security attributes to the data used by the tasks. Furthermore, by assigning security levels to the distinct hardware elements, we do not simply solve a mapping problem, but are also able to find a suitable platform configuration. Section III discusses the proposed approach in detail.

III. Proposed Methodology

Performing an optimal allocation of functionality to a predefined system architecture under consideration of security constraints needs a way of accurately defining tasks, architectural blocks, and security constraints. This section introduces the necessary components and describes the underlying constraint solving problem of the SADSE framework.

A. Representation of the System Functionality

According to [4], the functionality of a system is defined by a directed process or task graph in which the nodes represent functional elements, and the edges represent data transfers between those elements. This combined representation of data and functionality in one task leads to ambiguous results when attempting to define security requirements on it. Therefore, we split task functionality and data in our approach. The SADSE framework allows the definition of distinct security requirements on data entity without mingling it with the task's functionality. Each task is linked to a data entity by a set of operations. This more precise modeling of the control and data flow of the system enables the framework to perform a more comprehensive mapping. This explicits control and data modeling leaving less space for interpretation what a task is actually doing with its associated data. This is important when it comes to the decision of where to map tasks that handle secure data.

By splitting functionality and data each single data block can be attributed with security requirements, determining how the data must be secured. This assignment must be performed by a security expert based on a *Confidentiality-Integrity-Availability* (CIA) triad [8].Our approach focuses on the confidentiality, the integrity and the authenticity of the data entity. Therefore, the security requirement for a data unit is denoted as the tuple $sr = (conf, int, auth)$, where $conf$, int, and $auth$ can either be 0 or 1. Combining the definition of the security requirements (sr) with the operations, a data entity basically defines a set of operations and security requirements. For better readability, a task performing a set of operations on a set of data entities is defined as a process. The security requirements for each data entity must be determined by the designer and serves as an input to the SADSE framework.

Figure 2 shows the separation of task functionality and security attributed data connected by a range of operations. The system's functionality is represented as a directed process graph. The data flow in this graph consists of the set of all tasks operating on the same data entity. As each process operating on the same data entity is connected via an edge to its parent process, the data flow can be found by traversing all parent processes with the same data entity attribution.

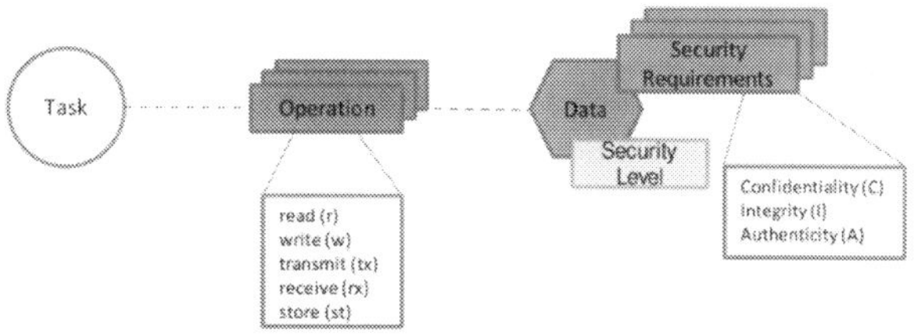

Figure 2. Representation of a process, consisting of a task, its associated data attributed with security requirements, and the task's operation performed on the data.

Considering the set of operations, the basic operations on the data entities, such as read (r), write (w), transmit (tx), receive (rx), and persistently store (st) are directly defined by the designer. This set of operations is represented by the tuple $op = (r, w, tx, rx, st)$, where each element can either be 0 or 1. The security related operations are derived from the basic operations and the data entity's security requirement. Additionally to the security requirement, each data entity is assigned a security assurance level, which must be evaluated by a domain expert. For simplification, these assurance levels are abstracted as an integer ranging from 0 to 3, with 3 representing the highest security level and 0 no security. Any task reading or writing confidential data must decrypt the data before processing it and encrypt it before passing it to another task. The same principle applies to the authenticity of data, which must be ensured by applying a signature or authentication code after writing and verified before reading. Transmitting and receiving of secured data does not enforce any security operation. These security operations $op_{sec} = (enc, sign, st_{sec})$ are derived according to (1). These operations and security assurance levels must be mapped to the security capabilities of the individual Processing Elements (PEs) which are explained in detail in the next section.

$$op_{sec}(op, sr) = \begin{pmatrix} (r \vee w) \wedge conf \\ (r \vee w) \wedge auth \\ st \wedge (auth \vee conf \vee int) \end{pmatrix} \quad (1)$$

B. Representation of the System Architecture

The hardware platform is represented by PEs, which are connected to each other via Hardware Bus Systems (HWBs). PEs can represent general purpose processors or application specific integrated circuits. PEs and HWBs are assigned distinct characteristics and attributes. The set of attributes for PEs are chip area, memory size and power consumption, whereas the attributes for HWBs are power consumption and transmission speed. PEs are further characterized by their security capabilities. They describe the PEs capability on cryptography ($crypt$), verification ($verify$), and tamper resistant storage (trs), which is described by the tuple $sec_{cap} = (crypt, verify, trs)$, where $crypt$, $verify$, and trs are abstracted by a security capability level ranging from 0 to 3, 3 being the highest security capability level and 0 meaning no security capability. These capabilities are implemented by additional hardware or software modules. The distinction of a software or a hardware implementation is performed by the attribution of the PE. A hardware implementation may increase the chip area, whereas a software implementation might shrink the available size of memory. Thus, a PE can be formalized as a set of modes, in which each mode defines $sec_{cap}s$ and the corresponding attributes. An HWB can be defined as a set of characteristics and modes. Furthermore, not all PEs are directly connected to one another. Any two PEs are connected via a hardware bus. With these definitions, an architectural platform can be described. Figure 3 depicts two PEs connected to one another by a hardware bus with their respective attributions.

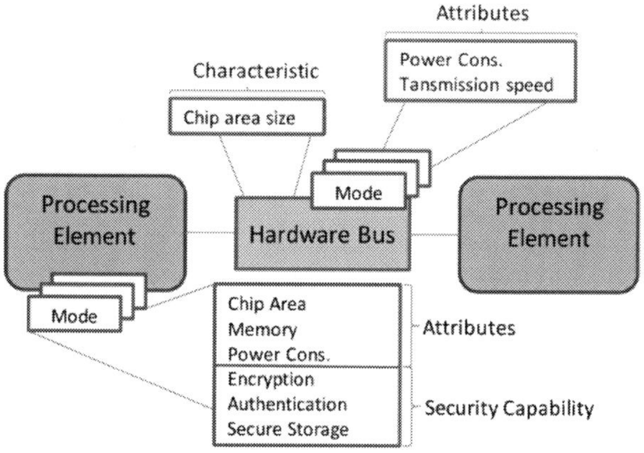

Figure 3. Hardware platform representation, consisting of PEs, connected by a hardware bus.

C. Attack Vectors

For determining the attack vectors on the system entities, we use the STRIDE analysis [9]. We focus on the attacker capabilities of spoofing (S), tampering (T), and information disclosure (ID), which can be either 0 or 1. These attack vectors, described by the tuple $av = (ID, S, T)$ can be directly mapped to sr, as spoofing affects the authenticity, tampering the integrity, and information disclosure compromises the confidentiality of the data. From the assets that can be attacked, we focus on processes, data stores, and data flows. In our approach, processes from the STRIDE analysis are simply processes p, data stores are represented by PEs, and data flows are the set of processes operating on the same entity of the data. Therefore, the av on a data flow is the combination of av of the involved processes. The susceptibility of the physical connections between the PEs is integrated into the attack vectors of the respective PEs. The attack vectors are defined by the designer.

The combination of the security requirements of the single data entities, the operations performed on the data entities by the processes, and the attack vectors form the basis on which the SADSE framework performs the mapping of the processes to PEs. Thereby, the SADSE framework considers the PEs' security capabilities. The mapping, and its influences on the overall system performance is explained in the next section.

D. Mapping Functionality to Architecture: A Constraint Satisfaction and Optimization Problem

Mapping the functionality of the system described by the process graph to the system architecture and selecting the optimal PE-modes is a typical application of combinatorial optimization. These classes of problems can be solved using CP. At the core of the CP method, a set of decision variables describes the problem at hand. Each of these decision variables has a certain domain of possible values. The variables depend on one another, described by the constraints. These constraints determine which combinations of values within the domain of the single variables are allowed. A constraint solver is used for finding an optimal mapping of the processes on PEs, satisfying all constraints [10]. The framework basically distinguishes between two types of design constraints - constraints to satisfy and to optimize.

Constraints to be satisfied are the security requirements and communication feasibility cf. The communication between two processes is only realizable, if either both processes are allocated on the same PE, or, if allocated on two different PEs, there is an HWB connecting them. The security constraints are a combination of av, sr, and op_{sec}. For each process mapped to a PE, the security constraints $sc = (sc_{enc}, sc_{auth}, sc_{store})$ are calculated according to (3). The attack vectors of the process and of the PE, on which the process is mapped, are denoted av_p and av_{PE}, respectively. OP_{sec}, defined in (2) is the result of all security operations performed by process p, and n is the number of all data entities p operates on. Furthermore, $asslvl_{sec} = (enc_{lvl}, sign_{lvl}, st_{lvl})$ stores the maximum security assurance level of the data entities these security operations are performed on.

$$OP_{sec} = \begin{pmatrix} enc_1 \vee \cdots \vee enc_n \\ auth_1 \vee \cdots \vee auth_n \\ st_{sec1} \vee \cdots \vee st_{secn} \end{pmatrix} \tag{2}$$

$$sc(av_{PE}, av_p, OP_{sec}) = \begin{pmatrix} (ID_{PE} \vee ID_p) \wedge enc \\ (S_{PE} \vee S_p) \wedge auth \\ (T_{PE} \vee T_p) \wedge st_{sec} \end{pmatrix} \tag{3}$$

$$sc_{lvl}(asslvl_{sec}, sc) = \begin{cases} enc_{lvl} & sc_{enc} > 0, \\ sign_{lvl} & sc_{auth} > 0, \\ st_{lvl} & sc_{store} > 0 \end{cases} \tag{4}$$

Equation (4) is use to calculate the security constraint levels for each process. For each level, there exists a sec_{cap} provided by the PE, which ensures the data's security requirement and mitigates the attack vector, satisfying the data's security levels. This mapping function map_{PE}^{p} is denoted by (5), and must be performed for all possible mappings of processes to PEs. Only if all mappings return 1, the security constraints are satisfied.

$$map_{PE}^{p}(sec_{cap}, sc_{lvl}) = (crypt \geq enc_{lvl}) \wedge (verify \geq sign_{lvl}) \wedge (trs \geq st_{lvl}) \tag{5}$$

Constraints to be optimized can be the power consumption of the overall system, the chip area size, as well as the system's performance. The performance is calculated considering the tasks' Worst Case Execution Times (WCETs). The WCETs reflect the processing delays of a process executed on a PE, for which an implementation exists or which can be estimated by the designer. More specifically, a process' WCET must be estimated or known for a PE's mode to be considered for the mapping by the SADSE framework. The security capabilities induce additionally computational overhead, which influences the overall execution time, depending on the process mapping the SADSE framework performs. Furthermore, the designer can specify different modes for each PE, which is also explored by the tool. Additionally to an optimal mapping of processes to PEs an optimal selection of the PE modes is done.

Depending on the situation and its requirements on execution time, power consumption, etc., one implementation would be preferred over the other. The framework performs an automatic and optimal mapping of the required functionality to the respective implementation alternatives, considering their performance, power consumption, needed memory, and gate size, and ensuring that the security hardness characterization fulfills the needed attack mitigation as defined by the designer.

E. SADSE Framework Implementation

As basis of the DSE tool, we used the work of Rosvall et al. [1]. The data blocks, operations, attack vectors, security requirements, security capabilities, and security levels were added to the platform and function graph representations. The network system was extended by a configurable bus system. The restrictions imposed by the bus system, and the security features were implemented as additional constraints and included into the CP model. The additional delay caused by the individual security features is added to the calculation of the overall execution time.

IV. USE-CASE EVALUATION AND RESULTS

The SADSE framework was evaluated by performing a performance optimized mapping of a keyless entry system. The system's functionality was derived from the systems described in [11] and [12]. The system consists of a lock and a device. The device's functionality and architecture is described in here. The device builds up a connection with the lock by receiving a request $requ_{chall}^{lock}$ from the lock. The device creates a challenge $resp_{chall}^{dev}$ using its master key key_{master} and sends it to the lock. The lock sends its own challenge $resp_{chall}^{lock}$ which is checked by the device, again using key_{master}. The device derives a long time key key_{lt} from key_{master} and sends an ready request $requ_{ready}^{dev}$ to the lock. It receives a response from the lock $resp_{ready}^{lock}$ stating that it is ready to open a session. The device informs the user, requesting an action $action_{user}$. It then derives a session key $key_{session}$ from key_{lt} and creates an open request $requ_{open}^{dev}$ using $key_{session}$.

The hardware platform considered for the analysis is represented by a device, consisting of an application processor, a secure element, a micro controller, and a Bluetooth Low Energy (BLE) radio. All components are connected with each other by a bus system. The functionality mapped to the device establishes an authenticated and secure connection between itself and an external lock. Therefore, it uses key_{lt} and $key_{session}$. The key_{lt} is negotiated between lock and device. It is used as long as lock and device are paired. The $key_{session}$, which is derived from key_{lt}, is used for the authentication between lock and device and is updated frequently. Hence, disclosure of the $key_{session}$ poses a less severe security impact to the access system. Figure 4 shows the system's task graph and hardware architecture. The mapping is performed based on the task's WCETs when running on the individual PEs, and their security constraints. The goal of the SADSE framework is now to find the optimal mapping of the tasks to the PEs, running in a specific mode, as well as an optimal selection of the PEs. This selection is optimal if the overall system's execution time is minimal and the security constraints are satisfied.

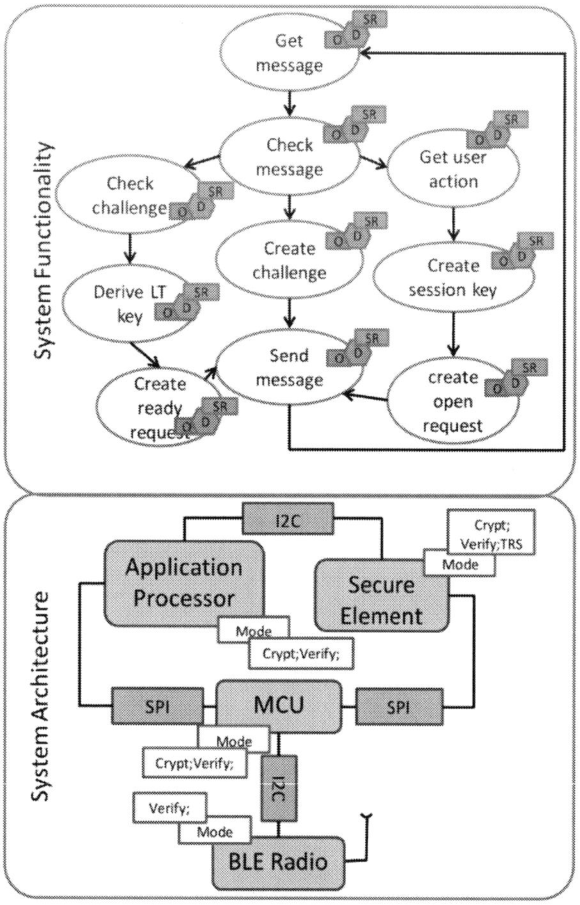

Figure 4. Evaluation example. Keyless entry system's simplified functionality which is to be mapped to a hardware platform. The PEs are connected via bus systems

The tasks of the system's functionality were attributed with the data blocks they are operating on. The attack vectors were attributed to the PEs of the system architecture. The SADSE framework was configured in such a way that the security constraints should be satisfied and the overall system' execution time should be minimized. Two runs with changing data operations on the session key, and a third run without any security constraints were performed. The security capabilities, the attack vectors, and the capability levels of the single hardware blocks are listed in Table I. The security capabilities of the components are based on existing hardware components. The Application Processor's (AP's) capabilities are derived from a *Snapdragon 410E* [13], the Secure Element's (SE's) capabilities from an *P6021* [14], the Micro Controller's (MCU's) capabilities from an *ARM A57* [15], and the BLE Radio's capabilitie's from an *HZX-51822-16N03* [16]. The components security capabilities define the security levels in each mode. E.g. the SE's encryption mechanism AES-256 is assigned a security level of 3, whereas an AES-128 gets a security level 2. A DES-112 is only assigned a security level of 1. For authentication functions, such as MAC and HMAC a similar classification is performed. Table II shows the attributions of the single data entities with security requirements, and their security assurance levels. Table III shows the attributions of the single tasks with data entities and operations.

TABLE I. ATTACK VECTORS AND SECURITY CAPABILITIES

HW	av	Sec_{cap}	m0	m1
AP	(S, T, I_D)	$(enc, verify)$	(1,1)	(2,2)
MCU	(T, I_D)	$(enc, verify)$	(2,2)	(3,3)
SE	(S, T, I_D)	$(enc, verify, sec_{store})$	(2,2,3)	(3,3,3)
BLE	(S, T, I_D)	$(verify)$	(1)	-

TABLE II. DATA BLOCK SECURITY REQUIREMENTS AND ASSURANCE LEVELS

Data Block	sr	$asslvl_{sec}$
$requ^{lock}_{chall}, action_{user}$	-	-
$key_{lt}, key_{master}, key_{session}$	$(Conf, Int)$	$(3, 3, 2)$
$resp^{dev}_{chall}, requ^{dev}_{open}, requ^{dev}_{ready}$	$(Conf, Auth)$	$(2, 2, 2)$
$resp^{lock}_{chall}, resp^{lock}_{ready}$	$(Conf, Auth)$	$(2, 2, 2)$

TABLE III. TASKS AND USED DATA BLOCKS

Task Name	Data Block	Operations
Get message	$resp^{lock}_{chall}, requ^{lock}_{chall}, resp^{lock}_{ready}$	rx, tx
Check message	$resp^{lock}_{chall}, requ^{lock}_{chall}, resp^{lock}_{open}$	rx, r
Create challenge	$resp^{dev}_{chall}$	w, tx
	key_{master}	r
Check challenge	$resp^{lock}_{chall}$	rx, r
	key_{master}	r
Derive LT key	key_{lt}	w, st
	key_{master}	r
Create ready request	key_{lt}	r
	$requ^{dev}_{ready}$	w, tx
Send message	$requ^{dev}_{open}, requ^{dev}_{ready}, resp^{dev}_{chall}$	rx, tx
Get User Action	$action_{user}$	r
Create session key	$key_{session}$	w, st
	key_{lt}	r
Create open request	$key_{session}$	r
	$requ_{open}$	w

The system's functionality and the hardware platform are presented in Figure 4. Table IV shows the full mappings of tasks to hardware components for the distinct runs. The tasks *Get message* and *Send message* have a fixed mapping to *BLE Radio*. As shown in Table IV, the framework was able to correctly map the security critical tasks to the respective hardware components and select the optimal modes regarding the overall performance of the system. To introduce the overhead of the respective security mechanisms of each mode, their computational overhead was derived using the work of [17]. For simplification, the WCETs of each process to PE mapping stays unchanged for the single PE's modes. Thus, the change in the system's performance is only induced by the selection of the security mechanisms.

To demonstrate the effect of the security requirements on the mapping, two runs. In the first execution, the configuration as described in the tables was chosen. In the second run, no security requirements were used. Table IV shows the optimal mappings of tasks to PEs in the respective runs. The PEs are numbered from 0 to 3: AP (0), MCU (1), SE (2), and BLE Radio (3). Each PE offers to possible modes, 0 or 1. The PE and mode mapping is abbreviated with [PE](mode). It can be seen, that the tool was able to correctly allocate *Derive LT key* and *Create session key* to the secure element in run *#1*. In run *#2*, the allocation changes completely, as no security constraints are to be solved. In run *#1*, 45 solutions were found in less than 400ms. In run *#2*, the SADSE framework found 5576 solutions in 27 seconds.

TABLE IV. MAPPING TASKS TO PROCESSING ELEMENTS

Task Name	mapping #1	mapping #2
Get message	[3](0)	[3](0)
Check message	[1](0)	[1](0)
Create challenge	[1](0)	[1](0)
Check challenge	[1](0)	[1](0)
Derive LT key	[2](1)	[1](0)
Create ready request	[1](0)	[0](0)
Get User Action	[0](1)	[0](0)
Create session key	[2](1)	[2](0)
Create open request	[1](0)	[3](0)
Send message	[3](0)	[3](0)

The keyless entry system example shows the correct functionality of the SADSE framework. It is able to find a valid solution which satisfies both the security constraints and has the fastest execution time. Considering the security constraints leads to a reduced number of found solution, which also speeds up the finding of the optimal solution for the keyless entry example.

V. Conclusion and Future Work

The SADSE framework allows to define security attack vectors and security requirements for system functionalities defined by designers. These security requirements and attack vectors are defined by security experts, following widely used approaches, such as STRIDE analysis or the CIA triad. Based on these requirements and the information about the assumed performance, the security levels, and power consumption of the single tasks executed on distinct hardware platforms, the SADSE framework finds an optimal mapping, under consideration of the security constraints. With this tool, security requirements can be regarded right at the beginning of the design phase. Thus, a greater awareness of security constraints is introduced into the early stages of product design.

Currently, the SADSE framework only regards abstract security levels, considering the capability of the components and the needed security levels of the data entities. These levels are mere placeholders and are to be replaced by real cost factors. To acquire these security costs, a novel method will be developed, helping designers to assess the right level of protection. Furthermore, we want to include distinct security communication protocols, as well as add key distribution mechanisms to the SADSE framework.

Acknowledgment

Project partners are NXP Semiconductor Austria GmbH and the Technical University of Graz. This work was supported by the Austrian Research Promotion Agency (FFG) within the project UBSmart (project number: 859475).

References

[1] K. Rosvall and I. Sander, "A constraint-based design space exploration framework for real-time applications on mpsocs," in Proceedings of the Conference on Design, Automation & Test in Europe, ser. DATE '14. 3001 Leuven, Belgium, Belgium: European Design and Automation Association, 2014, pp. 1–6.

[2] K. Rosvall, N. Khalilzad, G. Ungureanu, and I. Sander, "Throughput Propagation in Constraint-Based Design Space Exploration for Mixed-Criticality Systems," Proceedings of the 9th Workshop on Rapid Simulation and Performance Evaluation: Methods and Tools - RAPIDO '17, 2017, pp. 1–8.

[3] N. Khalilzad, K. Rosvall, and I. Sander, "A Modular Design Space Exploration Framework for Embedded Systems," IEEE Proc. Computers & Digital Techniques, vol. 152, 2005, pp. 183–192.

[4] B. Knerr, "Heuristic Optimisation Methods for System Partitioning in HW / SW Co-Design," Ph.D. dissertation, Vienna University of Technology, 2008.

[5] E. Kang, "Design Space Exploration for Security," no. April 2008, 2016, pp. 1–4.

[6] I. Stierand, S. Malipatlolla, S. Froschle, A. Stuhring, and S. Henkler, "Integrating the security aspect into design space exploration of embedded systems," Proceedings - IEEE 25th International Symposium on Software Reliability Engineering Workshops, ISSREW 2014, 2014, pp. 371–376.

[7] M. Hasan, S. Mohan, R. Pellizzoni, and R. B. Bobba, "A design-space exploration for allocating security tasks in multicore real-Time systems," Proceedings of the 2018 Design, Automation and Test in Europe Conference and Exhibition, DATE 2018, vol. 2018-Janua, 2018, pp. 225–230.

[8] M. Farooq, M. Waseem, A. Khairi, and S. Mazhar, "A Critical Analysis on the Security Concerns of Internet of Things (IoT)," International Journal of Computer Applications, vol. 111, no. 7, 2015, pp. 1–6.

[9] S. Hernan, S. Lambert, T. Ostwald, and A. Shostack, "Threat modeling-uncover security design flaws using the stride approach," MSDN Magazine-Louisville, 2006, pp. 68–75.

[10] P. Baptiste, C. Le Pape, and W. Nuijten, Constraint-based scheduling: applying constraint programming to scheduling problems. Springer Science & Business Media, 2012, vol. 39.

[11] J. Xu and et al., "Pairing and authentication security technologies in low-power bluetooth," Proceedings - 2013 IEEE International Conference on Green Computing and Communications and IEEE Internet of Things and IEEE Cyber, Physical and Social Computing, GreenCom-iThings-CPSCom 2013, 2013, pp. 1081–1085.

[12] H. Oguma, N. Nobata, K. Nawa, T. Mizota, and M. Shinagawa, "Passive keyless entry system for long term operation," 2011 IEEE International Symposium on a World of Wireless, Mobile and Multimedia Networks, WoWMoM 2011 - Digital Proceedings, 2011, pp. 1–3.

[13] "ARM Cortex®-A57 MPCore ProcessorCryptography Extension Technical Reference Manual," ARM Limited, Tech. Rep.

[14] "BSI-DSZ-CC-1072-2018 for NXP Secure Smart Card Controller P6021y VB *," 2018.

[15] "Qualcomm Snapdragon 410E Processor(APQ8016E) Technical Reference Manual," Qualcomm Technologies, Inc., Tech. Rep.

[16] Shen Zhen Huazhixin Technology Ltd, "HZX-51822-16N03 Bluetooth 4.0 Low Energy Module Datasheet," Tech. Rep., 2017.

[17] A.-K. Al Tamimi, "Performance Analysis of Data Encryption Algorithms."

Cellular Automata-based Wear Leveling in Resistive Memory

Sutapa Sarkar

Electronics & Communication Engineering
Seacom Engineering College
West Bengal, India
Email: sutapa321@gmail.com

***Abstract*—Due to *spatial locality of reference*, repetitive writes cause stress to few contiguous cache memory blocks. If the underlying technology is resistive memory, those blocks suffer with endurance problem and wear out at much faster rate than NAND/NOR Flash memories (10^5 to 10^6 program/erase cycles). In CMPs cache memory, uneven distribution of writes and/or *malicious attacks* cause system failures due to repetitive writes on a particular memory block. To avoid *wear out* of memory cells at premature stage, writes are distributed through *wear leveling* schemes. This work reports an efficient scheme of wear leveling in *resistive memory* using the concept of Cellular Automata (CA). Probably this is a unique effort of wear leveling, using Von Neuman's concept of cellular automata, that targets to make uniform writes throughout all memory blocks with *spatial access pattern predictions*. The contiguous *write-stressed* memory blocks are defined as a zone subjected to remapping. Two stage hierarchical Periodic Boundary Cellular Automata ($PBCA$) is used to perform *Density Classification Task (DCT)* to select the cache zone (remapping candidates). Thereafter, identified memory blocks are remapped to new addresses by an *algebraic* technique. This *access aware* write management policy can be worked along with fault tolerant design for implementation of a robust memory subsystem.**

***Keywords-Resistive memory*; *Spatial access characteristics*; *Wear leveling*; *Density classification task*; *Periodic Boundary Cellular Automata*.**

I. Introduction

Von Neuman's computing models of pipelining and super-scalar processor [25] [26] become performance limited by reduced throughput. Those processors are also not suitable for having their increased power budget exceeding the standard of Moore's law. Multicore architecture or chip multiprocessors (CMPs) has been considered as the proper replacement of single core architecture by integrating several processors in a single chip. But CMPs requires large *on-chip* cache, which covers an appreciable area of total chip die. Therefore, resistive memory (RRAM/ReRAM) is considered as replacement technology of DRAM/Flash memories for having the advantages of higher package density & scalability with lower energy consumption [1] [2]. But the main disadvantage of ReRAM lies with *write issues* related to endurance and reliabilty problem of resistive memory cells. Due to spatial locality of reference, few blocks are suffering from write stress where most of them are seldom written. In that scenario, *life time* may get hampered at least 20X faster than uniformly distributed writes for worn-out cells [12].

Wear leveling is a scheme that tries to make uniform distribution of writes applied to NAND Flash, as well as NVRAM technologies for the last few decades [11]. It can also be applicable in resistive memory but with little technology specific tunning. Remapping of write request of a memory block to another memory block is the process of achieving wear leveling [6]. *Wear leveling* schemes are categorized at two different levels: 1) cause of multiple writes on the memory blocks having unbalanced distribution of workload of CMPs or for malicious attacks, 2) depending on the technique of look up table based/algebraic method based. Different types of wear leveling schemes are compared in Table I, providing *workload/attack-based* and algebraic/table-based schemes.

Start gap scheme redirects write operation from one block to another neighbouring memory block if write count exceeds the threshold limit [3]. Write-stressed data blocks (*remapping candidates*) are found by assessing processor's nonuniform write access pattern to the hybrid memory composed of Static random-access memory (SRAM) & Spin-transfer Torque Magnetic Random-access Memory (STTRAM). Block address remapping is based on an algebraic (randomized) method which inserts a conversion step in between logical address and physical address. The remapping whereabouts of memory blocks are tracked by *Start & Gap* registers. The system lifetime is improved as compared to without *wear leveling* schemes but at the cost of increasing overhead in terms of latency, power and storage. In [4], inter-set and intraset remapping distributes writes between hybrid memory (SRAM & STTRAM). The property of locality of reference of write access is reviewed during selection of remapping candidates. Write counts are checked by cache line & cache set counter. But, the increased number of counters increases hardware overhead, as well as the design complexity.

Typical workload-based schemes are not capable of handling repetitive writes caused by malicious attacks that can also cause system failure within a very short time. *Practical Attack Detector (PAD)* is proposed in [7] to prevent cell failures due to malicious attacks by tracking the write streams within a short time frame. *Rancar* scheme is proposed to handle repeat address attack (RAA) through adaptive remapping in hybrid cache memory [9]. Translation of physical address to intermediate address for intraset/inter-set remapping is performed by swapping set index bits & tag bits. A table based (deterministic method) remapping scheme is proposed in [24] for resistive memory. Algebraic address remapping is proposed in [1] [3] [7] to fit within limited space overhead and to eliminate the requirement of look up table as it's size grows linearly with memory capacity.

Recently, Cellular Automata (CA) has become popular in different applications of cache systems like data migration, protocol processor design, fault tolerance circuit design, etc. [18] [19] [22]. In this paper, a CA-based approach is taken for workload based wear leveling in resistive memory. This research work attempts to increase the system lifetime [3] by enhancing the reliability

TABLE I. COMPARATIVE STUDY BETWEEN DIFFERENT WEAR LEVELING SCHEMES

Schemes	Memory technology	Granularity	Parameter reviewed	Remapping method	Limitation/Special feature
Start-gap [11]	PCM	Cache line	Spatial write activity	Algebraic method	This scheme is applicable for workload based stresses and malicious attacks.
Rancar [9]	Hybrid- DRAM & PCM	Cache Set	Repeated set attack	Algebraic method	It affects the spatial locality of reference adversely during remapping.
OWL [16]	NAND FLASH	Block	Temporal write activity	Table based	The scheme observes flip bits to ensure reduction of overwrites thereby eliminating redundancy of repetitive write operations.
WAPTM [10]	PCM	Page	Write-activity	Table based	Already used in Google Android 2.3 based on ARM architecture to reduce write activities to page table.
Software based wear-leveling [15]	Hybrid-PCM+DRAM	Memory address	Write activity	Integer linear programming formulation & polynomial-time algorithm	Hardware requirement is eliminated
PAD [7]	PCM	Cache line	Malicious attack	Not addressed	It can be effective to other memory technologies apart from PCM to detect malicious attacks by calculating attack density.
Ouroborous [12]	NVRAM-PCM/FeRAM/STT-MRAM	Local & global region	hybrid - both demand & attack	Hybrid scheme with both table & algebraic method based	It determines access pattern as well as demand prediction for wear leveling.

of resistive memory cells by redistributing writes. Write-stressed memory blocks as well as less written memory blocks are identified from access pattern.

Write distribution among the memory blocks shows program locality within few contiguous memory blocks termed as zone. The efficacy of any wear leveling scheme depends on the selection of the size of the zone. Here, in this paper, the small-sized source & target remapping zone is identified by parallel operation. Spatial locality of reference is utilized to predict precise and specific write-stressed & less written zone by two stage hierarchical DCT using $PBCA$. An algebraic address translation method is adopted to achieve local/global remapping (address translation of central memory address) of the zone. This simple but cost-effective scheme can be a suitable alternative of workload-based traditional wear leveling schemes [3] irrespective of memory technology.

Section II introduces a relevant theory of CA. CMPs cache architecture is explained with a typical example in Section III. An overview of the design is explained with a block in Section IV. Sections V and VI, describe a CA-based methodology for finding out the remapping candidates. The remapping equation is developed in Section VII. Section VIII deals with analysis of the current work and the paper is concluded with Section IX.

II. BASICS OF CELLULAR AUTOMATA (CA)

A cellular automaton consists of a number of cells evolving in discrete space and time according to some transition function (f_i). It can be viewed as an autonomous Finite State Machine (FSM) which is used to model a variety of physical systems [17] [21]. CA has been accepted as an attractive hardware structure for cache system modelling because of the following characteristics: 1) simple and identical/homogeneous structure, 2) modular, 3) restriction to local interactions among the states of left (S^t_{i-1}), centre (S^t_i) and right (S^t_{i+1}) cells. Each CA stores a discrete variable at time t and it refers to the present state (S^t_i) of the cell. In a two-state CA, the values of the states are '0' and '1'. In

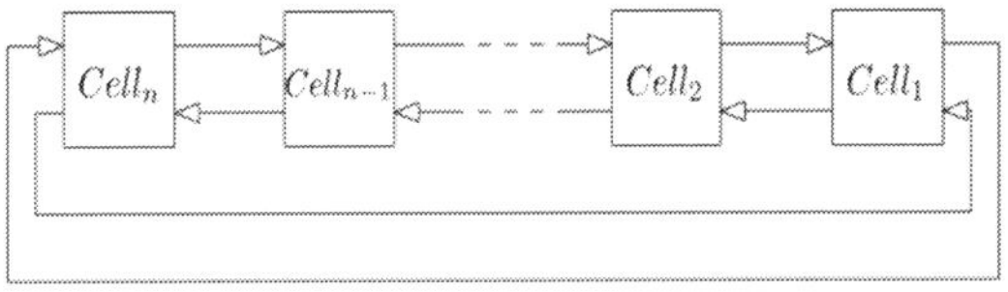

Figure 1. Block diagram of n cell periodic boundary CA.

one-dimensional 3-neighborhood CA, the next state of the ith cell is specified by the next state function (f_i) as given by the Eq. 1

$$S_i^{t+1} = f_i(S^t_{i-1}, S^t_i, S^t_{i+1}) \qquad (1)$$

CA cell is implemented with D Flip/Flop and a combinational logic circuit realizing f_i. Next state of the ith cell is expressed in the form as described in each row of Table II and the decimal equivalent of its NSs is referred as 'Rule' ('232', '184' & '226') as given in Table II. In a 3-neighbourhood CA, there can be a total of 2^8 (256) rules. The collection of the rules (R_is) applied to each cell of the set form rule vector R = $< R_1, R_2 \ldots R_n >$. For a linear CA, f_i employ only EXOR logic. Nonlinear CA employs logic functions (AND, OR, NOT, etc.). Whenever all the R_is of R are linear/additive, the CA is also referred to as Linear/Additive. A **nonuniform or hybrid CA** uses different rules for individual cells. Uniform CA is a special case of hybrid CA having $R_1 = R_2 = \cdots = R_n$. The state transition diagram shows the sequence of states during its evolution with time called CA behavior, as shown in Figure 8. A state transition diagram may contain single or multiple cycles and on that basis, CA can be categorized as reversible or irreversible CA. If $S_0 = S_n$ and $S_{n+1} = S_1$, the CA is referred to as **periodic boundary** CA, as shown in Figure 1. If $S_0 = 0$ (null) and $S_{n+1} = 0$, the CA is called **null boundary**. A one-dimensional binary CA is initialized with an IC (Initial configuration) or seed (random in nature) is

TABLE II. TRUTH TABLE

Present State	111	110	101	100	011	010	001	000	Rule
RMT	(7)	(6)	(5)	(4)	(3)	(2)	(1)	(0)	
Next State	1	1	1	0	1	0	0	0	232
Next State	1	0	1	1	1	0	0	0	184
Next State	1	1	1	0	0	0	1	0	226

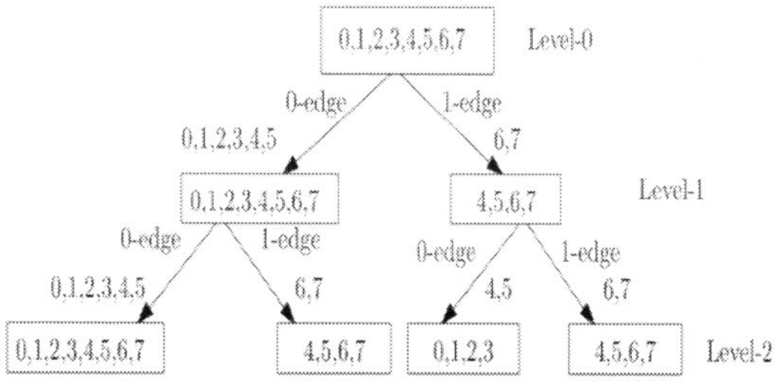

Figure 2. Reachability tree for <232,232,232>.

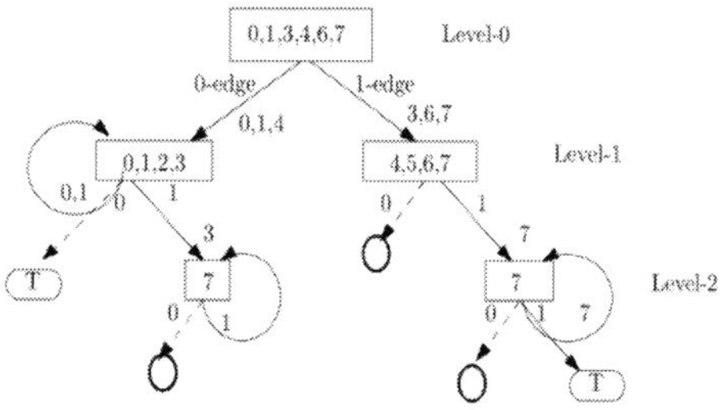

Figure 3. Reachability tree for attractor of hybrid rule <232,184,184,...>.

iterated for a maximum number of steps or until it reaches a fixed point attractor. One-dimensional and two-state CA can classify binary strings according to the densities of (1's or 0's). The ability of a particular elementary CA to solve the density classification task depends on the IC. ICs containing more ones or zeros are closer in hamming distance to one of the solution fixed points or attractors. If IC contains more ones (zeros) than zeros (ones), the CA settles to a fixed point of all ones (zeros). *DCT* may also be performed by realizing two different CA rules hierarchically. First rule is iterated for n_1 time steps and second rule is iterated for n_2 time steps on the resulting configuration [14]. In solving density classification task using $PBCA$, the following features are required [22]:

R_1: All 0s and all 1s two single length attractors

R_2: Binary string with more than 50% 1s (0s) fall on all 1s (0s) basin

R_3: No other attractors or multilength cycle

The number of reachable states of hybridized rule <232,184,184,184,184,184> is represented by a binary tree called reachability tree, as shown in Figure 3. Root node represents all possible RMTs. 0-edge (1-edge) presents RMTs those have next state value as '0' (1). Reachability tree can also be used to represent cycles/attractors, as shown in Figure 2.

III. CACHE ARCHITECTURE IN CHIP MULTI-PROCESSORS (CMPS)

To avoid bottleneck of off-chip interconnect, CMPs use *on-chip* two/three cache layers (L1 & L2 or L1, L2 & L3) which comprises of private cache (L1) of each core and last level cache (L2/L3) shared among the cores. Resistive memory (ReRAM) is available in variety types as Phase Change memory (PCM), Spin-transfer Torque memory (STTRAM), Magneto Resistive RAM (MRAM), Ferro-electric RAM (FRAM) and Memristors. It stores information in terms of low/high resistance to represent 0/1 logic states. Comparison of different types of memory technology is detailed in Table III. Hybrid cache composed of SRAM and other types of ReRAM are proposed in [1] [4] [5]. Four cores are connected to on-chip hybrid shared Last Level Cache (LLC) as shown in Figure 4. Cores are connected to LLC through bus, switch or a hybrid type of interconnect.

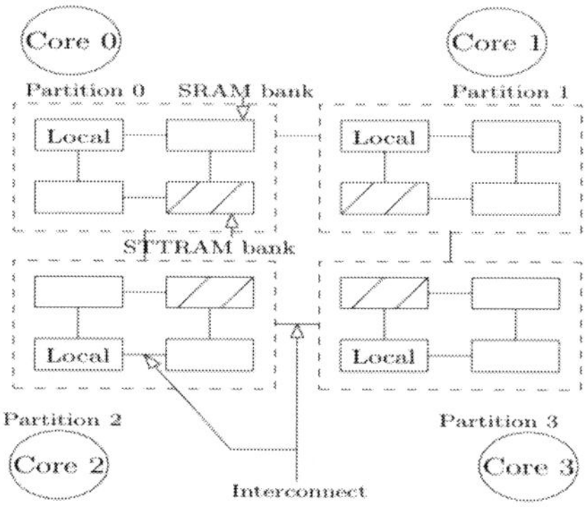

Figure 4. Partitioned hybrid cache architecture with STTRAM & SRAM.

IV. BLOCK DIAGRAM OF REMAPPING PROCESS

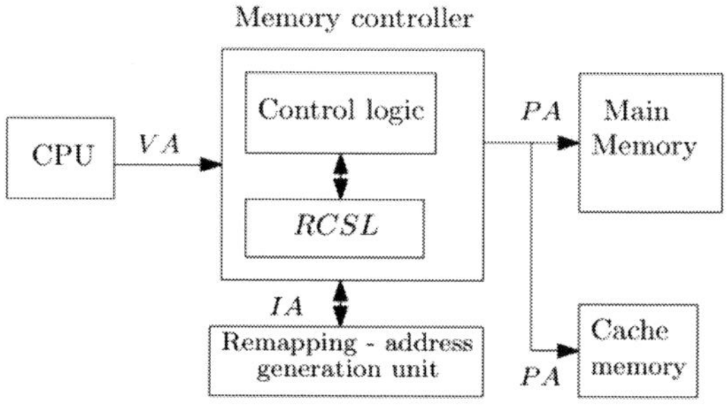

Figure 5. Block Diagram

In Figure 5, block diagram of a memory subsystem with in-built remapping address generation is described briefly. The

TABLE III. COMPARISON BETWEEN DIFFERENT TYPES OF RESISTIVE MEMORY.

Memory technology	FeRAM	MRAM	STT-RAM	PCM
Nonvolatility	Yes	Yes	Yes	Yes
Cell size	Large	Large	Small	Small
Package Density(ratio)	Low	Low	High	High
Read access time(ns)	20 to 80	3 to 20	2 to 20	20 to 50
Write access time(ns)	50	3 to 20	2 to 20	20
Write energy consumption	Mid	Mid-High	Low	Low
Cell lifetime (in terms of number of writes)	10^{12}	$> 10^{15}$	$> 10^{16}$	10^{12}

shared cache is assumed here with set-associative mapping policy. Cellular Automata based Remapping Candidate Selection Logic (*RCSL*) selects the write-stressed memory blocks with the help of *memory controller* and it is detailed in the next Section. Virtual Address (VA) is generated by the processor at compilation phase and which is translated to Physical Address (PA) by memory controller. But for the case of *write-stressed* memory block, the address is translated to Intermediate Address (IA) by remapping address generation unit. Further, IA is converted to PA for memory operation dictated by memory controller.

V. REMAPPING CANDIDATE SELECTION LOGIC (RCSL)

In CMPs, multiple processors may access an unpartitioned shared cache memory (L2 or L3) at any instant. Due to *spatial locality of reference*, few contiguous memory blocks are found written for multiple times. Let us assume, M number of processors P_1, P_2, P_3 ... P_M are integrated in a chip with 'N' number of *on-chip* cache lines. An access pattern vector (AP_v) is defined to collect write access information of each cacheline.

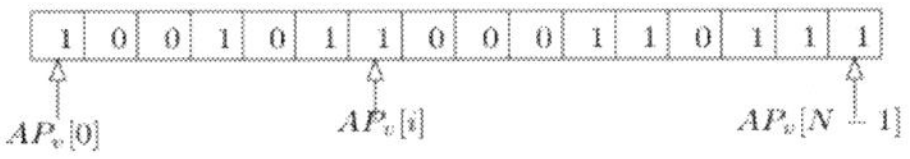

Figure 6. Vector representation of access pattern.

Therefore, length of AP_v is equal to the number (N) of cache lines. If there is a write access for i^{th} block (B[i] say) at any time instant, the value of that vector position $AP_v[i]$='1'or else the value will be '0' as shown in Figure 6. From AP_v, the write access of the cache lines are identified. According to write access pattern of memory block $B[i]$, it can be classified into two categories,

1) Write dominated zone and 2) Seldom written zone

Those blocks are seldom or never used can accept a write request redirected from write dominated blocks. When a less written block is found within the memory set itself, *intra-set* memory remapping is done. But when the memory request is transferred to another set, *inter-set* remapping is performed as per Eq. 4 described in Section VIII.

VI. DESIGN PROCESS

Total memory capacity is divided into groups by taking K number of memory blocks in each. Right/left half of the group (K/2 number of memory blocks) are the remapping zone. Let us take K=6 in this example, as shown in Figure 7. Two stage DCT is performed on AP_v to categorise the blocks. CA is loaded with initial configuration (IC or *seed*) and iterated for appropriate time steps so that it can settle down to an attractor having hamming distance closer to IC. The right/left half (three memory blocks) of six contiguous memory blocks are categorized as *write stressed* or *seldom written*.

Each memory block is represented by identical CA cells. 6 cell hybrid $PBCA$ and 3 cell uniform $PBCA$ are applied to perform DCT in two stages. Six-cell hybrid $PBCA$ with uniform rule set $<$ 232 184 184 184 184 184$>$ is iterated for t_1 time steps. States are having majority of '0' in their bit pattern, fall in '0' (000000) basin and those having majority '1' fall in basin '63' (111111). Almost uniformly distributed 0's and 1's states fall in alpha (α) basin '21' (010101) as given in Table IV. Check bit is the LSB bit of the attractor and saved in a register. For write-stressed block, the checkbit is '1' and zero for less written memory blocks. Therefore, states fall in all ones and alpha basin are both considered as write dominated blocks. Though uniformly distributed 1s and 0s fall on alpha basin violating the requirement R_3, it is not inserting any error in the design as the zone may be considered as write stressed.

Let us take an example according to Figure 7. The checkbits of

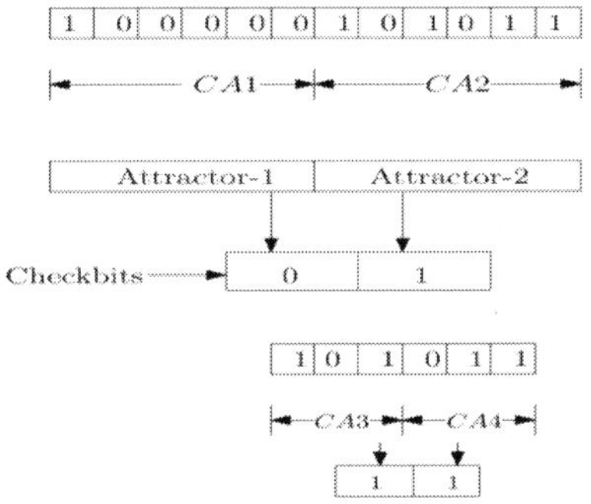

Figure 7. Example-1

CA-1 and CA-2 are found as '0' and '1'. Left half is considered as seldom written zone and right half as write stressed zone. To keep the remapping zone smaller, only three memory blocks is identified from the selected cache zone by making it divide by two. Two groups are iterated to perform DCT again. *3-cell* PBCA

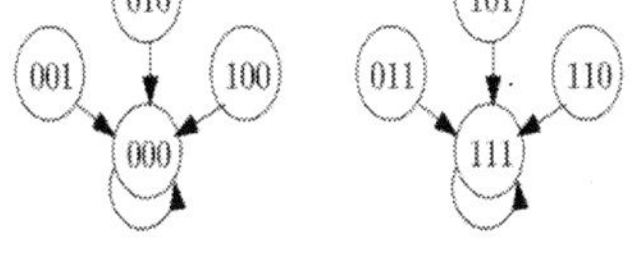

Figure 8. State transition diagram of 3 cell uniform PBCA.

with uniform rule set of $< 232, 232, 232 >$ is iterated for t_2 time steps in the second stage. *CA-3* and *CA-4* settle to any of these two attractors '000'/'111' within a single clock cycle as shown in Figure 8. According to the given example, both *CA-3* and *CA-4*

TABLE IV. STATE ANALYSIS REPORT

	Analysis of basin -'0	Analysis of basin -'63'	Analysis of basin -'α'
States	1, 2, 3, 4, 5, 6, 7, 8, 9, 10, 11, 12, 13, 14, 15, 16, 17, 18, 19, 20, 22, 24, 32, 34, 36, 40, 48 fall in zero basin	23, 25, 27, 29, 30, 31, 33, 35, 37, 39, 41, 43, 45, 46, 47, 49, 50, 51, 53, 54, 55, 57, 58, 59, 60, 61, 62, 63	19, 25, 26, 28, 38, 42, 44, 52, 56 fall in 21 basin
Loops	One single length loop 0→0	One single length loop 63→63	One multilength loop 21→42→21
Misprediction	15 (001111) as it falls on '0' basin having greater number of 1s	33 (100001) as it falls on '63' basin having less number of 1s	No unpredictable states

settles down to '111' attractor. Checkbit (LSB bit of the attractor) is 1 for LHS as well as RHS. The decision is taken as per decision rule illustrated in the Table V. Therefore, both RHS & LHS are *write dominated* and both are candidates of remapping as per decision rule. LSB bit of alpha basin is '1' and also considered as write-stressed zone. But few states with uniform distribution fall on zero basin. It will contribute a little bit error in the design.

VII. ADDRESS REMAPPING

Remapping candidates are write-stressed zone (with three contiguous memory blocks) that must be mapped to another less written zone (three contiguous memory blocks). $RCSL$ block identifies the write-stressed zone as well as less written zone through CA. Address generation block produces the remapped address by *algebraic* technique in communication with memory controller. *Intra-set* remapping is performed in between blocks of a set and termed as local wear leveling. *Inter-set* remapping or global wear leveling is performed between the sets of a memory.

Set-associative cache memory is studied in the current design where N number of sets with M equal number of blocks to each set is assumed. If G be a non-empty group with a defined operation * in it and H be a subgroup of G. The subset $\{ah : h \in H\}$ is called a left coset of H and denoted by aH. Here aH = Ha (right coset) for all 'a' and so H is a normal subgroup. G & H are represented by ($N_{Totalnumberofmemoryblocks}$, modulo operation) and ($N_{Totalnumberofsets}$, modulo operation). Therefore, the number of coset is given by Eq. 2 [23].

$$[G : H] = \frac{G_n}{H_n} \tag{2}$$

where order or number of elements of G and H are G_n and H_n respectively. The set of distinct cosets or partitions (P) represents the quotient group (Q) and given by the Eq 3.

$$Q = \{\{0 + H\}, \{1 + H\}, \dots, \{15 + H\}\} \tag{3}$$

Each elements of quotient group (Q) represents the sets (partitions) and the elements belonging to the partitions (sets) are the elements of the sets of *set associative* cache. Therefore, Block address is defined by the Eq. 4.

$$B_i = M * n + j \tag{4}$$

Here, i denotes the block index. Set index (j) and block offset (n) variables are remapping parameters those can be varied from 0 to N-1 and 0 to M-1, respectively, to adjust remapping offsets. To change within set or global wear leveling, change of set index (j) and for local wear leveling, block offset (n) has to be varied in the Eq. 4.

Let us take an example where total number of memory words or length of memory is 256. Number of sets and blocks are taken as 16 (N) & 16 (M). Group of all memory words (G) is $< Z_{256}, + >$ and $< Z_{16}, + >$ represents a subgroup (H). Therefore, the number of cosets is 16 as per Eq. 2. Distinct cosets/partitions are collection of blocks with index numbers are $C_1 = <0, 16, 32, 48, 64, \dots 240>$, $C_2 = <1, 17, 33, 49, 65, \dots 241>, \cdots C_{16} = <15, 31, 47, 63 \dots 255>$. Block of index number 17 can be written as B_{17} = 16*1 + 1. For global/interset mapping, the set index is changed from 1 to 5. So, the new block address will be 21 belonging to set five.

VIII. ANALYSIS

$SMPCache$ tool is developed to identify memory access traces (opcode read, data read/write) to the data blocks [8] for Symmetric (SMP/DSM) multiprocessors. Table VI illustrates a sample of memory *write access* on the memory blocks from traces of $WAVE$, $NASA7$ and SWM [27]. A typical CMPs architecture with eight cores and three levels of set-associative cache memory are used. To asses the fact of locality of reference, all processor's write access pattern is observed. CEXP, EAR, COMP, MDLJD, HYDRO and others are also considered in Table VII to capture access pattern that is collected from $SMPCache$ simulator. Total memory accesses, number of write accesses and total number of reused memory blocks of all trace files are computed. Observation reveals that distribution of writes are lumped within a very few cache blocks and other blocks are seldom written. So, locality of spatial reference is observed for contiguous memory blocks that can be considered for remapping candidates.

IX. CONCLUSION AND FUTURE WORK

In this paper, we have proposed wear leveling scheme to reduce write pressure on memory blocks and redistribute write requests within shared LLC of CMPs. Cache lifetime can be improved with local/global wear leveling at the cost of little hardware overhead. But this work addressed the non-uniformity of writes caused by workload distribution of CMPs by considering spatial write access pattern only. Therefore, it is not suitable for those write-stressed memory blocks subjected to malicious attacks. This CA based scheme can be extended for prevention of malicious attacks by capturing temporal as well spatial access patterns as a future work of the current research.

REFERENCES

[1] I. Lin and J. Chiou," High-Endurance Hybrid Cache Design in CMP Architecture With Cache Partitioning and Access-Aware Policies", *IEEE Transactions on Very Large Scale Integration (VLSI) Systems*, 2014.

[2] S. Mittal, Y. Cao and Z. Zhang, "MASTER: A Multicore Cache Energy-Saving Technique Using Dynamic Cache Reconfiguration", *IEEE Transaction on Very Large Scale Integration (VLSI) Systems, 2013.*

TABLE V. DECISION RULE

Checkbit-0	Checkbit-1	Decision	Remarks
0	0	Neither LHS or RHS is write dominated	Remapping is not required
0	1	RHS is write dominated	3 cells of RHS are remapping candidates
1	0	LHS is write dominated	3 cells of LHS are remapping candidates
1	1	Both LHS and RHS are write dominated	Remapping is required for all 6 cells

TABLE VI. MEMORY BLOCK'S WRITE ACCESS PATTERN

Block address	Processor	written for single/multiple times
3845	P_2, P_6	P_2-multiple, P_6-single
3844,3843	P_2, P_5, P_6	multiple
3596	P_0, P_4	multiple
3141,2045,2037	P_1, P_3	single
2044	P_1, P_3, P_7	single
2043	P_1, P_3, P_6, P_7	P_1, P_7-multiple & P_3, P_6-single
2039,2038	P_1, P_3,	multiple
2035	P_2, P_5	single
1522	P_0, P_4	single
1521	P_0, P_2, P_4, P_5, P_6	others multiple times except P_2
1520	P_0, P_4	multiple
1519,1518	P_0, P_4	single
1517	P_0, P_4	P_0-single, P_4-multiple
1516	P_0, P_4	P_0, P_4-multiple
1515	P_0, P_4	P_0-single, P_4-multiple
1493, 1416	P_0	single

TABLE VII. STATISTICS OF MEMORY BLOCK'S ACCESS

Trace	Total number of RD/WR Access	Number of Writes	Number of reused blocks
CEXP	20000	262	15
WAVE	3467	464	27
EAR	5308	262	33
COMP	2524	356	11
HYDRO	2127	284	27
MDLJD	20000	1175	31
NASA7	1825	270	21
UCOMP	2733	363	11

[3] M. K. Qureshi et al. "Enhancing lifetime and security of PCM-based main memory with start-gap wear leveling", "*In MICRO, 2009, pp. 14-23.*

[4] A. Jadidi, M. Arjomand and H. Sarbazi-Azad, "High-endurance and performance-efficient design of hybrid cache architectures through adaptive line replacement", *IEEE, 2011.*

[5] J. Li, C. Xue and Y. Xu, "STT-RAM based Energy-Efficiency Hybrid Cache for CMPs", *IEEE/IFIP 19th International Conference on VLSI and System-on-Chip, 2011.*

[6] L. P. Chang, "On efficient wear leveling for large-scale flash-memory storage systems", *in Proceedings of the 2007 ACM symposium on Applied computing. ACM, 2007, pp. 11261130.*

[7] M. K. Qureshi, A. Seznec and L. A. Lastras, "Practical and Secure PCM Systems by Online Detection of Malicious Write Streams", *17th International Symposium on High Performance Computer Architecture, 2011.*

[8] M. A. Vega Rodr guez, J. M. S Prez, R. Mart n de laae Monta a, and F. A. Zarallo Gallardo, "Simulation of Cache n Memory Systems on Symmetric Multiprocessors with Educational Purposes.", *International Congress in Quality and in Technical Education Innovation,volume 3, pages 4759, 2000.*

[9] G. Wu, H. Zhang, Y. Don, and J. Hu, "CAR: Securing PCM Main Memory System with Cache Address Remapping", *18th International Conference on Parallel and Distributed Systems, IEEE, 2012.*

[10] T. Wang, D. Liu, Z. Shao and C. Yang, "Write-activity-aware page table management for PCM-based embedded systems", *17th Asia and South pacific conference, IEEE, 2012.*

[11] M. K. Qureshi, M. Franchescini, V. Srinivasan, L. Lastras, B. Abali and J. Karidis, "Enhancing Lifetime and Security of PCM-Based Main Memory with Start-Gap Wear Leveling", *in Proceedings of the 42nd Annual IEEE/ACM International Symposium on Microarchitecture ACM.*

[12] Q. Liu and P. Varman, "Ouroboros Wear-Leveling: A Two-Level Hierarchical Wear-Leveling Model for NVRAM", *IEEE*, 2015.

[13] C. Stone and L. Bull, "Solving the Density Classification Task Using Cellular Automaton 184 with Memory", *2009.*

[14] H. Fuks, "Solution of the density classification problem with two cellular automata rules", *Phys. Rev. E 55, R2081(R) Published 1 March 1997.*

[15] J. Hu, M. Xie, C. Pan, C. J. Xue, Q. Zhuge and E. H. Sha, "Low Overhead Software Wear Leveling for Hybrid PCM + DRAM Main Memory on Embedded Systems", *IEEE Transactions on Very Large Scale Integration (VLSI), 2015.*

[16] C. Wang and W. Wong, "Observational Wear Leveling: An Efficient Algorithm for Flash Memory Management", *2012.*

[17] C. Lee, "Synthesis of a Cellular Universal Machine using 29 state Model of von Neumann ", *Automata Theory Notes, The University of Michigan Engineering Summer Conferences,* 1964.

[18] M. Dalui and B. K. Sikdar, " A cellular automata based self-correcting protocol processor for scalable cmps", *Microelectronics Journal 62 (2017) 108119.*

[19] S. Sarkar, M. Saha and B. K. Sikdar, "Multi-bit fault tolerant design for resistive memories through dynamic partitioning", *EWDTS, IEEE Computer Society, Novisad, Serbia, 2017, pp. 16.*

[20] J. Thatcher, "Universality in Von Neumann Cellular Automata.", *In Tech Report 03105-30-T,ORA, University of Michigan.*, 1964.

[21] J. V. Neumann., "The theory of self-reproducing Automata.", *In Tech Report 03105-30-T,ORA, University of Michigan.*, 1964.

[22] B. Das, M. Dalui, S. Kamilya, S. Das and B. K. Sikdar, "Synthesis of Periodic Boundary CA for Efficient Data Migration in Chip-Multiprocessors", *IEEE, 2013.*

[23] J. Nicholoson, "The Development and Understanding of the Concept of Quotient Group", *HISTORIA MATHEMATICA(1993), 68-88*

[24] W. Wen, Y. Zhang and J. Yang, "Wear Leveling for Crossbar Resistive Memory", *In Proceedings of the 55th Annual Design Automation Conference DAC '18, ACM.*

[25] K. Asanovic, J. Beck, B. Irissou, B.Kingsbury and J. Wawrzynek, "A Single-Chip Vector Microprocessor with Reconfigurable Pipelines", *In the Proceedings of the 22nd European Solid-State Circuits Conference, Sept. 1996.*

[26] N. N. Sirhan and S. I. Serhan, "Multi-core Processors: Concepts And Implementations", *International Journal of Computer Science & Information Technology (IJCSIT), Vol 10, No 1, February 2018.*

[27] M. A. Vega-Rodrguez, J. M. Snchez-Prez, R. M. de la Montaa and F. A. Zarallo-Gallardo, "Simulation of Cache Memory Systems on Symmetric Multiprocessors with Educational Purposes", *Proc. of the I International Congress in Quality and in Technical Education Innovation, vol. III, pp. 47-59.*

Development of Extended-STIL Pattern Compiler for Test Programming Environment

Seong-Jin Kim
Dept. of Computer Science and Engineering
Sangji University
Wonju-si Gangwon-do, Republic of Korea
Seongjin.gim@gmail.com

Kwang-Man Ko
Dept. of Computer Science and Engineering
Sangji University
Wonju-si Gangwon-do, Republic of Korea
kkman@sangji.ac.kr

***Abstract*—In this paper, we extended the blocks that can generate analog signals in the Alternating Current (AC) Instrument board along with the basic blocks provided by the Standard Test Interface Language (STIL) standard. We developed a compiler that extracts test information by analyzing STIL files by block. In order to verify the accuracy of the test information extracted by the compiler, experimental results using Automatic Test Equipment (ATE) are presented.**

***Keywords*—STIL pattern compiler; Standard test interface language; test pattern**

I. INTRODUCTION

Standard Test Interface Language (STIL) is a standard test interface language that allows one to define test patterns and waveforms, which are generated when simulating digital integrated circuits, in one language. STIL provides an interface between digital test generation tools and the test equipment [1]. It can be created directly as a test generation tool's output language or used as an intermediate format for processing a specific stage. Therefore, STIL is ideal for exchanging data between a Computer-Aided Design (CAD) or a simulator and a test environment. Test programs written in STIL generally consist of seven blocks that define STIL, Signals, SignalGroups, Timing, PatternBurst, PatternExec, and Pattern. Each block is created based on the design description of the chip to be tested [2].

In this paper, we expanded the functions of STIL by adding blocks that can be applied to AC test instruments board along with the basic blocks provided by the STIL standard and have developed a compiler that extracts and saves the necessary test information by interpreting the file created with the extended STIL. In addition, we utilized the digital instrument board for open/short test which is a DC parameter test. We also experimented for gross function test to verify the truth table for Texas Instruments' SN74LS00N chip in order to validate the test information extracted by the compiler.

II. BACKGROUNDS AND MOTIVATIONS

A. *Standard Interface Language and Block*

STIL is a standard language that provides an interface between digital test generation tools and test equipment. It is either created directly in the output language of the test generator or is used as an intermediate format for specific stage processing. In addition, STIL is well suited as data exchanged between a CAD or simulator and a test environment [3][4].

STIL files generated by an ATPG or simulator are used as inputs to a converter or a compiler to classify and store test information for each component. Among the stored information, the test vector is loaded into the memory of the target tester when necessary. The test vector is the most important element defined in the STIL language. It is used to detect defects and is usually similar to the truth table type and consists of input data and output data. The test vectors and patterns are used in combination and are used to measure the logic functions and AC/DC functions of semiconductor products. The STIL file is also used as an input to the STIL manipulation tool and can be used as an output to generate STIL files with specific rules and commands added. STIL allows tester-dependent programs to be applied to specific ATE systems and directly connects ATPG tools such as CAD/CAE to the ATE environment. A test program written in this STIL is generally composed of 7 blocks, and each block is created based on the design specification of the chip to be tested.

B. *Motivations and Contributions*

Developers of ATE (Automatic Test Equipment) that can test and evaluate digital devices and provide an easy-to-access debug-able test program environment for users to test various devices. Users who write test programs are required to become familiar with the structure and behavior of test languages and ATE, and it is especially important to write and maintain test patterns used to evaluate and test DUT (Device Under Test) during testing. Since the use of a test description language is essential to easily create and manage these test patterns, many ATE vendors are using STIL standards that can easily describe the structure and test patterns of DUTs. Therefore, it is essential that the STIL standard used in the test description language is software that classifies and stores test information for each component by analyzing STIL files so that it can be interpreted by the test equipment [5].

Typically, the ADVANTEST SoC test systems T2000 and V93000 generate STIL files of patterns, timing, and level information generated by ATPG as shown in the Figure 3, and provide STIL Reader to convert the generated STIL files to the test system. TERADYNE's mixed-signal SoC test systems, UltraFLEX and J750, also provide IG-XL Test Software, which converts STIL, WGL (Waveform Generation Language) and VCD (Value Change Dump). The use of the STIL standard is essential for testing a variety of devices using ATE, and a compiler for interpreting and categorizing files written in the STIL standard is a must-have tool [6].

III. EXTENDED STIL

A. Abbreviations and Acronyms

The SourceWave block is a block that allows the user to create waveforms by defining eight kinds of information, such as period, frequency, and amplitude for four types of waveforms such as Sine, Ramp, Pulse, and Staircase. To do this, we define keywords and token groups that can be defined in the SourceWave block. A total of 15 keywords can be used in the SourceWave block and four types of waveforms can be defined by the user. The waveforms are divided into five token groups according to the attributes of the keywords. The division of a keyword into token groups is a way to make it as simple and easy to use as possible when defining a grammar.

B. SourceWave Definition

Fig. 1 shows the BNF representation of the SourceWave block syntax and how it can actually be defined based on these BNF representations.

```
source_wave ::= SourceWave source_wave_name "{"
                    [outer_wave_item_list]
                    signal_wave
                "}"
source_wave_name ::= identifier
outer_wave_item_list ::= outer_wave_item
                    | outer_wave_item_list outer_wave_item
signal_wave ::= signal_name "{"
                  wave_type "{"
                    [inner_wave_item_list]
                  "}"
                [Operation type_operand]
                "}"
inner_wave_item_list ::= inner_wave_item
                    | inner_wave_item_list outer_wave_item
outer_wave_item ::= outer_current_type type_operand ";"
inner_wave_item ::= `inner_current_type type_operand ";"
outer_current_type ::= Period | Frequency | Sample
inner_current_type ::= Period | Amplitude | Offset
                    | Repeat | Phase | Invert
                    | MaximumRise
type_operand ::= integer | float
signal_name  ::= identifier
wave_type    ::= Sin | Ramp | Pulse | Staircase
```

Fig. 1. BNF Representation of SourceWave Block

In Fig. 1, the SourceWave block can define a signal wave with one or more outer wave items and only one signal name, either the signal or the signal name defined in the SignalGroups block. In the "outer wave" item, we can declare a type and type subject with three keywords: period, frequency, and sample. In the waveform definition of the signal, we can declare 8 attributes and 4 waveforms in total.

IV. STIL PATTERN COMPILER

The STIL Pattern Compiler implemented in this study receives a STIL file composed of basic blocks provided by the STIL standard as input. The STIL Pattern Compiler analyzes the file and stores the necessary test information. In addition, the functions were extended by defining additional blocks applicable to AC/DC instruments, and an intermediate file that can be recognized by the test program and the instrument is generated through the linker and the loader.

A. Overall Structure

The overall structure of the STIL Pattern Compiler is shown in Fig. 2. The STIL Pattern Compiler is divided into Small Vector Compiler, Small Vector Linker, and Small Vector Loader. Small Vector Compiler and Linker operate in conjunction with Test Program which defines a STIL file, and Loader works in conjunction with Test OS to send test data to the instrument.

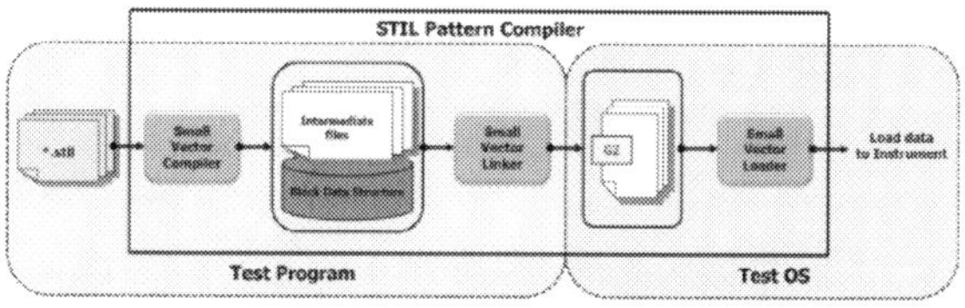

Fig. 2. The Structure of STIL Pattern Compiler

First, the Small Vector Compiler receives a STIL file as an input, classifies and analyzes the data by blocks, stores the analyzed data in a block data structure, and generates an intermediate file as the input of the linker. Second, the Small Vector Linker receives the intermediate file generated by the Small Vector Compiler as input and generates an input file of the Small Vector Loader. The intermediate files received as inputs at this time contain pattern and block information. Finally, the Small Vector Loader receives a compressed file generated by the Small Vector Linker as input and loads the test data in the actual instrument.

B. Small Vector Compiler

The main purpose of the STIL Pattern Compiler is to analyze and classify incoming STIL files and provide the required test data to the Test OS and Instrument. The structure of Small Vector Compiler designed and implemented in this study to perform this function is shown in Fig. 3.

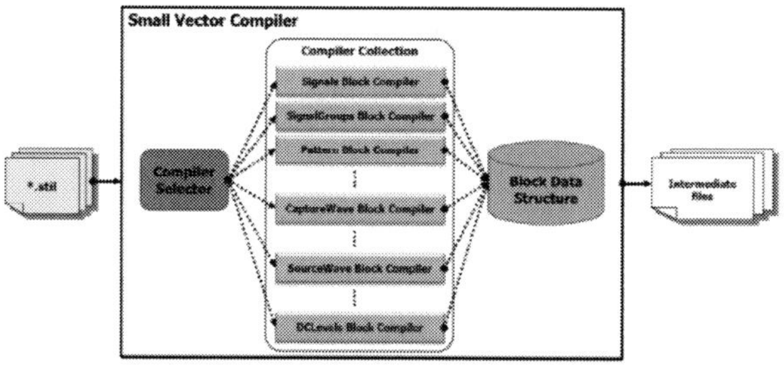

Fig. 3. The Structure of Small Vector Compiler

Small Vector Compiler is divided into Compiler Selector that receives STIL files as inputs and calls corresponding Compiler, Compiler Collection area that analyzes and stores STIL blocks, and Block Data Structure that stores test data. First, the Small Vector Compiler delivers the user-defined STIL files received as inputs to the Compiler Selector. Compiler Selector divides the received STIL files into blocks and calls the corresponding Block Compiler in the Compiler Collection area consisting of 18 Block Compilers to analyze the Block contents. The called Block Compiler extracts the test data while analyzing the block contents, stores it in the block data structure, and generates an intermediate file for storing the pattern in-formation and the test data. The Block Data Structure stored by the Small Vector Compiler contains a lot of test data which is used as very important data in the Test OS. The intermediate file is used as the input of the Small Vector Linker. The core of the Small Vector Compiler implemented in this study is the Compiler Collection area, which is a set of block compilers that analyze each block and store test data.

C. *Block Compiler*

Block Compiler in the Compiler Collection area basically analyzes the corresponding STIL file and stores necessary data, and has the structure shown in Fig. 4 to perform such functions.

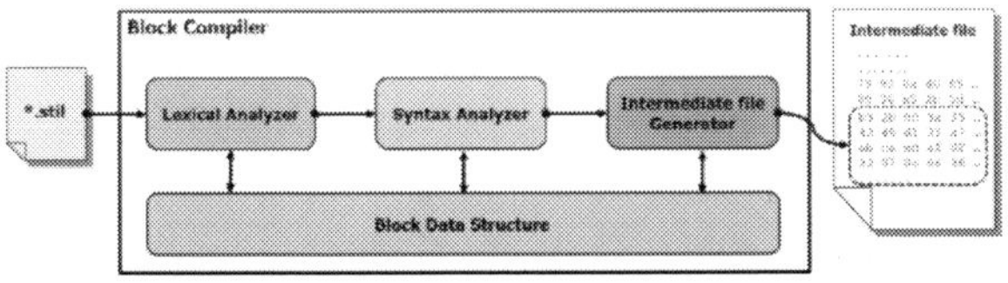

Fig. 4. The Structure of Block Compiler

Block Compiler, which receives a STIL file as an input, first divides it into tokens, which are grammatically meaningful minimum units, through a lexical analyzer. In order to do this, we have defined regular expressions and state transitions, and implemented a recognizer to identify all the tokens that are needed in the STIL file that was received as input. In the next step, the parser receives the tokens identified in the lexical analysis step, checks errors against the syntax defined in the STIL file, and extracts the test data information if there is no error. At this time, the extracted data is stored in the Block Data Structure and is input to the intermediate file generator. In the final step, the inter-mediate file generator generates an intermediate file, which is the input of the Small Vector Linker, in a specific format based on the test data information analyzed by the parser.

V. Experiments and Results

In order to verify the operation of the STIL Pattern Compiler implemented in this study and the accuracy of extracted test data, open/short test, which is a DC parameter test, and gross functional test were performed for verification of defects in the circuit using the Digital Instrument Board [7], which is used in ATE [8], with SN74LS00N, which is a 4 channel NAND gate IC of Texas Instruments. For this purpose, STIL and a test program for chip operation were prepared, compiled, and loaded into TestOS and the instrument board, and the results of the two tests were obtained. In addition, the information extracted from STIL was verified using the STIL Viewer Tool of TestOS.

A. *Test Program Configuration*

In order to drive and test the chip, it is necessary to write and compile the test program. For this, the STIL must be defined first based on the chip specification. Fig. 5 shows the pin configuration, logic diagram, and truth table among the chip specifications used for the experiment in this study.

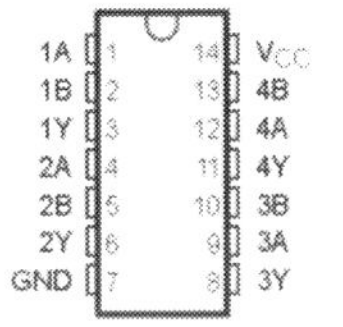

(a) Package

(b) Logic diagram

FUNCTION TABLE
(each gate)

INPUTS		OUTPUT
A	B	Y
H	H	L
L	X	H
X	L	H

(c) Function table

Fig. 5. The Specification of SN74LS00N

In this figure, the SN74LS00N consists of 14 pins (8 inputs, 4 outputs, Vcc, and GND) and 4 NAND gates. The output has a low value only when the inputs are all high.

```
STIL 1.0;
Signals {
  "ina0"  In; "ina1" In; "outa" Out;
  "inb0"  In; "inb1" In; "outb" Out;
  "outc" Out; "inc0" In; "inc1"  In;
  "outd" Out; "ind0" In; "ind1"  In;
  "vcc"   In;
}
SignalGroups {
  ainput = 'ina0 + ina1';
  binput = 'inb0 + inb1'; .
  cinput = 'inc0 + inc1';
  dinput = 'ind0 + ind1';
  input  = 'ainput + binput + cinput + dinput';
  output = 'outa + outb + outc + outd';
  all = 'input + output';
}
Timing "timeNormal" {
  WaveformTable "ts0" {
    Period '100ns';
      Waveforms {
        all {
          P { '1.0ns' P; }
          0 { '0.0ns' N; '1.0ns' D; }
          1 { '0.0ns' N; '1.0ns' U; }
          L { '0.0ns' Z; '81.0ns' L; }
          H { '0.0ns' Z; '81.0ns' H; }
          X { '0.0ns' Z; '81.0ns' X; }
          T { '0.0ns' Z; '81.0ns' T; }
          Z { '0.0ns' Z; }
          2 { '0.0ns' 2; }
        } // end all
      } // end waveforms
  }  // end WaveformTable
} // end Timing
PatternBurst "burst" {
  PatList {
    "gross";
  }
}
PatternExec "exec" {
  Timing        "timeNormal";
  PatternBurst "burst";
}
Vector gross {
  Signals ("all");
  W ts0;
  > XX XX XX XX X X X X;
  loop_start 1000
  > 00 01 10 11 H H H L;
  > 01 10 11 00 H H L H;
  > 10 11 00 01 H L H H;
  > 11 00 01 10 L H H H;
  > 10 11 00 01 H L H H;
  > 01 10 11 00 H H L H;
  loop_end;
  stop;
}
```

Fig. 6. The Definition of STIL for SN74LS00N

Base on this, the STIL for chip test was defined as shown in Fig. 6. First, the signal name and type for the input and output pins of 4 NAND gates were declared in the signal block and the signals defined above were classified into seven groups in the SignalGroups block for convenience. In the Timing block, a WaveformTable with the name ts0 was defined with nine WaveformChars for a period of "100ns" and "all" groups. In addition, timing and pattern names to be used were described in the PatternBusrt and PatterExec blocks. Finally, in the Vector (block) block, the operation of actual signals was defined using the signal and timing block information.

B. Experimental Environment

After compiling the STIL file and test program created in Section 4.1 and loading the test data to TestOS and the Digital Instrument Board, the experimental environment as shown in Figure 16 was constructed to test the characteristics and defects of the corresponding device using the device verification tool.

Fig. 7. The Experimental Environment

First, TestOS is connected to the Digital Instrument Board to load the compiled test program and test data. The Digital Instrument Board used in the experiment has 64 I/O channels with basic 200Mhz/400Mbps speeds and provides 32 timing sets and 4 edges per channel. Next, an interface board was used for connection between the Digital Instrument Board and the DUT as shown Fig. 8. A total of five devices can be connected to this interface board and two SN74LS00N chips were connected in this study.

Fig. 8. The Connection Configuration: Instrument board and Interface board

C. Experiment Result

In the first experiment, open/short test, which is a DC parameter test, was per-formed to verify that the DUT operates normally in the specified environment. TestCenter Tool, an engineering tool for device verification, was used to execute the test defined in the test program and analyze the characteristics of the device. The result of the experiment is shown in Figure 18. From the result, we can see that the measured values of all the signals defined in the STIL file are between -0.2 and -1.5 V, con-firming that all the pins of the two tested devices are normal.

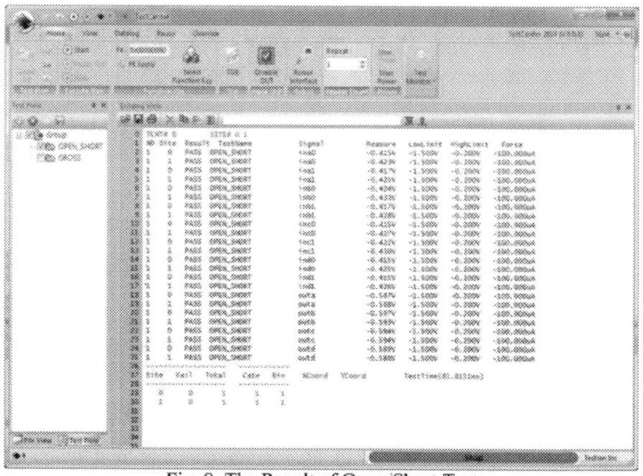

Fig. 9. The Result of Open/Short Test

In the second experiment, a gross functional test was performed to verify the presence of defects on the DUT circuit. To obtain the execution result of the test, we used the Pattern Tool which shows the pattern information defined in the PatternExec block and the actual execution result of the pat-tern and the waveform of each signal. The result of the experiment is shown in Fig. 10. The yellow line in the result signifies the response data output from the DUT, and the blue line signifies the expected data to be compared with the DUT output. The green line is the baseline of the data, and the upper side of the line signifies HIGH and the lower side LOW. Figure 10(a) and 10(b) show the wave-forms of the response data output by each DUT and the expected data for output signals, verifying that the waveform of the response data from each DUT matches that of the expected data. There-fore, the two tested devices have no problem in the circuit.

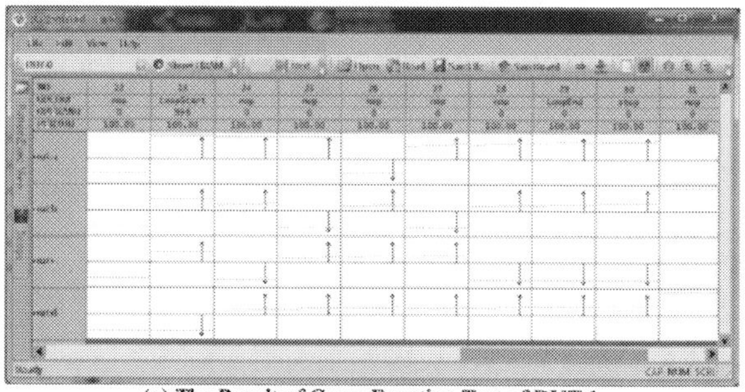

(a) The Result of Gross Function Test of DUT 1

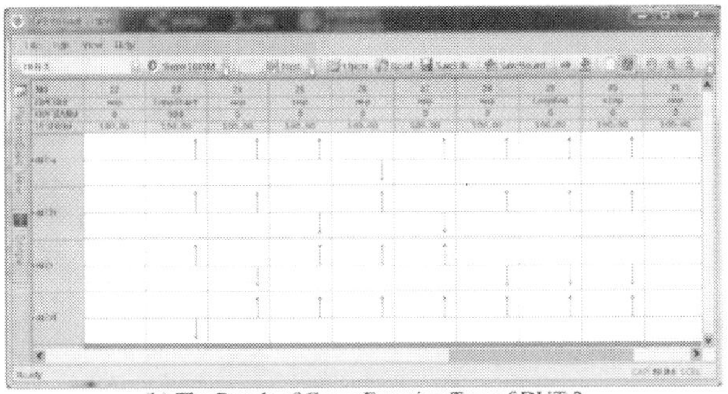

(b) The Result of Gross Function Test of DUT 2

Fig. 10. The Result of Gross Function Test

Finally, the information extracted by the STIL Pattern Compiler was confirmed by using the STIL Viewer Tool of TestOS, as shown in Fig. 11. The Viewer Tool shows block information such as Signal (Fig. 11(a)), SiganlGroup (Fig. 20(b)), and Timing (Fig. 20(c)) information defined in the STIL, and it can be seen that the test information extracted by the compiler is normally stored.

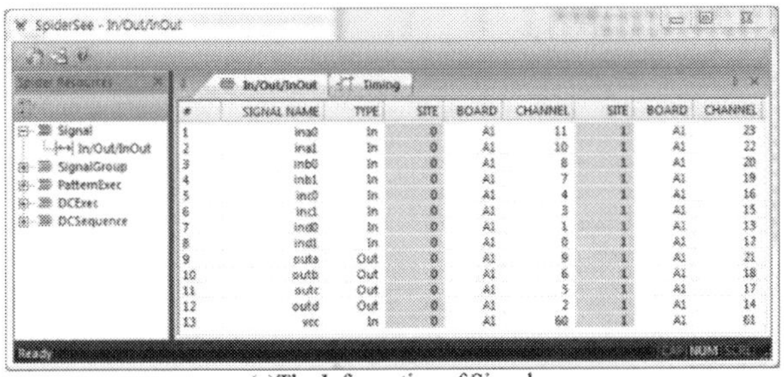

(a)The Information of Signal

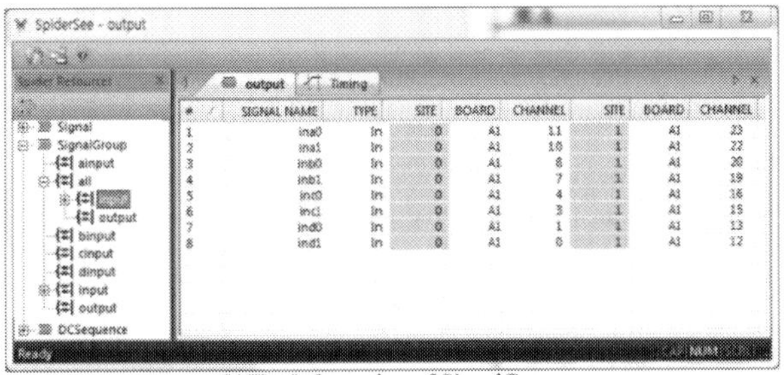

(b)The Information of SignalGroup

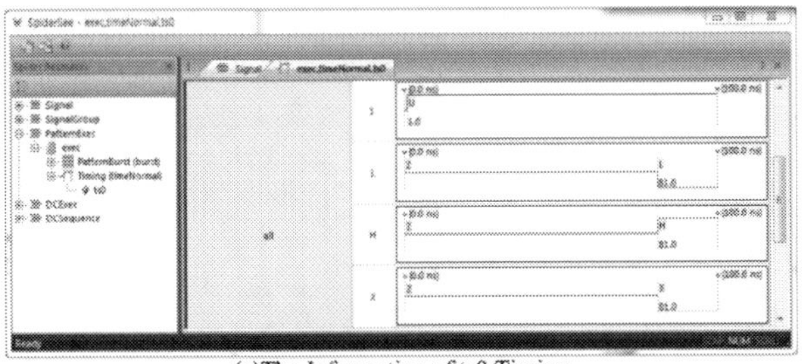

(c)The Information of ts0 Timing

Fig. 11. The Information of STIL Viewer Tool

VI. Related Works

STIL-based pattern generation tools eliminate the process of switching to a specific format of the tester by directly connecting ATPG tools with ATE [9]. Compatible with the ADVANTEST T2000 system, OPENSTAR ™ has established an efficient communication link between the Electronic Design Automation (EDA) system and the ATE platform. In addition, they applied the same standards as STIL, Core Test Language (CTL), and Standard for Embedded Core Test (SECT) to support common solutions [10]. Teradyne's Ultra FLEX digital instruments were applied to the Test Insight Tool Suite [11]. Test Insight is the primary partner for Teradyne and Advantest, offering a variety of tools for testing and validating test conversions, testing programs [12]. In particular, ATEGEN, a test program generator, generates tester program files for various ATE formats such as general IC tester, J750, and 93K for files written in WGL and STIL. STILVerify, the STIL Checker for Mentor Graphics Tessent®, is commercially available as a tool for parsing and verifying files written in the STIL standard. STILVerify provides Verilog test bench functionality by checking that files written in STIL are syntactically correct, and by running them in the Verilog simulator to verify the contents and behavior of the code [13]. Synopsys' TetraMax ™ ATPG provides test patterns in STIL format and is a tool that automatically generates high-quality test patterns to reduce mistakes in test patterns created to test complex logic [14]. The STIL Director of Toshiba Microelectronics Corporation is a system tool for building test environments based on the STIL standard and is available as a Toshiba STIL design kit. Because it is an open system, it can be easily applied to specific system environment by plug-in method and can be customized in various environments by using Access interface [15].

VII. Conclusion

In this study, we defined the blocks provided by the STIL standard and extended the functions of STIL by adding blocks applicable to the AC/DC test instruments. We also developed the STIL Pattern Compiler, which can extract and save the necessary test information, by analyzing the file created by STIL. Open/short test and gross functional test were performed on the SN74LS00N chip of Texas Instruments to verify the operation of the implemented compiler and the extracted test information. For the verification experiment, first, the STIL file and the test program were created. Second, the experimental environment was constructed using the Interface Board which connects the Digital Instrument Board, DUT and Digital Instrument Board used in TestOS and ATE. Finally, open/short test and gross functional test were conducted by loading a test program from TestCenter, a device verification tool. The logs provided by the TestCenter and the results of the Pattern Tool confirmed that all pins of the two tested devices were normal and that there were no defects in the circuit.

ACKNOWLEDGEMENT

This research was supported by Basic Science Research Program through the National Research Foundation of Korea (NRF) funded by the Ministry of Science, ICT and Future Planning (20173030223).

References

[1] IEEE Computer Society, IEEE Standard Test Interface Language (STIL) for Digital Test Vector Data Language Manual IEEE Std. 1450.1999, IEEE New York (1999)

[2] D. Fan et al, Case Study-Using STIL as Test Pattern Language, NPTest, Inc. LLC, ITC International Test Conference, pp. 811-817, 2003.

[3] P. Wohl and N. Biggs, P1450.1: STIL for the simulation environment, VLSI Test Symposium, 18th IEEE, 2000.

[4] A. Pramanick, R. Krishnaswamy, M. Elston, T. Adachi, Harsanjeet Singh, B. Parnas, and L. Chen, Test programming environment in a modular, open architecture test system, ITC 2004 International, 2004

[5] M. Sato, H. Wakamatsu, M. Arai, K. Ichino, K. Iwasaki, and T. Asaka, Tester Structure Expression Language and its Application to the Environment for VLSI Tester Program Development, Journal of Information Processing Systems pp.121-132, 2008.

[6] ADVANTEST, STILReader, [online] https://ebiz.advantest.com/aac/EProductSheets/viewDatasheets.html?id=36&menu=soctab

[7] TESTIAN, TA15 (AC Test Instrument Board), [online] http://www.testian.co.kr/eng/_products_05.htm

[8] TESTIAN, Spider Nano (Desktop ATE), [online] http://www.testian.co.kr/eng/_products_02_1.htm

[9] H. Lang, B. Pande, and H. Ahrens, Automating test program generation in STIL-expectations and experiences using IEEE 1450 [standard test interface language], The Eight IEEE European, pp. 99–104, 2003.

[10] Y. Ma, "Open Architecture Software for OPENSTAR™ Test Platform," IEEE Future of ATE (FATE) Workshop, Charlotte, N.C., 2003.

[11] TERADYNE Teradyne Software Solutions, [online] http://www.teradyne.com/services/software

[12] Test Insight, ATEGen, http://www.testinsight.com/products/design-to-tester-conversion/test-program-generator.aspx

[13] Mentor Graphics, STIL Checker, [online] https://www.mentor.com/products/silicon-yield/request?&fmpath=/products/silicon-yield/stil_checker&id=73528dbf-95b3-41cc-b9d6-a114a4286ecc

[14] Synopsys, TetraMAX ATPG, [online] https://www.synopsys.com/implementation-and-signoff/rtl-synthesis-test/test-automation/tetramax-atpg.html

[15] Toshiba Microelectronics, STILDirector, http://www.tosmec-web.toshiba.co.jp/stildirector/eng/products/stildirector1.html

Method for Classification of Textures Based on Histogram and Random Events Analysis

Vladimir Iliev
Technical University - Sofia
Faculty of Industrial Technology
Sofia, Bulgaria
vladimir.iliev@fit.tu-sofia.bg

Alexander Tzokev
Technical University – Sofia
Faculty of Industrial Technology
Sofia, Bulgaria
alextz@tu-sofia.bg

Tzanko Georgiev
Technical University - Sofia
Faculty of Automation
Sofia, Bulgaria
tzg@tu-sofia.bg

Anton Mihaylov
Technical University - Sofia
Faculty of Industrial Technology
Sofia, Bulgaria
amm@tu-sofia.bg

***Abstract*— An image histogram is a set of parameters commonly used to automatically evaluate the image during processing or recognition. When comparing or classifying different images, the histogram data can be analysed as it presents the overall colour or intensity composition of the image. This is very important in case of texture classification as the system must provide sufficient accuracy. In this paper, we present an approach and algorithm for visual analysis of images with different histograms, which can be easily implemented as a software application, improving substantially the image classification after non-destructive testing of vehicle tire's sidewall. The main contribution of this work is a software product for automated defect detection against a series of images, generated by laser shearography in a tire factory.**

Keywords-image analysis; pattern recognition; image processing.

I. INTRODUCTION

Histogram analysis [4] is often used to automatically evaluate an image during its recognition process.

Previous researches show that it is possible to use the histogram of grayscale images generated by laser shearography [6] for non-destructive testing of vehicle tires, together with Multi-Layer Perceptron neural network assisted calculations for pattern classification [3]. After further analysis, that method demonstrated some disadvantages, as some of the textures, which have obvious defects, were skipped while others, being part of the non-affected surface, were highlighted as defects. Also, another finding was that some of the images' histograms were identical due to similar samples (same model tires) in the automated shearography approach. Even if the position of a pixel or a set of pixels within the image is changed, the histogram will remain the same. That problem created the need to introduce a new flexible approach. The basic requirements led to the implementation of an algorithmic type, allowing parallel calculations and processing as well as high performance, even with limited hardware resources.

The rest of the paper is structured as follows. In Section 2, we present the algorithm step by step. An example of detected defects in images of tire carcasses is included. The conclusions and comparison with another approach for pattern recognition are presented in Section 3.

II. DESCRIPTION OF THE METHOD

The analyzed image color pattern is in grayscale. Initial conversion to 8 color grayscale takes place to additionally optimize the calculations. Each single pixel has a color code and is described by an elementary random event. All elementary random events $\omega_1, \omega_2, \ldots, \omega_b$ generate an event sequence with length b, where b is the number of all different color codes discovered within the given image. For example: If the different codes are $\omega_1 = 0$, $\omega_2 = 32$, s$\omega_3 = 64$, $\omega_4 = 96$, $\omega_5 = 128$, $\omega_6 = 160$, $\omega_7 = 192$, $\omega_8 = 224$, then $b=8$.

Sequences of k simple events are introduced and each sequence allows recurrence. The relocation of two simple events will cause the production of a new sequence. A number collates to each sequence

$$\varphi(\omega_1, \ldots, \omega_k) = \sum_{i=1}^{k} (\omega_i - 1) b^{k-i} + \omega_k \rightarrow [1, b^k] \quad (1)$$

where $\omega_i = i$, $i = 1, \ldots k$.

Introduction of the unique sequence outlines the dependency between all simple random events, which can be described simultaneously by relation, regression and correlation between simple random events.

Considering the above definitions, we can present the image as a row vector of all simple random events. Following (1), starting from left to right and using a step with length 1 (single simple random event) and for pre-selected k-tuples, we calculate a number that corresponds to a class in the histogram. That is how the frequencies of the selected k-tuples are defined.

Figure 1 shows an image of a vehicle tire, the result of non-destructive control based on laser shearography, after initial conversion to 8 color grayscale. The image size is 64x64 pixels.

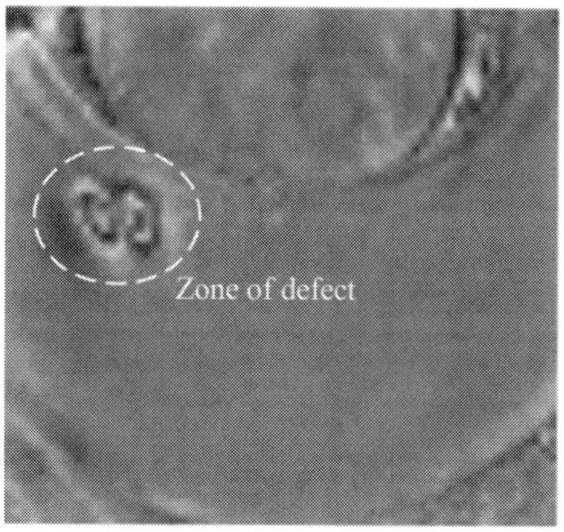

Figure 1. 64x64 pixels image, representing defect in vehicle tire carcass based on laser shearography.

For Figure 1, it was calculated that ω_1 **= 0,** ω_2 **= 32,** ω_3 **= 64,** ω_4 **= 96,** ω_5 **= 128,** ω_6 **= 160,** ω_7 **= 192,** ω_8 **= 224** and ***b=8.*** The 2-tuples (k=2) are taken into consideration, which generates b^k classes, or 64 classes in the given example.

The histogram is calculated according to (1) and is illustrated in Figure 3.

An approach for generation of an arranged dataset based on the pixel information (symbols) is to scan the image in predefined direction (i.e. rows and columns) and to generate an array of k consecutive symbols – the so called "k-tuples". After all k-tuples are generated, their histogram can be calculated for subsequent classification analysis. Figure 2 presents the process of generating the k-tuples; if k=3, the scan step is 1 and the directions is a row, followed by a column.

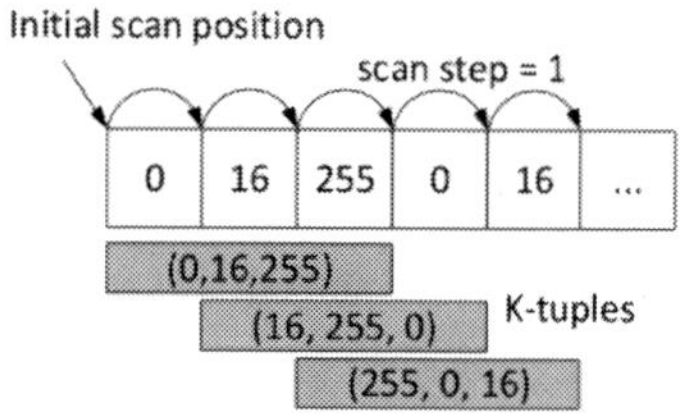

Figure 2. Example of k-tuple generation (k=3, scan step=1)

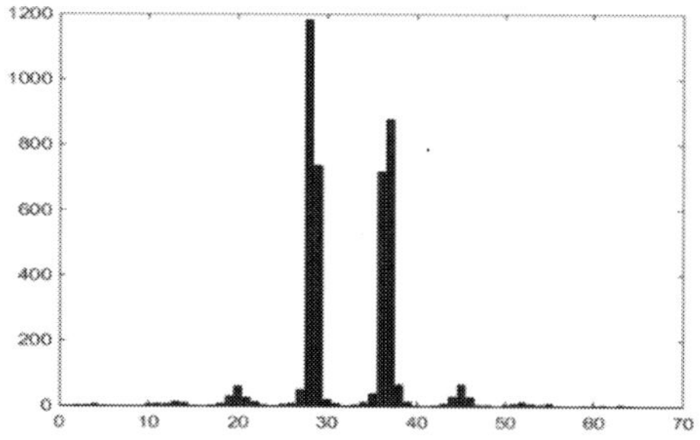

Figure 3. Histogram of 2-tuples, calculated for the image, shown in Figure 1

The same process with k=3 is shown in Figure 4.

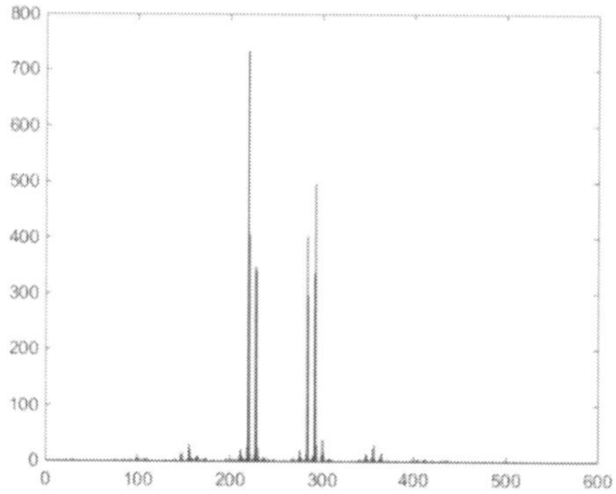

Figure 4. Histogram of 3-tuples, calculated for the image, shown in Figure 1

The histogram in Figure 3 shows the frequency of appearance of separate 2-tuples within the image and gives an opportunity for the initial image preparation to take place. It is known that the optimal selection of classes in a given histogram defines the expected frequency of a class between $N^{(2/5)} - N^{(3/5)}$, where N is the count of the simple random events (N=4096 for the current example) [1]. That is why N=147 is chosen.

All the classes from Figure 2 meeting the above requirement and having a count less than 147 are presented in Figure 5.

Figure 5. Selected pixels for N=147

Figure 5 shows the pixels of the classes with frequencies less than N.

The dependency between simple random events is defined by calculating the relation, regression and correlation between them. The definitions of relation, regression and correlation are given in [2].

The relation between simple random events $\boldsymbol{\delta}$ is calculated by the sections $\boldsymbol{P}$ [2]:

$$\boldsymbol{\delta}(\omega_i, \omega_j) = \boldsymbol{P}(\omega_i \cap \omega_j) - \boldsymbol{P}(\omega_i)\boldsymbol{P}(\omega_j) \qquad (2)$$

where

$$\delta(\omega_i,\omega_j) \neq \delta(\omega_j,\omega_i) \quad (3)$$

Figure 6 illustrates the relation between simple random events, as per Figure 2.

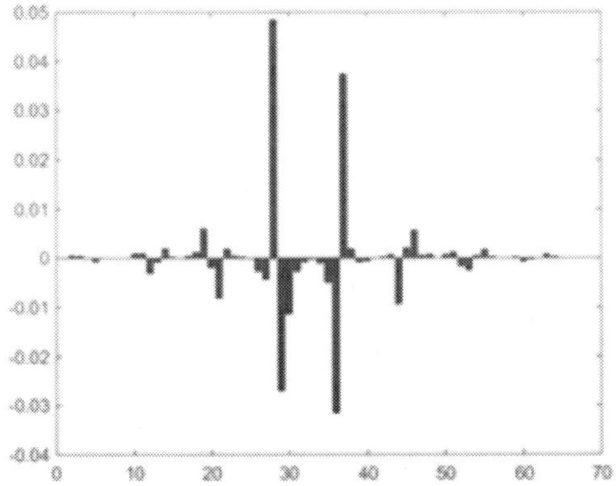

Figure 6. Relation between simple random events, calculated by (2) and (3) for the selected pixels, shown in Figure 5

A limiting constant (1/64) is selected. The constant is defined by the number of the classes – 8^2. In this way, each random event's probability is 1/64. If random events are equipropable, then the relation between them is going to be 0, according to (2). So, the classes with relation less than 1/64 are selected and the results are displayed in Figure 7.

Figure 7. Selected pixels for relation less than 1/64, based on the image, shown in Figure 1.

The coefficient of regression R of a simple random event ω_i according to the simple random event ω_j is defined as a difference between conditional probabilities following (4) [2].

$$R_{\omega_j}(\omega_i) = P(\omega_i|\omega_j) - P(\omega_i|\overline{\omega_j}) \quad (4)$$

Condition (3) of asymmetry defines that there are two ways to calculate R, against indexes i and j. The numeric values are shown in Figure 8.

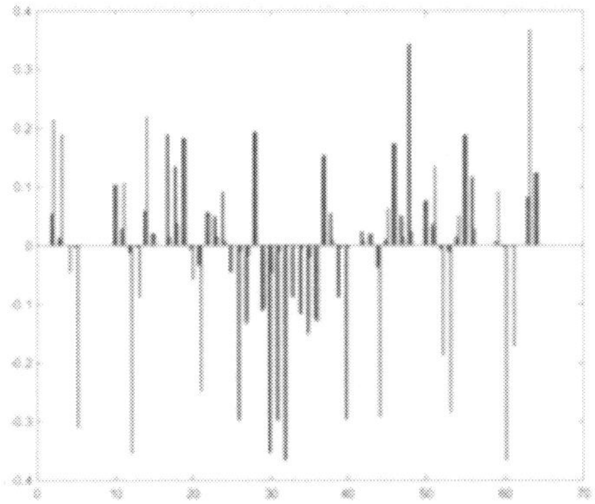

Figure 8. Coefficient of regression for (3), calculated for the relations, presented in Figure 7

A limiting constant (1/39) greater than (1/64) empirically is used for the examined set of images.

In Figure 9 are displayed the classes having regression coefficient less than (1/39).

Figure 9. Classes with limiting constant less than (1/39)

The correlation coefficient between two simple random events is given by (5) [2].

$$C(\omega_i,\omega_j) = \pm\sqrt{R_{\omega_j}(\omega_i)R_{\omega_i}(\omega_j)} \quad (5)$$

where ω_i and ω_j are simple random events.

For the analysis of Figure 1, C is illustrated in Figure 10.

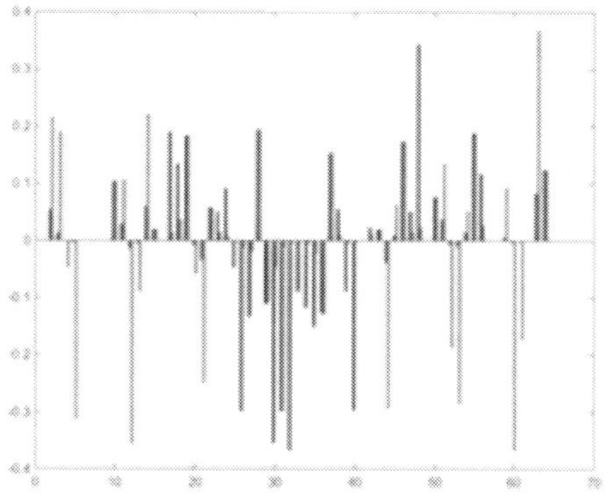

Figure 10. Coefficient of correlation calculated for the relations, given in Figure 7

The selected classes, according to the calculated value of C, are illustrated in Figure 11.

Figure 11. Selected classes according to the correlation

The value of the limiting constant is the same to compare relation, correlation and regression numeric values and their effect over the pattern classification.

Based on the proposed method, the following algorithm can be summarized:

1. Conversion of the image to 8 color greyscale
2. Definition of k-tuples
3. Calculation of the histogram
4. Calculation of the relation between simple random events
5. Calculation of the regression between simple random events
6. Calculation of the correlation between simple random events
7. Display of the detected defects

Figure 12 shows the detected defect for 20 of the test images. The analysis time for the images is 100 ms/img.

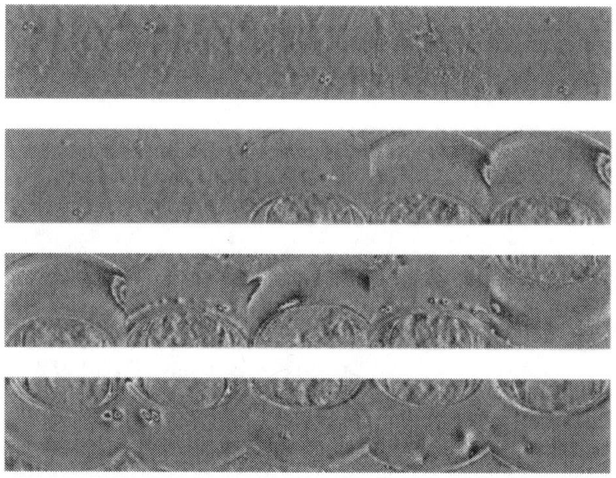

Figure 12. Detected defects in 20 images of vehicle tire carcass, based on laser shearography

III. Conclusions

The described method has been applied to over 50 grayscale images, result of shearography based, nondestructive testing in a tire factory. The number of the detected defects was 50 (100%), which proves the approach as reliable for detecting defects or abnormal differences in the texture (of the tire carcass). Compared to the X-ray based approach presented in [7], it proves its effectiveness and simple implementation, eliminating the potential endless loop if different types of defects exist in a single image. The proposed method can distinguish two or more visually different images with same histograms. Also, the required user decisions and manual interventions, that can potentially cause errors, are less than in the approach given in [7]. Due to its algorithmic structure, it was implemented easily as an experimental software and demonstrated fast processing combined with satisfactory results. It is robust against images with identical or similar histograms due to the implementation of the unique sequence logic. Potentially, the approach can be applied to all kinds of textures in grayscale images and its further development can be beneficial. As a future improvement, it could be beneficial the calculations to be executed over Graphics Processing Unit [5], to increase the parallel processes handling capabilities. The defining of the limiting constant, based on the user's expectation, is a weakness of the method and something that will be researched further. Future researches and development should include a wider overview of the most recent approaches applied to pattern classification in images, resulted of nondestructive testing.

ACKNOWLEDGMENT

This work was supported by the European Regional Development Fund within the Operational Program "Science and Education for Smart Growth 2014 - 2020" under the Project CoE "National center of mechatronics and clean technologies" BG05M2OP001-1.001-0008-C01

REFERENCES

[1] W. T. Eadie, D. Dryard, F. E. Jamse, M. Roos and B. Sadoulet, Statistical Methods in Experimental Physics, North – Holland Publishing, Amsterdam, London, 1971 (In Russian, 1976).

[2] B. Dimitrov, Some Obreshkov Measures Of Dependence And Their Use, Comptes rendus de l'Acad´emie bulgare des Sciences, Tome 63, No 1, 2010.

[3] G. Pass and R. Zabih, Comparing images using joint histograms, Multimedia Systems, May 1999, Volume 7, Issue 3, pp 234-240.

[4] H. G. Schaathun, Machine Learning in Image Steganalysis, Oct. 2012.

[5] D. B. Kirk and Wen-Mei W. Hwu, Programming Massively Parallel Processors: A Hands-on Approach, Jan. 2010

[6] Y. Y. Hung "Shearography: A New Optical Method For Strain Measurement And Nondestructive Testing," Optical Engineering 21(3), 213391 (1 June 1982).

[7] G. Zhao and S. Qin, "High-Precision Detection of Defects of Tire Texture Through X-ray Imaging Based on Local Inverse Difference Moment Features," Sensors (Basel). 2018;18(8):2524. Published 2018 Aug 2. doi:10.3390/s18082524

The Use of Image Processing Techniques for Detection of Weed in Lawns

Lorena Parra [1], [2], Virginia Torices [3], José Marín [3], Pedro Vicente Mauri [2], Jaime Lloret [1]

[1] Instituto de Inv. para la Gestión Integrada de Zonas Costeras (IGIC), Universitat Politècnica de València (UPV). C/ Paranimf, 1, 46730 Grau de Gandia, Gandia

[2] Instituto Madrileño de Investigación y Desarrollo Rural, Agrario y Alimentario (IMIDRA), Finca El Encin, Autovía del Noreste A-2, Km. 38.200, 28805 Alcalá de Henares, Madrid

[3] Universidad Politécnica de Madrid. Escuela Técnica Superior de Ingeniería Agronómica, Alimentaria y de Biosistemas. Av. Puerta de Hierro, 2, 28040 Madrid

Email: loparbo@doctor.upv.es, virtorices@gmail.com, jmarin@areaverde.es, pedro.mauri@madrid.org, jlloret@dcom.upv.es

Abstract—**The presence of weed plants in lawns disrupts their behavior and correct growth. Moreover, it implies a lack of uniformity, which is one of the most important factors of the lawns. The early detection of weeds is crucial to minimize the need for phytosanitary products. Image processing techniques and machine vision are widely used in many different areas such as agriculture, industry, or object identification. In this paper, we propose the use of image processing techniques to detect undesired grass species in the lawn. We utilize a drone with an Arduino module to take pictures. The obtained images are used to determine the best option to detect the presence of weeds. Pictures from different grass species with and without undesired weed species are used. The Red, Green and Blue (RGB) layers of each picture are mathematically combined in order to obtain a new raster layer to automatically detect the weed. Two different methods are used. Different equations offer different results depending on the weed species. We can detect two big groups of weeds with the first or with the second method, according to their color. Finally, the proposed formulas are verified with pictures taken with different solar conditions. An aggrupation method to minimize the false positives is shown.**

Keywords-grass lawns; weed plants; image processing; RGB bands; drone.

I. INTRODUCTION

In order to maintain a great appearance for grass surfaces, certain requirements need to be addressed. Due to the activities that are carried out on the grass or around it, the grass suffers from compaction and the leaves are broken. Some of the activities performed on the lawns are: certain sports, entertainment, and enjoyment in residential areas or in public gardens. The users of the lawns demand a series of requisites, being the most important one the visual aspect of the lawns. The visual aspect can be expressed as the uniformity of the lawn, the greenness of the grass and the absence of grassless patches.

The existence of weeds in lawns is a problem. On the one hand, the weed presence implies a lack of uniformity on the surface. This lack of uniformity is the first cause of users' disappointment. On the other hand, the weeds will generate competition between them and the grass species. For this reason, it is necessary to carry out specific actions to solve the weed problem as soon as possible.

It is crucial to detect the appearance of weeds during the first days. Otherwise, the weed can infest huge areas of the lawn and it will be more difficult to eradicate. Nowadays, the best available techniques to detect weeds are the aerial images of the visual inspection of the lawns. The first option, the use of satellite images, offers multispectral images. Nonetheless, they have small spatial resolution and small temporal resolution. Thus, when we detect the weeds with the satellite image it may be too late and would be necessary to apply the phytosanitary treatment to a large area. The second option, the visual inspection, is useful for small areas as a private garden. Nevertheless, for big areas such as golf camps or big public gardens, this solution is not applicable. Therefore, the use of pictures obtained with drones and their analysis can be a solution for large surfaces. The use of image processing is widely used in many different areas and for countless purposes. In agriculture, it has been used for illness detection [1] and for fruit maturity evaluation [2]. In aquaculture, it has been used for feed falling detection [3]. Moreover, it is used for face detection [4] and car license plate identification [5].

The aim of this paper is to present the use of image processing techniques for detecting the presence of weeds in lawns. Thus, a series of pictures were obtained from different lawns with the presence and absence of weed. All the pictures were taken under the same solar conditions. Different grass species and different weed species appear in the pictures. Part of the pictures will be used to train our system and the rest of them to verify our findings. The goal is to use this methodology to automatize the monitoring of lawns in terms of weed detection. Therefore, it will be possible to detect the weed and apply the phytosanitary products only in the affected area.

The rest of this paper is organized as follows. Section II presents the related work. Section III describes the proposal. Section IV addresses the obtained results. Section V summarizes the conclusion and future work.

II. RELATED WORK

In this section, we are going to compare other techniques utilized to detect weed in different crops.

The detection of weeds is an important issue for agriculture. Therefore, many scientists have work on their identification using pictures. The use of drones has increased the possibilities, and, in recent years, several papers have been published.

The use of image processing to determine the presence of weeds in maize fields was presented by X. P. Burgos-Artizzu in 2011 [6]. They detail a computer vision system that can be used with videos. They test their system under different light conditions. The system detects 95% of the weeds and 80% of the crops. A. Paikekari et al. presented in 2016 [7] an image processing methodology for weed detection. First, they use color to differentiate soil and grass. Then, the resultant image is converted into a greyscale picture to apply an edge detection technique. Finally, the resultant image of the edge detection is divided into 25 blocks. The analysis of each block determines if it contains weed with narrow leaves, weed with wide leaves, or crop. In 2018, J. Gao et al. [8] presented the use of aerial picture with an ultra-high resolution to detect intra and inter-row weed. They use a semi-automatic object-based image analysis with random forests. In addition, they use techniques to classify soil, weed, and crop. The authors applied this proposal to maize crop fields. The utilized pictures show the maize in the first days of growth. Their results have a coefficient of correlation of 0.895 and a squared mean error of 0.026. J. Marín et al. in 2017 applied simple image processing techniques in different publications to detect the grass coverage in lawns [9][10]. They work with the histograms of the grass pictures to determine the weight of the grass and the level of coverage (high, low, very low).

On the other hand, there are other types of studies focused on identifying different leaves affections. One example is the work developed by V. Khanaa and K. P. Thooyamani in 2017 [11]. They proposed an algorithm based on image processing. Their algorithm was able to detect different leave diseases, such as bacterial pith necrosis, early blight, white trail, and target spot among others.

III. Proposal

In this section, we detail the proposed system for lawns monitoring. The system is composed of a drone that flies over the lawn and takes photos. Then, the pictures are evaluated to determine where there are weeds in the lawn to program the application of phytosanitary products.

A. Drone

Our system uses a drone to take pictures of the lawn [12]. As long as we need that spatial resolution of 1mm, we should select a drone with a high spatial resolution flying at height altitude or drone with lower spatial resolution flying at a lower height. In order to calculate the flying height according to the camera resolution, we can use the equations proposed by Marin et al. in [10]. We are going to use an Arduino camera with 640X480 pixels and the flying height will be 2.3m.

It is important to note that for our proposal we are going to use a drone with no camera. We will add the above-mentioned camera connected to an Arduino node. The Arduino node will be in charge of taking pictures and analyzing them. On the other hand, the flying issues will be operated by the drone processor, not by the Arduino node. Thus, we can split the task into different processors and our system can be adaptive to different situations.

B. Image processing

Once the pictures were gathered by the drone, the node analyzes them. As we need a fast analysis because the processor should analyze the data during the flight, it is necessary to focus on simple image processing techniques. Therefore, we reduce our possibilities to the operations involving the RGB data of each pixel in the picture. These types of operations are common when we work with satellite images, which are multispectral images. Our challenge is to detect weed plants in the lawns with the combination of only 3 picture bands. The proposed system is shown in Figure 1, where one can see the different obtained bands and their names. Red, green and blue bands are named as Band 1, 2 and 3.

The first issue to be considered is that it is not possible to work with threshold values of only one of the layers because these values are greatly affected by sun exposure, the presence of clouds, and even the day of the year. Thus, we need to work with a mathematical combination of different bands to avoid this problem. The second issue is related to the values of the pixels. Each pixel has a value between 0 and 255 in each one of the bands. This value has no decimals and can only have a positive value. When we apply the mathematical combination, these rules are maintained, the resultant value of each pixel will be a positive value with no decimals. The last issue is the need of finding a way to assign values of 0 to the pixels that contain soil of dead grass. This should be done in order to avoid having false positives.

C. Studied lawns

The proposed system was tested in Finca El Encin, research facilities of the Instituto Madrileño de Investigación y Desarrollo Rural, Agrario y Alimentario (IMIDRA) in Spain. There are small experimental plots where other scientists are testing multiple grass combinations. During their research, different weed plants appear in their lawns. We use their experimental plots to take pictures of different types of lawns with and without the presence of weed plants. By using this experimental plot, we ensure that we will have lawns with different types of grass and under different environmental conditions.

IV. Results

In this section, we show the obtained pictures and their processing to determine the presence or absence of weeds. First, we show the process to obtain the equations to detect the weed. Finally, we present its verification.

D. Image processing: soil removal

The image processing method is shown in this subsection. First, Table 1 presents the RGB pictures in four different cases. The first one is a lawn with low grass coverage and with the presence of weeds at the top-center part. The weed has darker coloration than the grass. Furthermore, it presents higher relative values in the blue band, compared with the rest of the grass. Picture 2 is taken in a lawn with high grass coverage. There is a weed plant at the bottom-left of the picture. As in the previous case, the weed plant has more bluish coloration.

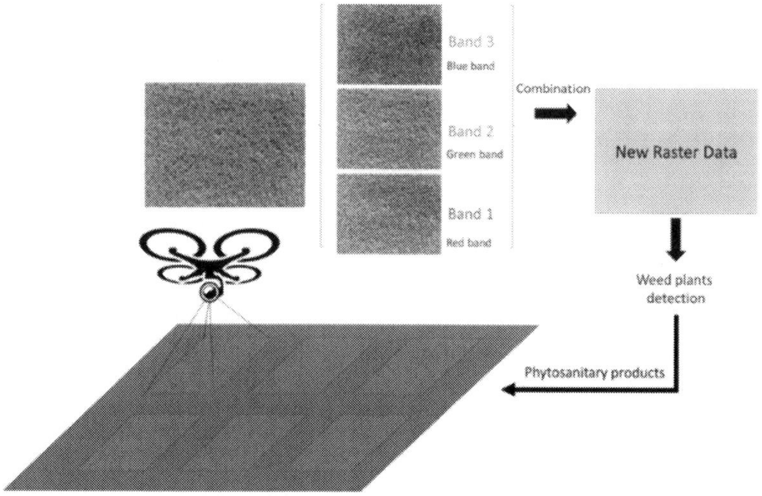

Figure 1. System description.

In picture 3, we can see a lawn with low grass coverage and with the presence of the weed plant in the bottom right of the picture. In this case, the weed plant has more yellowish coloration, compared with the grass. Finally, picture 4 represents typical lawns with no weed plants; but, under light water stress. Thus, there are some parts of the grass that have yellowish coloration due to the lack of water.

The first issue that we can pay attention to is the fact that the soil has higher values of brightness in the red band than in the green band. Therefore, considering that the values of the pixels only can be positive and without decimals, we divide the green band into the red band obtaining a new raster, which gives us information about the soil/plant coverage, see (1). The result of this mathematical relation between bands can be seen in Table I. Grass pixels have values higher than zero and are colored in green. The soil pixels have values of zero and are colored in yellow.

Unfortunately, the grass that is stressed or has been strongly compacted has a similar color as the soil and it is classified as soil. For our application, it is not a problem, because the important part for us is the green grass and the green weeds.

$$Soil\ removal = {}^{Band\ 2}/_{Band\ 1} \qquad (1)$$

A. Image processing: weed detection

The next step is to find a mathematical relation, which gives, as a result, a new raster with different values for pixels of grass and pixels of weed.

As we have two different types of weed, the ones with more bluish color, and the ones with more yellowish color than the grass. Consequently, we will need two different equations to detect the presence of weeds. One equation for the bluish weed, the ones that appear in pictures 1 and 2 of Table 1, and another equation for yellowish weed as the one that appears in picture 3 of Table I. The first equation, (2), will be used to detect the bluish weed. This resultant raster after applying (2) will have high pixel values where there is a bluish weed. Thus, the equation has to maximize the data of pixels with higher relative blue values. Then, the data from blue band should be divided under the data from red and green band. As in the dividend of the equation (Blue brightness value of the pixel) has lower values that the divisor (Green x Red brightness values of pixels), and the pixels can only be a natural number almost all the pixels have the value of zero. Thus, no differences were found. In order to increase the value of the dividend, we square the dividend. Nevertheless, the value of the dividend is still lower than the value of the divisor in the majority of the cases and most of the pixels have a value of zero in the resultant raster. Finally, we cube the divisor. Then, we obtain a new raster with different values for different coverage surfaces. The last step is to apply (1) to the used formula. The obtained raster combination that is used to detect bluish weeds can be seen in (2).

On the other hand, we have the picture with yellowish weed. To detect them we should use the opposite steps that in the preceding paragraph, we have to use the data from green and red bands for the dividend and the data from the blue band for the divisor. As in this case, the values of the dividend are always higher than the values of the divisor, it is not necessary to neither square nor cube any of them. As in the previous case, it is necessary to add the soil/plant coverage correction factor. Therefore, the proposed formula that can be used to detect the yellowish weed is given by (3).

$$Weed = \left({Band\ 3^3}/{Band\ 2\ \times Band\ 1}\right) \times \left({Band\ 2}/{Band\ 1}\right) \quad (2)$$

$$Weed = \left({Band\ 2\ \times Band\ 1}/{Band\ 3}\right) \times \left({Band\ 2}/{Band\ 1}\right) \quad (3)$$

The result of applying (2) and (3) to the pictures of Table I can be seen in Table II. We apply both formulas to all of the pictures to show the effectiveness of each formula for generating a new raster that contains information about weed presence. The different colors represent different values in the raster. The pixels with yellow tones have lower pixel values. On the contrary, the pixels with purple and blue colors have the highest values. In the RGB picture, the weeds position is indicated with red circles. As it is expected, the pixels that contain bluish weeds (Picture 1 and Picture 2 in Table I and Table II), present higher values in the resultant raster after apply (2) than the pixels that contain grass or soil. The pixels of the resultant raster that have higher brightness values are represented in purple and blue colors. Meanwhile, the pixels with low brightness values are colored in yellow and light yellow. We can see that in Pictures 1 and the resultant raster of (2) present higher pixel values, colored in blue, in the area where there are weed plants. The resultant raster of (3) presents highest values in the pixels, which represents one of the grass species in Picture 1. In Picture 2, there is no specific area that contains pixels with high values.

For Picture 3, we can see that the pixels of the raster obtained with (2), which have the highest values, are not related with the presence of weeds. However, in the raster obtained with (3) we can clearly identify the presence of the weed plant. We can see that one of the grass species present in the lawn of Picture 3, are giving high values (red color). But the purple and blue colors are only related with the weed presence.

Finally, the resultant raster of the picture from the lawns without weed do not present any areas with high values. In the case of resultant raster of (2) there are some pixels with high values but they appear along the raster, not joined in one area as in the other cases. Meanwhile, in the raster of (3) almost all the pixels present low values and few pixels have high values.

TABLE I. FIGURES UTILIZED TO OBTAIN EQUATIONS FOR WEED DETECTION

Picture n°	1	2	3	4
RGB picture	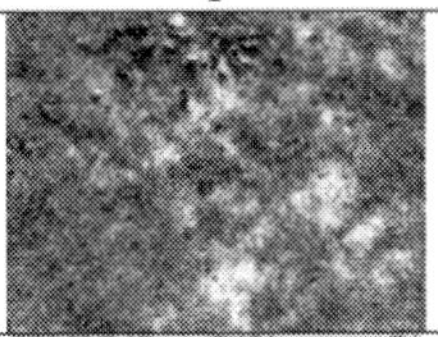	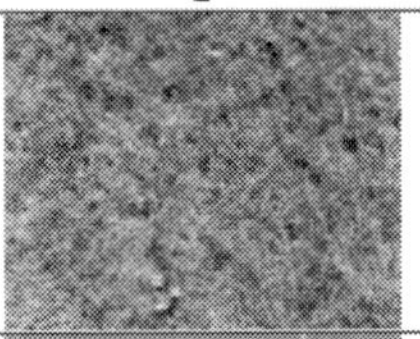	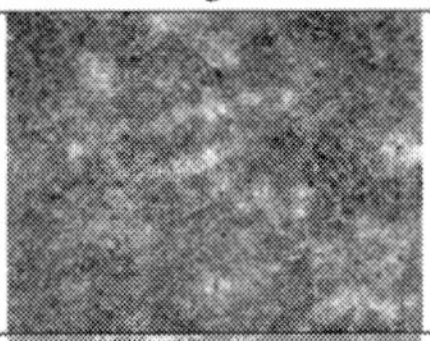	
Soil/Grass Coverage	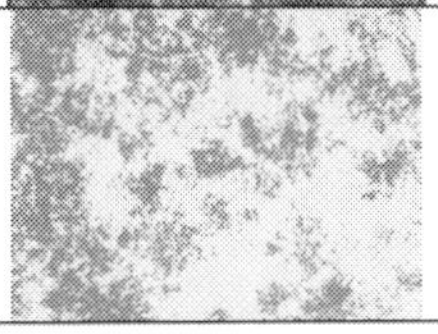	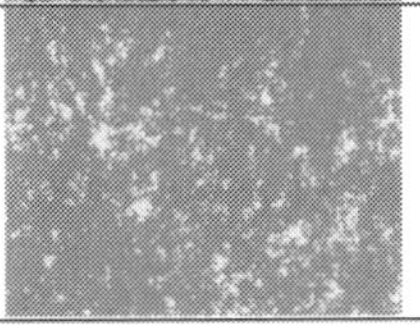	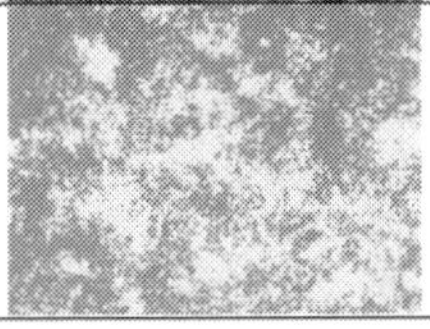	

TABLE II. RASTER OBTAINED AFTER APPLY THE FORMULAS OF (2) AND (3) FOR WEED DETECTION

Picture n°	1	2	3	4
RGB picture	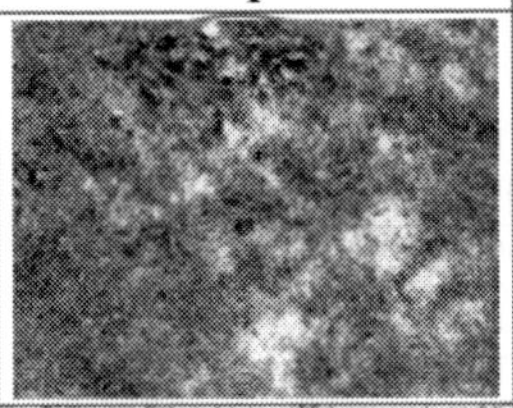	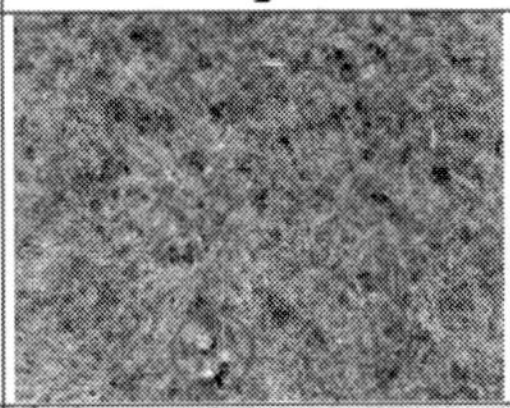	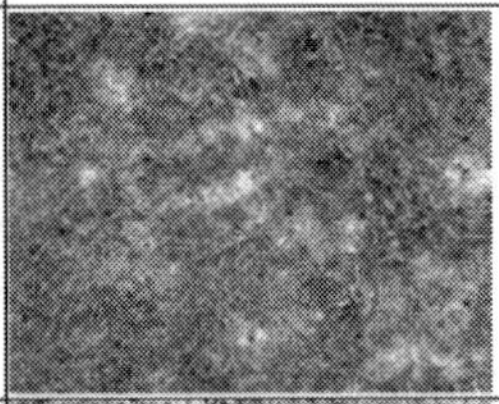	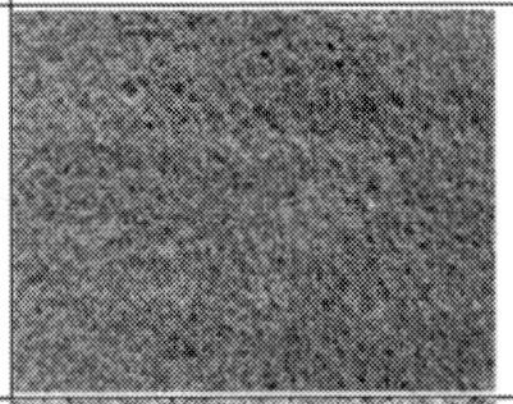
Result of apply (2)	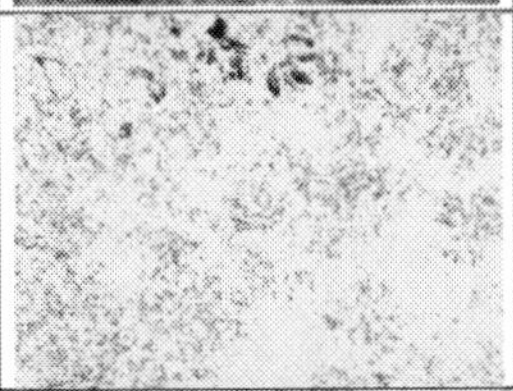	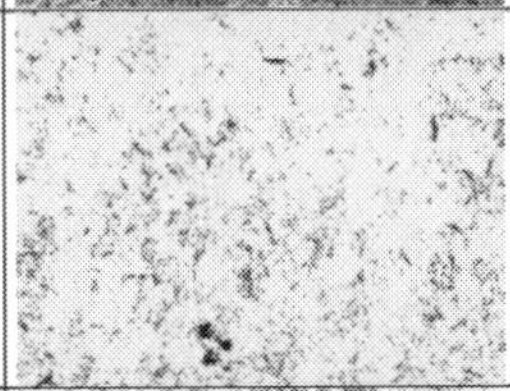	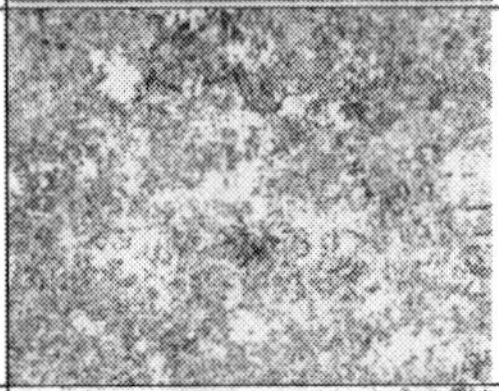	
Result of apply (3)	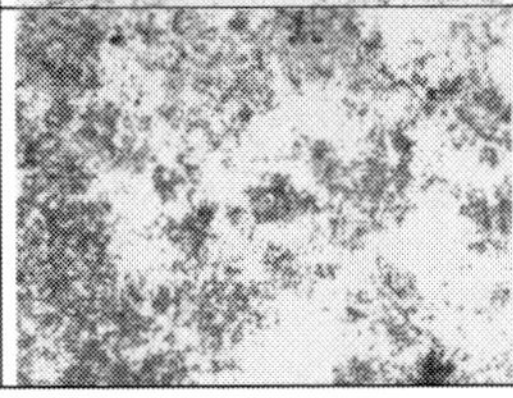	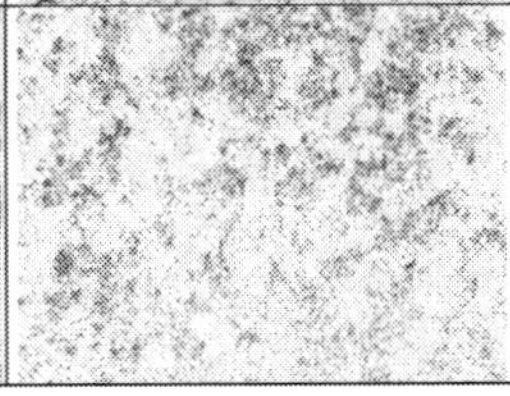	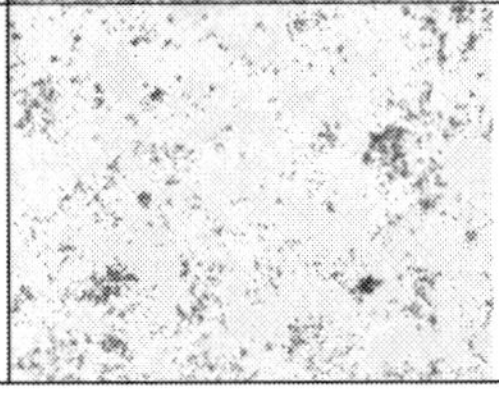	

In all the cases, there are some pixels that do not belong to weed that have high values and may be considered as a false positive. However, as long as these pixels are isolated and their neighbors have low values it can be easily solved by using smoothing techniques.

As the higher values indicate the presence of weeds, in the verification test we are only going to consider the pixels with the highest values. We will use the natural breaks, jenks, to divide the pixels into 5 groups and only the last group will indicate the presence of weeds.

E. Verification process

One of the major advantages of the proposed system is that its results should not be affected by changes in the solar exposition. Thus, we are going to verify the obtained formula with pictures gathered in another time period with different environmental conditions. Moreover, in the verification test, we are going to evaluate the use of the smooth technique to reduce the false positives.

To smooth the resultant raster we are going to aggregate the data. There are different available options in terms of the cell factor and in terms of the aggregation technique. In our case, we are going to test cell values of 5 and 10, and aggregation techniques of minimum, mean, and media.

The used pictures and the results of the verification can be seen in Table III. Again, the position of weed is indicated with a red circle in the RGB picture. Picture 5 was gathered on a sunny day and represents a lawn with low grass coverage, with two types of soil (light and dark brown) and the presence of a lot of weed plants. Some of the weeds of Picture 5 are a bluish weed, then, the results are after apply (2). Picture 6 was done a day with less solar radiation. The picture represents a lawn with some grass patches and the presence of yellowish weed at the bottom of the picture. Therefore, the verification is done with (3). Finally, Picture 7 represents a lawn with regular grass coverage on a cloudy day. In Picture 7, no weed plants are present, the results are obtained with (2). We select (2) because it is the one that gives more false positives in the previous test.

The results with the cell value of 10 have not been presented because they were not representative. We are going to present in Table III the results of the aggregation with a cell value of 5. First, we present the results of the aggregation technique that uses the mean as a result. This technique is quite accurate in terms of identifying the leaves of the weed plants. However, there are still some false positives, which identifies as a weed plant normal grass leaves. The false positives are more visible in the case of Picture 7, where there was no weed. The aggregation technique that uses the median, as a result, has less false positives. But, it is less precise in terms of weed plant leaves identification. Finally, if we use the minimum as a result, there are no false positives. Nevertheless, this results with this technique have some false negatives.

Thus, depending on the application and the produces effects on the case of false positives and false negatives, we can use one aggregation technique or other. For our application, as the point is to maximize the grass quality by minimizing the phytosanitary products usage, we prefer to have false positives than false negatives. Therefore, we propose to use the aggregation technique that uses the median as a result.

V. CONCLUSION

In this paper, we have presented our proposal for weed detection in lawns using image processing. The objective is to detect the weed plants to apply the phytosanitary products just to the affected area and not to the entire lawn.

We use a mathematical combination of the RGB layers to obtain new raster data that can be used to detect the weed. First, we found a formula that can be used to remove the soil from the pictures. Then, after analyzing the RGB values of the weed plants and the grass, we realize that there are two big groups of weed plants. The ones with a bluish coloration and the ones with a yellowish coloration, compared with the grass. Thus, we need to use two different formulas to detect the weed. Finally, we verify the proposed method of two equations and apply aggregation techniques to minimize the number of false positives.

The future works will be related to the identification of different weed species. Moreover, we will work with other image processing techniques including the boundary detection and its combination with our current findings.

ACKNOWLEDGMENT

This work is partially found by the European Union with the Fondo Europeo Agrícola de Desarrollo Rural (FEADER) – Europa invierte en zonas rurales, the MAPAMA, and Comunidad de Madrid with the IMIDRA, under the mark of the PDR-CM 2014-2020" project number PDR18-XEROCESPED.

REFERENCES

[1] J. Lloret, I. Bosch, S. Sendra, and A. Serrano, "A wireless sensor network for vineyard monitoring that uses image processing", Sensors, 2011, vol. 11, no 6, pp. 6165-6196.

[2] P. D. Surya and K. J. Satheesh, "Assessment of banana fruit maturity by image processing technique", Journal of food science and technology, 2015, vol. 52, no 3, p. 1316-1327.

[3] L. Parra, L. García, S. Sendra, and J. Lloret, "The Use of Sensors for Monitoring the Feeding Process and Adjusting the Feed Supply Velocity in Fish Farms", Journal of Sensors, 2018, vol. 2018.

[4] H. Li, Z. Lin, X. Shen, J. Brandt, and G. Hua, "A convolutional neural network cascade for face detection", Proceedings of the IEEE Conference on Computer Vision and Pattern Recognition. 2015. pp. 5325-5334.

[5] G. Maria, E. Baccaglini, D. Brevi, M. Gavelli, and R. Scopigno, "A drone-based image processing system for car detection in a smart transport infrastructure", Electrotechnical

Conference (MELECON), 2016 18th Mediterranean. IEEE, 2016. pp. 1-5.

[6] X. P. Burgos-Artizzu, A. Ribeiro, M. Guijarro, and G. Pajares, "Real-time image processing for crop/weed discrimination in maize fields", Computers and Electronics in Agriculture, 2011, vol. 75, no 2, pp. 337-346.

[7] A. Paikekari, V. Ghule, R. Meshram and V. B. Raskar, "Weed detection using image processing", International Research Journal of Engineering and Technology (IRJET), 2016, vol. 3, no 3, pp. 1220-1222

[8] J. Gao *et al.* "Fusion of pixel and object-based features for weed mapping using unmanned aerial vehicle imagery", International journal of applied earth observation and geoinformation, 2018, vol. 67, pp. 43-53.

[9] J. F. Marín Peira, *et al.* "Automation in the characterization of the cultivation of lawns in urban grasslands", Proccedings of the IX Congresso Ibérico de Agroengenharia, Braganza, Portugal, 4 – 9 Sept. 2017.

[10] J. F. Marín Peira et al. "Urban Lawn Monitoring in Smart City Environments". Journal of Sensors, 2018, vol. 2018.

[11] V. Khanaa and K. P. Thooyamani, "An Efficient Weed and Pest Detection System", Indian Journal of Science and Technology, 2015, vol. 8, no 32.

[12] C. C Baseca, J. R. Díaz, J. Lloret, Communication Ad Hoc protocol for intelligent video sensing using AR drones, 9th International Conference on Mobile Ad-hoc and Sensor Networks (MSN 2013), Dec 11 - 13, 2013. Dalian, China

TABLE III. PICTURES AND OBTAINED RASTERS IN THE VERIFICATION PROCESS

Picture nº	**5**	**6**	**7**
RGB picture		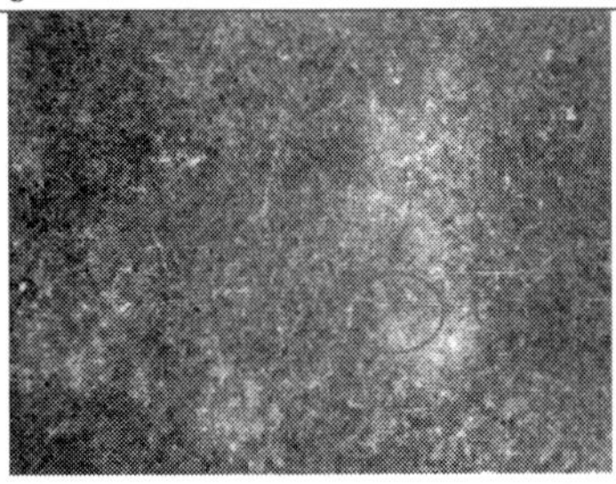	
Aggregate data: Cell size 5 Aggregation type: Mean	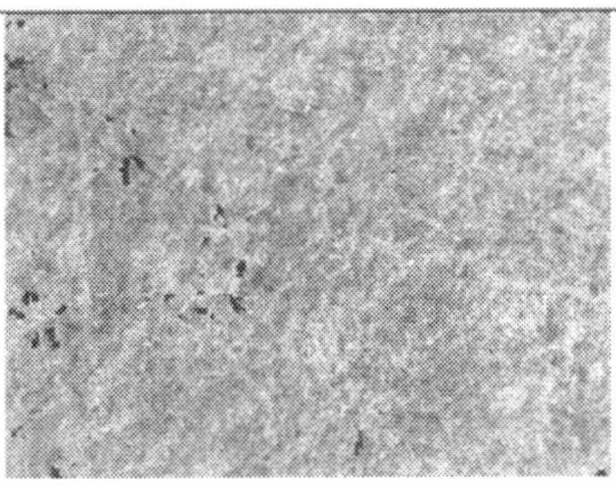	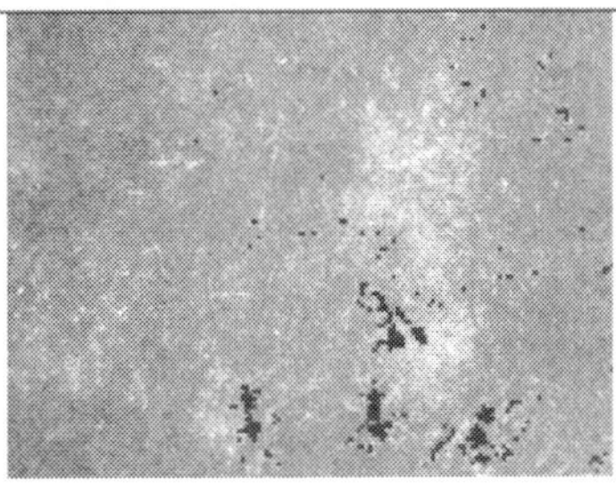	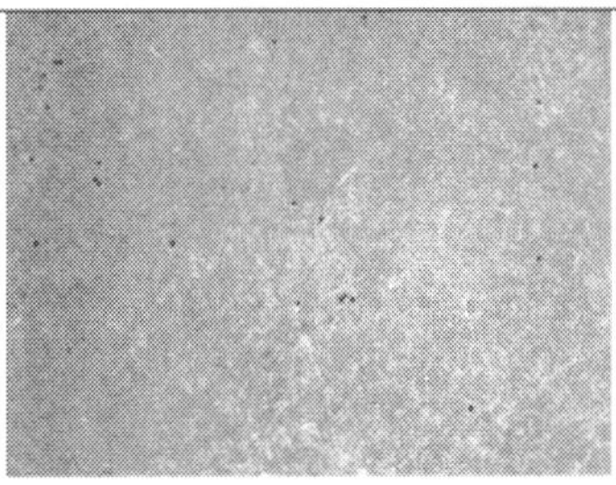
Aggregate data: Cell size 5 Aggregation type: Media	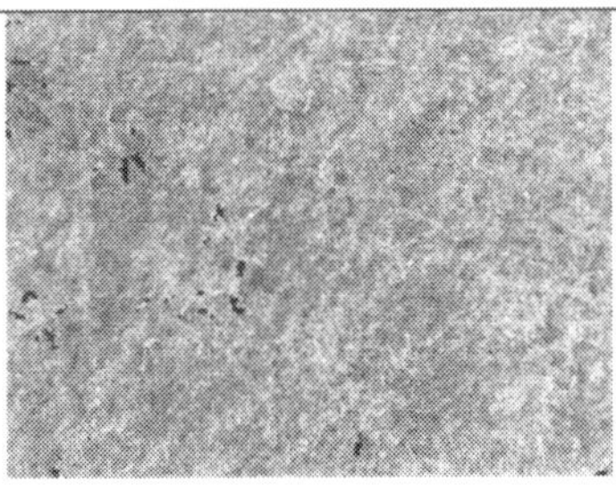	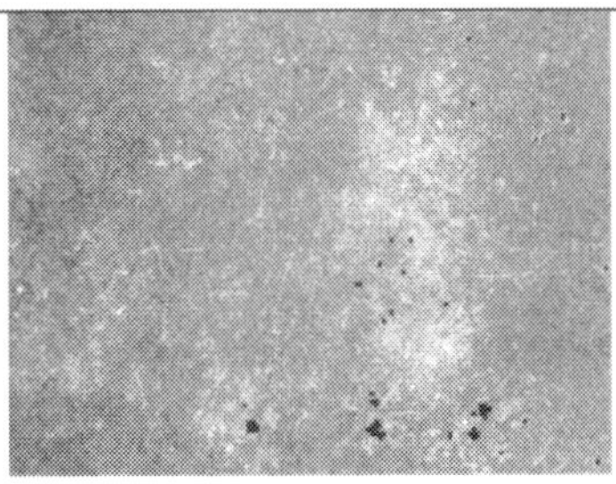	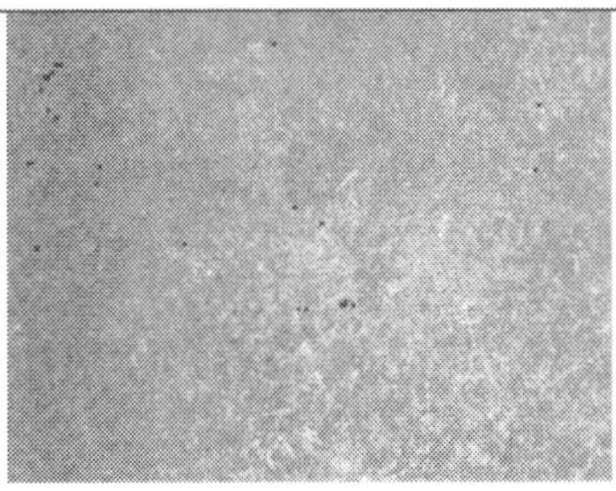
Aggregate data: Cell size 5 Aggregation type: Minimum	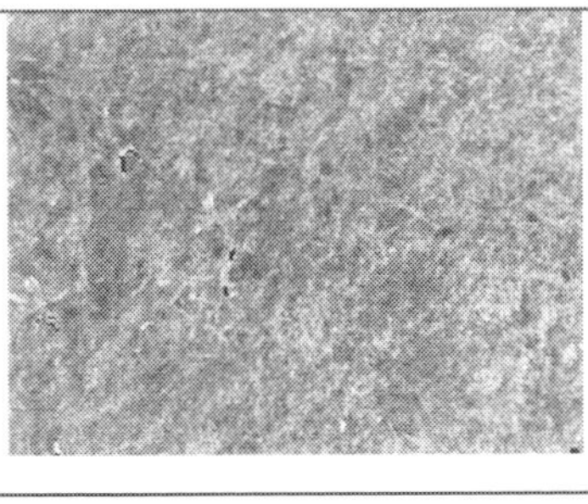	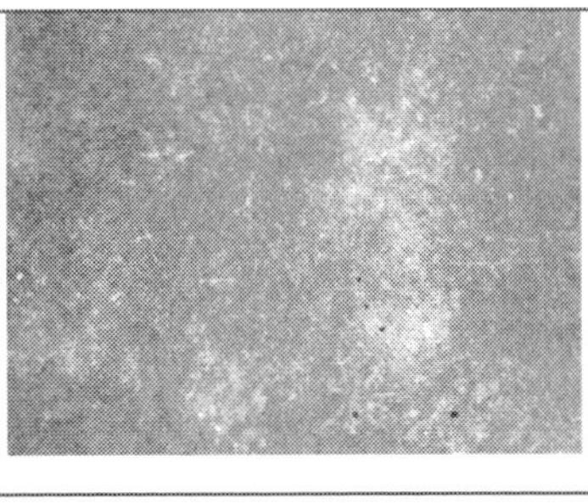	

Automatic Ship Detection on Inland Waters: Problems and a Preliminary Solution

Tomasz Hyla
Marine Technology Ltd.
Szczecin, Poland
e-mail: t.hyla@marinetechnology.pl

Natalia Wawrzyniak
Institute of Geoinformatics, Faculty of Navigation
Maritime University of Szczecin
Szczecin, Poland
e-mail: n.wawrzyniak@am.szczecin.pl

Abstract—**Marine ship traffic is usually monitored using a combination of Automatic Identification System (AIS) and radar networks. Video monitoring is often used to control vessel traffic on rivers, in ports, and other restricted areas. Despite the many means used, the task of automatic detection and identification of vessels on inland waters is not trivial. In this paper, the problem of automatic ship detection using the video surveillance system is analyzed and discussed primarily in the context of systems' performance. In the proposed solution, we assume that detection uses only video streams from the existing monitoring system without any additional hardware or special configuration or placement of cameras. In addition, the detection must work in real time and the system must detect all moving vessels, including small boats and kayaks. The main contributions of this work consist in presenting the results from several performance tests using different background subtraction algorithms as well as discussing problems that make moving vessels difficult to detect.**

Keywords- ship; detection; video surveillance; fixed camera.

I. INTRODUCTION

Ship traffic is usually monitored using a combination of radar networks and AISs. Moreover, video monitoring systems are common to monitor the traffic on inland or coastal waters. From a technical perspective, video monitoring is a passive system in contrast to a radar and AIS, which can be treated as active sensors. Therefore, traffic monitoring using a video monitoring system can be seen as a more cost efficient system that does not require additional hardware and additionally is more reliable in recognizing, e.g., terror threats, than a radar or AIS. On the other hand, automatic vessel detection is a complex task that requires to consider many scenarios.

The ship in a video stream can be detected using two basic approaches. The first one is to use a pixel-based detection method that allows detecting any moving object on constant or slightly changing background. The second approach is to use object-based detection using some kind of classifier. The second approach is better when it is possible to find a distinctive property of a class of objects, e.g., mast of a sailing vessel, because it usually provides better detection result.

One of the possible solutions to the ship detection problem was presented by Ferreira et al. [1]. The authors use two cameras: one camera with low resolution that detects movement and another camera with high resolution that is used to take a photo when the first camera detects movement. Their solution is designed to detect fishing vessels. They achieved the best results when using object-based detection based on Histogram of Oriented Gradients (HOG) classifier [2]. In contrast, Hu et al. [3] used pixel based detection in their visual surveillance scheme for cage aquaculture that automatically detects and tracks ships. They used the median scheme to create a background image from previous *N* frames with some additional improvements that allowed to reduce the influence of sea waves. The problem of ship detection in the presence of waves was also addressed by Szpak and Tapamo [4]. They present techniques that solve a problem of moving vessels' tracking in the presence of a moving dynamic background (the ocean). Other works related to the problem of ship detection include [5][6] and a survey [7].

This short paper is a part of an ongoing research in Ship Recognition (SHREC) [8], which concerns automatic recognition and identification of non-conventional (according to International Convention for the Safety of Life at Sea (SOLAS)) ships in areas covered by RIS (River Information System) and Vessel Traffic Service (VTS) systems. In this paper, we analyze the problem of ship detection on inland and coastal waters, provide a preliminary solution and test its performance. In the proposed approach, we assume that detection uses only video streams from an existing monitoring system without any additional hardware or special configuration of cameras. In addition, the detection is performed in real time with the use of only one processor working at not more than 25% of its maximum load for one video stream. This requirement is caused by the need to perform also other operations for the video stream from one camera, i.e., ship classification and identification. The system must detect all moving ships, including small boats and kayaks, which is the main difference from existing solutions that mostly focus on only one vessel type. The main contributions of this work consist in presenting the results from several performance tests using different background subtraction algorithms as well as discussing problems that make moving vessels difficult to detect.

The rest of this paper is organized as follows. Section 2 describes the most popular background subtraction algorithms. Section 3 presents the problem of ship detection on inland waters using existing video monitoring. Section 4 presents the results of performance tests of different background subtraction algorithms. We conclude the paper in Section 5.

II. Background Subtraction Algorithms

Moving objects can be detected using a background subtraction algorithm or, to be more precise, using a background/foreground segmentation algorithm. The task of selecting foreground objects in a scene is easy in indoor environments, but in outdoor environments it is more difficult because of many factors that must be considered. The easiest approach is to save a reference (first) frame and then calculate the difference to this frame (algorithm FF). More advanced algorithms use around 100 to 200 frames from which they try to model a background. Many such algorithms exist and it is very difficult to show which one is the best, because their accuracy depends on a chosen benchmark. Additionally, better performance might require more processing power or memory. Storing 200 decompressed frames of a full high definition video requires around 1.2GB of memory and 4K video requires around 4.8GB. The background subtraction algorithms were evaluated by [9] and compared by [10].

Several background subtraction algorithms are implemented in the OpenCV library [11]. To begin with, Gaussian Mixture-based Background- Foreground Segmentation (MOG) algorithm (that uses a mixture of K (K=3 to 5) gaussian distributions to model each background picture. The probable values of background pixels are the ones that are more static and present in more previous frames [12]. Next, Gaussian Mixture-based Background-Foreground Segmentation Algorithm version 2 (MOG2) [13] is available, which is an improved version of MOG. The algorithm selects the appropriate number of gaussian distributions for each pixel. It works better in scenes that change often, e.g., due to illumination changes caused by clouds. Shadows can also be detected using this algorithm.

The algorithm Godbehere-Matsukawa-Goldberg (GMG) [17] uses by default 120 frames for background modelling and per-pixel Bayesian segmentation. New frames have more weight to support variable lightning conditions. The unwanted noise is removed using morphological operations like closing and opening. Another algorithm, 'CouNT (CNT) was designed by Sagi Zeevi [14] to reflect the human vision. It is designed for variable outdoor lighting conditions and it works well on Internet of Things (IoT) hardware. Other algorithms include: k Nearest Neighbours (KNN) that implements K-nearest neighbors background subtraction from [15], the algorithm created during Google Summer of Code (GSOC) [11], and Background Subtraction using Local SVD Binary Pattern (LSBP) [16].

III. Ship Detection

Detection of a foreground object is an easy task when background and lightning are constant at the scene and the camera is fixed. However, in our system, there are small background changes and the lighting changes over time. The basic assumption of our system is that the system uses fixed cameras, which are part of an existing surveillance system and therefore must use video streams from different camera' views.

Figure 1. A screenshot from the application used to test different algorithms of background subtraction.

The main problems that were identified during observations of different video streams are as follows:

1) the camera is usually not directed only at the water and several other moving objects are present in the frame:
   a) trees, other plants and movement depend on wind speed and direction;
   b) object on land: cars, bikes, people, and even trains;
2) animals: especially birds, but also dogs and jumping fish;
3) different water state (waves) – however, less than at sea and waves after fast moving boats;
4) different camera angles, waterway crossroads;
5) obstacles blocking the view, e.g., pillars of bridges, street lamps, mast of moored ships, threes, buildings;
6) multiples ships coming in different directions simultaneously and overlapping with each other;
7) different lightning during different time of the day and of the year.

Our preliminary method for ships detection consists of three main steps as in most standard solutions used for object detection. The first step is the pre-processing in which video is decoded to frames in a bitmap format. The frame rate is reduced to 25 or 30 frames when a video file contains 50 or 60 frames per second. Then, the frames are resized to 1280x720 or 940x540 resolution and converted to grayscale. Additionally, all 25 or 30 frames are used as an input for the background subtraction algorithm.

The second step is foreground extraction that results in a mask. The mask is a black-white bitmap where white color means a foreground object. In this step, one of the background subtraction algorithms is used. Depending on the algorithm, an input frame might be blurred and the morphological opening and closing might be used on the output mask.

The third step is the ship distinction from all moving objects. This step is the most difficult as all artefacts must be removed. The step contains edge detection, creation of bounding boxes, removing objects from pre-configured non-water regions (e.g., regions that contains trees), removing objects with small area or dimensions, and removing objects that appeared for the first time (using a few seconds history).

IV. EXPERIMENTAL RESULTS

The first step in creating the ship detection method was to test how different background subtraction algorithms with different parameters will behave on different video samples. The first decision was making pixel-based detection obligatory due to the fact that the system must detect all types of vessels including leisure units. The tests have been carried out using a test application (Figure 1) that allows testing video samples using different foreground extraction algorithms.

Figure 1 shows detection using the simplest method for foreground extraction, i.e., blurring image and calculating difference to the reference frame containing only background. It contains detected ships with some artefacts that can be easily removed in further steps.

One of the main problems related to real time detection is the performance that limits possible options, especially when the input stream is the high quality 4K stream. Therefore, the first test was a performance test. The test application is written in C# and is using Emgu CV version 3.4.3 (C# wrapper for OpenCV). Two test computers (A - Intel Core i5-8250U, 32GB RAM, SSD 512GB; B - Intel Core i7-8700K, 32GB RAM, SSD 1TB, NVIDIA Quadro P4000) were used in the test. In the test, the explicit Compute Unified Device Architecture (CUDA) OpenCV functions were not used, so it was possible to test only the impact of the algorithm on Central Processing Unit (CPU). Three samples from our database were chosen to the test:

1) Sample 1, low quality High Definition (HD) stream from webcam (1280x720, 18 fps, bitrate: 596kb/s, Advanced Video Coding (AVC) Main@L3.1, duration 90s);
2) Sample 2, medium quality Full High Definition (FHD) (1920x1080, 25 fps, bitrate: 20 Mb/s, AVC Baseline@L4, duration: 90s);
3) Sample 3, high quality 4K (3840x2160, 30fps, bitrate: 48Mb/s, AVC High@L5.1, duration 90s).

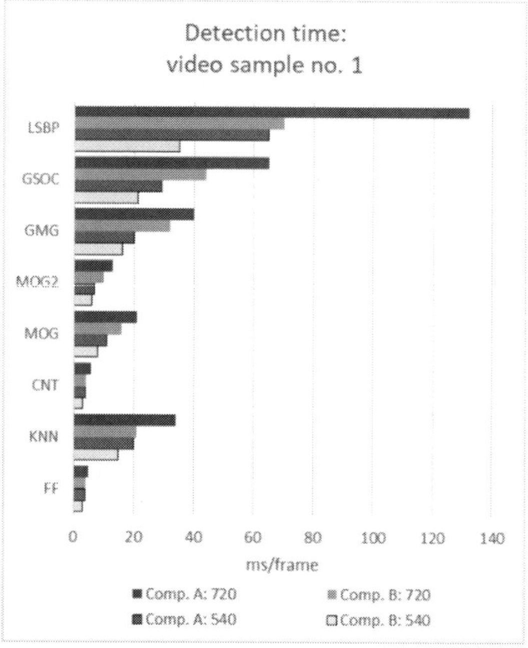

Figure 2. Detection performance - video sample no. 1.

In all the tests, samples were kept in the original size (except 4k resolution, as initial tests have shown, uses to much CPU and does not give better detection results, than stream resized to FHD resolution) or resized to resolutions 1920x1080, 1280x720, and 960x540. The test includes seven different background subtraction algorithms from OpenCV (MOG [12], MOG2 [13], GMG [17], CNT [14], KNN [15], GSOC[11], LSBP [16]) and a simple algorithm that calculates difference to frame with background only (FF).

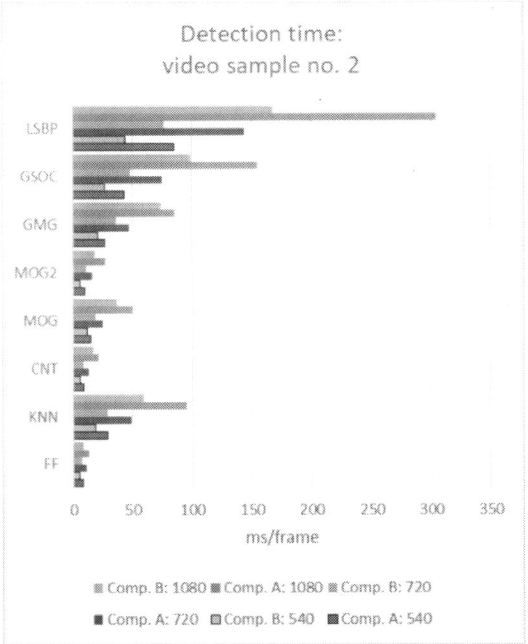

Figure 3. Detection performance - video sample no. 2.

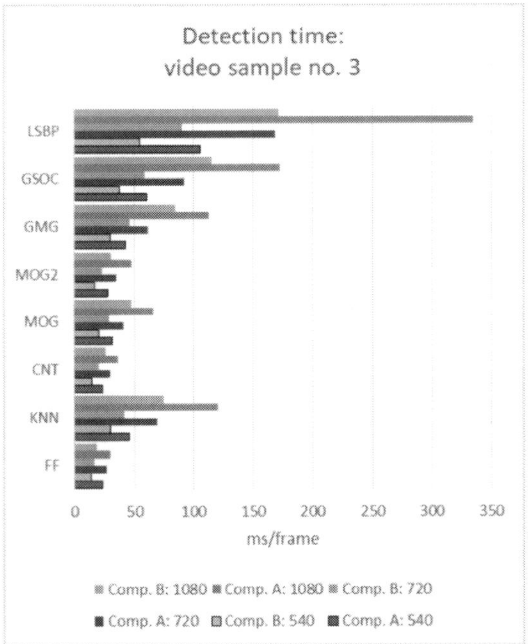

Figure 4. Detection performance - video sample no. 3.

The test results (see Figures 2-4) confirm that detection using 1920x1080 resolution takes significantly more time than using 1280x720 and 960x540 resolutions when using a more advanced algorithm. The maximum detection time must be below 40 ms to enable real time processing using the 25 fps video. In all three video samples, LSBP substractor was the slowest, where processing of 1080p frame took between 150-300 ms (depending on the test computer and input resolution). The fastest was MOG2 substractor and the simple algorithm (but ineffective in dynamic scenes) that subtracts a current frame from a first frame that contains only background (FF) with frame processing time between 3 and 30 ms. The tests have shown that the size of the input has a little impact on processing time. It is mainly, because decoding H.264 stream is fast, for the reason that AVC codec internally uses hardware acceleration and a frame resizing operation is rather simple and therefore swift.

Additionally, a second experiment was carried out to check how background subtraction algorithms affect the ship detection result. During the test, different video samples were viewed by our research team members. This was an initial experiment that allowed us to narrow down algorithms for further quality tests. The main conclusion from the experiment is that higher resolution does not always provide better detection results, mainly because higher resolution also mean more details and noise. The preliminary observation from the test is that GSOC algorithm returns the smallest number of erroneous artefacts.

V. Conclusion and Future Work

In the SHREC system, a detection phase is one of the steps that must be calculated in real time by a single processor for one camera. The test shows that a time less than 100 ms per frame can be achieved using most of the algorithms when resizing to 720p or 540p resolution is used. This time is acceptable, because no more than 3 frames (probably 1) per second will be used for detection purposes.

The main problem with background subtraction algorithms is that often, when on a scene problem described in Section 2 emerges, they do not correctly recognize a foreground object (a ship). Most of the artefacts (incorrectly recognized objects) can be easily removed, but when an object (a ship) is incorrectly subtracted from a background, it is difficult to correct it in further steps. For example, sometimes the presence of waves causes that a background subtraction does not correctly detect a slowly moving ship. The first tests on quality of detection indicate that the best algorithms are GSOC and CNT.

Future works include improving the proposed detection method. The works will be carried out in two paths. In the first path, the algorithm that returns bounding box containing detected ships will be improved based on experimental results. In second one, the method will be further optimized by shifting most of the computation to a graphic processing unit.

The method will be tested on two larger data sets that contain more than 200 video samples each. The first dataset was recorded for the purpose of the project on the waterways near Szczecin. The second contains video files recorded from several public webcams that shows different waterways in Europe. After the test, if results are not satisfactory, the algorithm that uses two background subtraction algorithms at once or one of optical flow methods will be used. The optical flow methods were not tested on the beginning due to their high performance requirements for FHD or 4K video files [18].

ACKNOWLEDGEMENT

This scientific research work was supported by National Centre for Research and Development (NCBR) of Poland under grant No. LIDER/17/0098/L-8/16/NCBR/2017) and under grant No. 1/S/IG/16 financed from a subsidy of the Ministry of Science and Higher Education for statutory activities.

REFERENCES

[1] J. C. Ferreira, J. Branquinho, P. C. Ferreira, and F. Piedade, "Computer vision algorithms fishing vessel monitoring—identification of vesselplate number," Ambient Intelligence– Software and Applications – 8th International Symposium on Ambient Intelligence (ISAmI 2017), J. F. De Paz, V. Juli´an, G. Villarrubia, G. Marreiros, and P. Novais, Eds. Cham: Springer International Publishing, 2017, pp. 9–17, 10.1007/978-3-319-61118-1_2.

[2] R. K. McConnell, "Method of and apparatus for pattern recognition", US Patent 4,567,610, 1986.

[3] W.-C. Hu, C.-Y. Yang, and D.-Y. Huang, "Robust real-time ship detection and tracking for visual surveillance of cage aquaculture," Journal of Visual Communication and Image Representation, vol. 22, no. 6, 2011, pp. 543–556, doi:10.1016/j.jvcir.2011.03.009.

[4] Z. L. Szpak and J. R. Tapamo, "Maritime surveillance: Tracking ships inside a dynamic background using a fast level-set," Expert Systems with Applications, vol. 38, no. 6, 2011, pp. 6669–6680, doi: 10.1016/j.eswa.2010.11.068.

[5] N. Kaido, S. Yamamoto, and T. Hashimoto, "Examination of automatic detection and tracking of ships on camera image in marine environment," 2016 Techno-Ocean (Techno-Ocean), Oct. 2016, pp. 58–63, doi:10.1109/Techno-Ocean.2016.7890748.

[6] Y. J. Kim, Y. K. Chung, and B. G. Lee, "Vessel tracking vision system using a combination of kaiman filter, bayesian classification, and adaptive tracking algorithm," 16th International Conference on Advanced Communication Technology, Feb. 2014, pp. 196–201, doi:10.1109/ICACT.2014.6778948.

[7] R. da Silva Moreira, N. F. F. Ebecken, A. S. Alves, F. Livernet, and A. Campillo-Navetti, "A survey on video detection and tracking of maritime vessels," International Journal of Research and Reviews in Applied Sciences, vol. 20, no. 1, July 2014, pp. 37–50.

[8] N.Wawrzyniak and A. Stateczny, "Automatic watercraft recognition and identification on water areas covered by video monitoring as extension for sea and river traffic supervision systems," Polish Maritime Research, vol. 25, iss. s1, June 2018, pp. 5-13, doi.org/10.2478/pomr-2018-0016.

[9] S. Brutzer, B. Höferlin and G. Heidemann, "Evaluation of background subtraction techniques for video surveillance," CVPR 2011, Colorado Springs, CO, USA, 2011, pp. 1937-1944, doi: 10.1109/CVPR.2011.5995508.

[10] Y. Benezeth, Y. Benezeth, Pierre-Marc Jodoin, Pierre-Marc Jodoin, Bruno Emile, Bruno Emile, Helene Laurent, Helene Laurent, Christophe Rosenberger, Christophe Rosenberger, "Comparative study of background subtraction algorithms," Journal of Electronic Imaging vol. 19, no. 3, July 2010, pp. 1-30, https://doi.org/10.1117/1.3456695.

[11] "Emgu CV Library Documentation version 3.4.3," http://www.emgu.com/wiki/files/3.4.3/document/index.html, 2018, [retrieved: February, 2019].

[12] P. KaewTraKulPong and R. Bowden, "An Improved Adaptive Background Mixture Model for Real-time Tracking with Shadow Detection," Boston, MA: Springer US, 2002, pp. 135–144, doi: 10.1007/978-1-4615-0913-4_11.

[13] Z. Zivkovic, "Improved adaptive gaussian mixture model for background subtraction," in Proceedings of the Pattern Recognition, 17th International Conference on (ICPR'04) Volume 2 - Volume 02, ser. ICPR '04. Washington, DC, USA: IEEE Computer Society, 2004, pp. 28–31, doi:10.1109/ICPR.2004.479.

[14] S. Zeevi, BackgroundSubtractorCNT Project, https://sagi-.github.io/BackgroundSubtractorCNT/, [retrieved: February, 2019].

[15] Z. Zivkovic and F. van der Heijden, "Efficient adaptive density estimation per image pixel for the task of background subtraction," Pattern Recognition Letters, vol. 27, no. 7, 2006, pp. 773–780.

[16] L. Guo, D. Xu and Z. Qiang, "Background Subtraction Using Local SVD Binary Pattern," 2016 IEEE Conference on Computer Vision and Pattern Recognition Workshops (CVPRW), Las Vegas, NV, 2016, pp. 1159-1167, doi: 10.1109/CVPRW.2016.148.

[17] A. B. Godbehere, A. Matsukawa, and K. Goldberg, "Visual tracking of human visitors under variable-lighting conditions for a responsive audio art installation," in 2012 American Control Conference (ACC), June 2012, pp. 4305–4312, doi:10.1109/ACC.2012.6315174.

[18] J. Huang, W. Zou, J. Zhu, and Z Zhu, "Optical Flow Based Real-time Moving Object Detection in Unconstrained Scenes," arXiv e-prints, July 2018, http://adsabs.harvard.edu/abs/2018arXiv180704890H, [retrieved: February, 2019].

Monte Carlo Tree Search for Optimizing Hyperparameters of Neural Network Training

Karolina Polanska, Wiktoria Dywan, Piotr Labuda, Leszek Koszalka, Iwona Pozniak-Koszalka, and Andrzej Kasprzak
Dept. of Systems and Computer Networks
Wroclaw University of Science and Technology
Wroclaw, Poland
Email: {209108, 218457, 218740}@student.pwr.edu.pl, {leszek.koszalka, iwona.pozniak-koszalka, andrzej.kasprzak}@pwr.edu.pl

Abstract—In tasks related to machine learning, the right selection of hyper-parameters can significantly impact training time and quality of the obtained results. Often, iterative search algorithms are used. In this paper, we propose an approach, based on our own modification of Monte Carlo Tree Search. The new algorithm is designed to work on discrete hyper-parameter spaces, and uses feedback from training process to learn and adjust its subsequent outputs. In the paper, the properties of the algorithm are studied, in particular for training Multilayer Perceptron. Moreover, three search algorithms are compared: Grid Search, Random Search and the proposed Monte Carlo Tree Search. As it is shown, the Monte Carlo Tree Search can give promising results and can be treated as fair competition to the off-shelf solutions.

Keywords-algorithm; Monte Carlo approach; Tree search; hyperparameter; neural network.

I. INTRODUCTION

In the recent decades, a lot of improvements were made in the area of known computing technologies, which had an essential impact on popularizing machine learning, leading to new, and more computationally complex algorithms being created [1]. Despite many advantages of machine learning as we know it nowadays, the high complexity of these methods translates to the time needed by a given model to learn what is desired; hence, a lot of attention given to developing the best way of automatically tuning hyper-parameters can be observed [2].

Hyper-parameters of a neural network are parameters of the learning process itself, such as learning rate, activation function, loss function or number of layers [3]. Their selection can significantly impact training time and results and therefore choosing hyper-parameters for neural network is an optimization problem [4][5]. There is a variety of available methods, for instance based on Bayesian approaches [6], or Sequential Model-based Algorithm Configurations (SMAC) [7]. Their performance varies with the type of network and çhosen data. Monte Carlo Tree Search (MCTS) proposed in [8] is a heuristic search algorithm for decision processes; this method is often used in game play [9]. Notable example of usage is AlphaGo, an artificial intelligence application to play Go [10]. It is believed that using Monte Carlo Tree Search could bring satisfying results in hyper-parameter optimization process [8]. The main objective of this work is to improve Monte Carlo Tree Search algorithm so that it finds the best set of neural network hyper-parameters by executing the minimal amount of iterations and to compare the proposed method with two known algorithms, namely Grid Search and Random Search.

Grid Search searches the multidimensional grid of hyper-parameters by giving a trial to every node of the grid. This algorithm requires to manually specify the set of possible values for each parameter. The algorithm moves through the grid in iterative manner. This approach makes Grid Search suffer from the curse of dimensionality as the amount of nodes grows exponentially with the number of hyper-parameters [11].

Random Search is more effective in optimization for high dimensional spaces as it draws subsequent sets of parameters. For discrete parameter collection, Random Search moves over grid nodes, but, unlike Grid Search, in random order [12].

We introduce our method that involves Monte Carlo Tree Search to optimize hyper-parameters. Also, the proposed MCTS algorithm itself can be described along with the applied optimizations and method limitations.

The proposed experimentation system allows the comparison of MCTS with Grid Search and Random Search with regards to the obtained accuracy in subsequent trials. It was decided to focus on classification problems, particularly on Convolutional Neural Network (CNN), Multilayer Perceptron (MLP) and Support Vector Machine (SVM) [13], to confirm that MCTS algorithm can be applied to various machine learning techniques, not only neural networks.

All tests presented in this paper were conducted on Modified National Institute of Standards and Technology dataset (MNIST) [14], which is the biggest available collection of handwritten digits. It consists of about 60 000 samples in shape of matrices 28x28 pixels.

The rest of the paper is organized as follows. Section II contains a short review of important scientific papers in the area. In Section III, the problem is formulated. The core of the paper is Section IV with the presentation of the proposed algorithm. The designed and implemented experimentation system is described in Section V. This section contains experiment design, the obtained results and comments. The conclusion and plans for further research appear in the last Section VI.

II. RELATED WORK

Traditionally, a manual search (meaning an approach based on empirical research) has been used for finding the most satisfying hyper-parameters [15]. While this approach can be enough for some researchers while training simple models, it still requires constant conscious management of chosen hyper-parameters values as even the slightest change in data used for learning can make them insufficient for achieving satisfactory results.

Several methods of automated choosing values of hyper-parameters were proposed over the years. One of the most common approaches is known as Grid Search, which looks for the best combination of parameters within whole space of previously defined fixed values, thus it can become time-consuming for a large space of potential solutions [16].

One of the most popular approaches, Random Search, is also one of the simplest. As suggested by its name, combinations of hyper-parameters values are chosen randomly until a satisfactory result of learning process is received. As presented in [12], Random Search can achieve the same results as Grid Search, but without the need to check every possible combination, i.e., it is relatively faster.

The Monte Carlo approach is applied to support solving many problems in artificial intelligence area [17], in particular in optimization of reinforcement learning process [18]. Very new and interesting review of applications of Monte Carlo Tree search can be found in [19].

III. PROBLEM STATEMENT

Given an artificial neural network N, with variable vector of hyper-parameters V, let a(V) be the accuracy of the vector V, defined as the highest accuracy reached by network N, trained with hyper-parameters V, among all the accuracies reached in a 10-fold cross-validation.

Let S be an algorithm searching through the possible space of hyper-parameter vectors V. During its operation, algorithm S produces the number of m hyper-parameter vectors. Accuracy of the algorithm A(S,-m) is defined as the highest $a(V_i)$, where $i = 1, 2, \ldots, m$.

As training a neural network can be a computationally expensive operation, the optimization task lies in finding an algorithm S such that A(S, m) is maximized, while m is minimized at the same time.

IV. PROPOSED METHOD AND ALGORITHM

The proposed method of exploring the hyper-parameter space is based on a modified Monte Carlo Tree Search approach. We introduced several changes that allowed the approach to be used for exploring a discrete hyper-parameter space.

A. *Building the tree*

For each neural network, the hyper-parameter space to be explored is defined as a discrete set of possible values for each of hyper-parameters taken into consideration. When transforming the space into a tree data structure, the following approach was used:

First, hyper-parameters are ordered according to their number of possible values, from lowest to highest. The ordered list of hyper-parameters is marked as HS.

The root node of the tree represents the beginning of the decision process. For each possible value of first hyper-parameter in the list HS, a child node is added to the root node, representing the choice of that value for a given hyper-parameter. Then, for each possible value of the second hyper-parameter in the list HS, a child node is added to all of the level 2 nodes. The process repeats itself until there are no more hyper-parameters on the list HS to further expand the tree.

The resulting tree has every possible combination of chosen values represented as a leaf node, and represents the whole space of hyper-parameters as a multi-staged decision process.

B. *The algorithm*

The modified version of the MCTS algorithm follows a standard model:

Selection - Expansion - Simulation - Backpropagation.

Each node (except the root) in the tree has a value representing expected accuracy of a neural network trained using hyper-parameters represented by leaf descendants of a given node. This value is assigned and updated by the MCTS algorithm during its operation.

a) Selection: As long as the node the algorithm is in has children nodes of known value, the algorithm chooses a node of highest value and moves to it.

b) Expansion: If the node has no children of known value, a node is chosen at random for the Simulation phase.

c) Simulation: To complete the set of hyper-parameter values the algorithm chooses remaining values at random. A neural network of choice is constructed and trained using this set of hyper-parameters, and its accuracy, measured as a result of 10 k-fold cross-validation, is assigned as a value of the node the algorithm started from.

d) Backpropagation: After all child nodes created during expansion phase are assigned a value, the value of their parent node is updated to the mean of their values. The process propagates recursively, updating the parent nodes value until the root is reached.

C. *Optimisation*

As the search algorithms are compared on what was their best proposed solution after N trials (one trial being equal to one 10 k-fold validation of a given set of hyper-parameters), three optimizations were introduced to maximize the algorithms performance within the three allowed trials described below.

a) Hyper-parameter sorting: As described in Section IV-A, hyper-parameters are ordered from the one with least possible values to the one with the most. The algorithm will, therefore, always have to start by expanding the root node of the tree. If the initial expansion requires a small amount of simulations, the algorithm can start making more informed decisions sooner, relying less on random choice and more on past values of the nodes.

b) Node exclusion: The algorithm can find itself in a local maximum of accuracy when the entire set of hyper-parameters is chosen based on node values and not random chance. In that case the leaf node of this solution is marked as excluded and cannot be included in any following set of hyper-parameters. This forces the algorithm to consider other options, and due to backpropagation will gradually push the algorithm to the global maximum as the number of generated solutions tends to infinity.

c) Result caching: Due to random choice, it might occur that an algorithm generates the same solution multiple times. For that reason, all previously generated solutions and their respective accuracy are stored, and can be used to substitute the training process when such case occurs. Since this does not count as a generated solution, the MCTS can generate overall better results within a given solutions limit.

D. Limitation

Due to its nature, MCTS is significantly harder to execute in parallel than Random Search or Grid Search. Due to the fact that next set of hyper-parameters is known only after training the network on previous sets, the execution has to be done sequentially. Only during the expansion phase several sets of hyper-parameters to test are known in advance and the order of their testing does not matter. Alternatively, the algorithm could be modified to test several promising nodes of the tree at once - however, this hypothetical method is beyond the scope of this paper and poses several questions about potentially redundant work.

V. EXPERIMENTATION SYSTEM

The main goal of the research was checking whether the proposed method of exploring hyper-parameter space is useful while solving the classification task. In addition, the results of comparative research aimed in comparison of the accuracy of known algorithms and the accuracy of a new algorithm based on Monte Carlo tree search are presented.

A. Experiment Design

In order to conduct research, the Python application has been created. Its components have been written with usage of Keras, TensorFlow and Scikit libraries [13][20].

The classification of the MNIST dataset [14] has been chosen as the task to train the network on. It is a popular set of handwritten letters and digits represented as bitmap. It was chosen with regards to its size of around 60 000 samples. A Multilayer Perceptron classifier was trained, and several parameters of the training process and network's structure were chosen as the hyper-parameter space to compare the search algorithms. Table I presents the hyper-parameters and their values used in experiments.

TABLE I. HYPERPARAMETERS

Hyper-parameter	Possible Values
Learning rate	0.1, 0.01, 0.001
Activation function	tanh, relu, sigmoid
Hidden layer units	1, 30, 100, 800
First dropout	0.1, 0.25, 0.7, 0.9
Second dropout	0.1, 0.3, 0.5, 0.9

Three search algorithms, Random Search, Grid Search, and our own, were tested at finding the best set of hyper-parameters in as few guesses as possible.

B. Results

The obtained results of the number of sixteen experiments, conducted on Multilayer Perceptron, are shown: in Figure 1, produced by Grid Search, in Figure 2, produced by Random Search, and in Figure 3, produced by our Monte Carlo Tree Search.

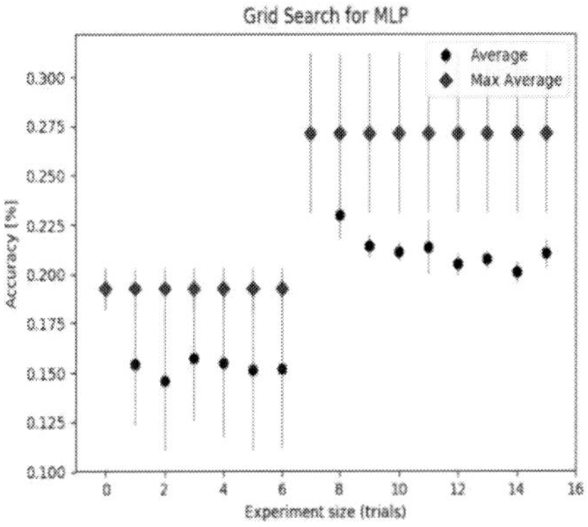

Figure 1. Results of the experiment with Grid Search.

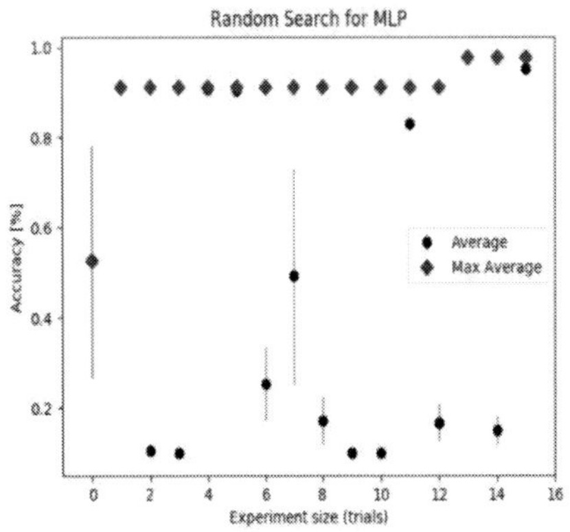

Figure 2. Results of the experiment with Random Search.

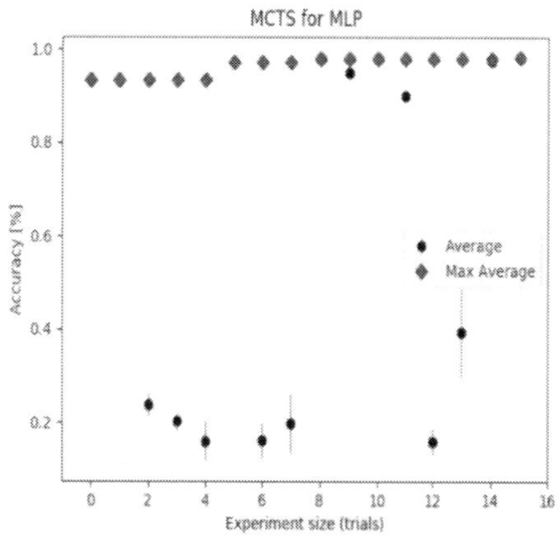

Figure 3. Results of the experiment with Monte Carlo Tree Search.

C. *Comments*

As shown in Figure 1 and Figure 2, the known search algorithms are susceptible to a sudden spike of precision due to accidental finding of a good solution. Contrary, as it can be observed in Figure 3, our Monte Carlo Tree Search algorithm is able to make small incremental changes from session to session.

VI. CONCLUSION

The presented approach to exploring hyper-parameters space, in particular the proposed Monte Carlo Tree Search algorithm can be considered as an interesting alternative for the off-shelf solutions. Its computational overhead is significantly higher than in the case of Grid Search or Random Search but negligible compared to the typical task of training artificial neural networks.

In the near future, we plan to conduct more research using the proposed approach on Convolutional Neural Network and Support Vector Machine. Also, we are in the process of some improvement consisting in implementation of the multistage experimentation system along with the rules described in [21].

ACKNOWLEDGMENT

This work was supported by the statutory funds of the Department of Systems and Computer Networks under grant no. 0401/0132/18, Faculty of Electronics, Wroclaw University of Science and Technology, Wroclaw, Poland.

REFERENCES

[1] G. Montavon, G. Orr, and K-R. Muller, "Neural Networks: Tricks of the Trade," LNCS, vol. 7700, Springer, 2012.

[2] W. Koehrsen, "Automated Machine Learning Hyper-Parameter Tuning in Python," https://towardsdatascience.com/automated-machine-learning-hyperparameter-tuning-in-python-dfda59b72f8a [retrieved: January 2019].

[3] A. Honchar, "Neural Networks for Algorithmic Trading. Hyper-Parameters Optimization," https:/medium.com/@alexrachnog/neural-networks-for-algorithmic-trading-hyperparameters-optimization-cb2b [retrieved: January 2019].

[4] R. Bardenet, M. Brendel, B. Kegl, and M. Sebag, "Collaborative Hyper-Parameter Tuning," Proc. of ICML, 2013, pp. 199-207.

[5] P. Sharma, "Improving Neural Networks – Hyper-Parameter Tuning,," analyticsvidhya.com/blog/2018/11/neural-networks-hyperparameter-tuning-regularization-deeplearning [retrieved: January 2019].

[6] N. Srivastava, G. Hinton, A. Krizhevsky, I. Sutskever, and R. Salakhutdinov, "Dropout: A Simple Way to Prevent Neural Networks from Overfitting," Journal of Machine Learning Research, vol. 15, 2014, pp. 1929-1958.

[7] F. Huffer, H. H. Hoos, and K. Leyton-Brown, "Sequential model Based Optimization for General Algorithm Configuration," Learning and Intell. Optim., Springer, 2011, pp. 507-523.

[8] G. M. J-B. Chaslot, " Monte Carlo Tree Search," PhD Thesis, Maastricht University, 2010, Dissertation Series No. 2010-41, ISBN 978-90-8559-099-6.

[9] T. Cazenave and N. Jouandeau, "A Parallel Monte Carlo Tree Search Algorithm," Proc. Comput. And Games, LNCS, vol. 5131, 2008, pp. 72-80.

[10] H. Bajer and M. H. Winands, "Beam Monte Carlo Tree Search" Proc. IEEE Conf. Comput. Intell. Games, 2012, pp. 227-233.

[11] J. Bergstra, R. Bardenet, Y. Bengio, and B. Kegl, "Algorithms for Hyper-Parameter Optimization," Advances in Neural Information Processing Systems 24 (NIPS 2011), pp.2546-2554.

[12] J. Bergstra and Y. Bengio, "Random Search for Hyper-parameter Optimization," Journal of Machine Learning Research, vol. 13(1), 2012, pp. 281-305.

[13] S. Raschka, "Python Machine Learning," Packt Publishing, 2016.

[14] Yann.lecun.com/exdb/mnist, [retrieved: November 2018].

[15] P. Koch, B. Wujek, O. Golowidov, and S. Gardner, "Automated Hyper-parameter Tuning for Effective Machine Learning," 2017, SAS514-2017.

[16] S. Li and M. Tan, "Tuning SVM Parameters by Using-Hybrid CLPSO-BFGS Algorithm," Journal of Neurocomputing, vol. 73, June 2010, pp. 2089-2096.

[17] H. Akiyama, K. Komiya, and Y. Kotani, "Nested Monte Carlo Search with AMAF Heuristic," Proc. Int. Conf. Tech. Applica. Artif. Intell, 2010, pp. 172-176.

[18] J. Asmuth and M. L. Littman, "Learning Planning Near Bayes Optimal Reinforcement Learning via Monte Carlo Search," Proc. Conf. Uncert. Artif. Intell., 2011, pp.19-26.

[19] J. N. van Rijn and F. Hutter, "Hyper-parameter Importance Across Datasets," Proc. 24th ACM SIGKDD International Conference on Knowledge Discovery & Data Mining, 2018, pp. 2367-2376.

[20] Stackshare.io/stackups/keras-vs-scikit-learn-vs-tensorflow [retrieved: January 2019].

[21] M. Hudziak, I. Pozniak-Koszalka, L Koszalka, and A. Kasprzak, "Multiagent Pathfinding in the Crowded Environment with Obstacles," Journal of Intelligent and Fuzzy Systems, vol. 32(2), 2017, pp. 1561-1573.

Automatic Ship Identification Approach for Video Surveillance Systems

Natalia Wawrzyniak
Marine Technology Ltd.
Szczecin, Poland
e-mail: n.wawrzyniak@marinetechnology.pl

Tomasz Hyla
Marine Technology Ltd.
Szczecin, Poland
e-mail: t.hyla@marinetechnology.pl

***Abstract*—Existing methods and systems for ships identification are mostly tailored for large, commercial vessels. Nowadays, a need to automatically identify smaller craft emerged, especially in coastal, port or busy river waters. This paper presents a proposal of automatic vessel identification method using video streams from existing marine and inland surveillance systems that are part of vessel traffic services. The identification uses image processing methods to detect and classify ships, as well as recognize vessel plates. The results of these processes are then matched with vessels hull data from internal and external data bases. Fuzzy logic and historical analysis are used to assess identification certainty. The proposed preliminary solution is described and visualized with the use of systems logic schema.**

Keywords-ship identification; marine systems; image processing; video surveillance.

I. INTRODUCTION

Identification of vessels taking part in marine and inland ships traffic is a complex and difficult task. Especially now, in turbulent times, when the risk of pirates or terror attacks is rising, fast and reliable identification of ships in coastal, port, and busy river areas has become a crucial task for traffic information services systems. Existing solutions differ in assumptions, used sensors and scale of operation depending on reasons why such identification must be undertaken. Nevertheless, in each situation, identification means comparing results of object detection and recognition with some reliable sort of source information on existing vessels.

Identification of vessels not covered by International Convention for the Safety of Life at Sea (SOLAS) [1] convention is the biggest challenge, because such vessels are not required to own and use Automatic Identification System (AIS) or Long-Range Identification and Tracking (LRIT) transponders, which allow to identify ships automatically and at least passively. These non-conventional ships are small, but they are the most numerous group of units present on inland waterways. The group includes leisure crafts, motorboats, yachts, authorities' vessels, specialized port units, etc. Due to this fact, video surveillance plays a very important role in restricted areas both marine and inland (inland waterways class 4b, ports, and others) [2]. The surveillance is usually a part of traffic information systems - Vessel Traffic Services (VTS) on marine waters and River Information Services (RIS) on inland waters [3]. However, video monitoring and ship identification is done manually by an operator, which is time consuming, resource intensive and insufficient at the same time. Usually, all other information in such systems (built mostly using Service Oriented Architecture (SOA)) is pushed via Simple Object Access Protocol (SOAP) to different traffic participants and to other systems (e.g., authorities). Hence, the need for automation of identification in such systems is urgent.

In this paper, we propose an initial solution for conducting automatic ship identification using video streams from existing surveillance systems on areas covered by vessels traffic information systems, such as RIS or VTS. We propose the scheme for ships identification and discuss its evaluation method. The research is done as a part of Automatic Recognition and Identification System for Ships in Video Surveillance Areas (SHREC) project [4]. SHREC is a system that is going to use multiple existing video streams to identify passing ships. The system does not require specialized cameras and has modular and scalable architecture that allow connecting many surveillance cameras.

The rest of this paper is organized as follows. Section II describes the problem of identification and current state of the art. Section III presents the identification approach used in SHREC system. Section IV describes our approach to system evaluation. The conclusion closes the article.

II. BACKGROUND

There are four main approaches to track and monitor ships traffic: AIS, LRIT, Vessel Monitoring System (VMS), and via already mentioned VTS and RIS traffic services. The first two are imposed by the SOLAS convention, and therefore, work for large international voyaging ships, passenger crafts, offshore drilling units, etc. Moreover, AIS [5] is a passive way of identification, because ships for a variety of reasons can turn off their transponders or send false messages. VMS is used in commercial fishing for environmental and regulatory purposes and uses a variety of sensors. Nowadays, more and more of such systems use airborne and satellite-borne imaging sensors. In the detection and tracking domain, the main research is going in two ways: (i) using optical sensors [6][7] and (ii) Synthetic Aperture Radar (SAR) [8]. Still some additional information must be used to identify units. Usually, the identification is based on data provided by AIS [9] or some other referenced data, e.g., Ship Arrival Notification System [10].

The problem of detection and identification of small, noncommercial crafts remains a challenge. VTS and RIS systems, besides AIS (when possible) and radars (for detection and tracking), use video monitoring [11] as a way to visually identify units. Surveillance is used by a system operator to observe current traffic or to make an assessment of archival situations. Detection, recognition and identification of units based only on surveillance in coastal and inland areas are very complicated due to many factors including scene characteristics: illumination changes, reflections, existence of high frequency background objects [12], etc., as well as the lack of unification of ships markings [4].

Contrary to data in other VTS/RIS subsystems, information on ships identification is not processed in any way, nor passed to other receivers in the system. RIS and VTS systems were developed to primarily exchange information between its centers and other external systems (e.g., authorities or shipowners). On the other hand, there is no standardized marking system for vessels side marks, which could possibly facilitate remote craft identification.

In image or video stream analysis, the identification process is usually the third step after objects detection and recognition (or classification). The identification itself is to compare results of classification/recognition and match it with actual knowledge from systems own information on vessels or some external data source (e.g., Hull Data Base in RIS). In order to identify objects, a number of image processing algorithms must be executed to analyze video streams. There is vast ongoing research on this matter. Detection can be done using multiple approaches [13][14]. Many times, classification, besides traditional image processing approach (Feature-based template Matching, pattern matching, etc.), uses artificial intelligence methods like neural networks or other deep learning algorithms [8][15]. Moreover, from systems' performance perspective, it is much more difficult to execute these methods in close to real-time mode. They use more resources, take more time to execute and training database must be large and well-structured. Interestingly, recognition of vessel plates (side marks) can be very helpful [16].

III. Identification in SHREC system

SHREC is being developed as a system that can be easily integrated with existing RIS or VTS systems. The core of SHREC system is the ships recognition and identification method. It will need an access to any number of video streams in order to run image analysis and to systems vessel database to be able to perform identification. The simplified schema of SHREC identification process is shown in Figure 1.

The system can be divided into four layers. The video capture layer is responsible for receiving and decoding of video streams into series of bitmap. Each stream is decoded separately and forwarded to corresponding frame analysis module in detection and recognition layer. This module consists of three different submodules responsible for ship detection, ships classification and text (vessels plate) recognition. After a ship is being detected, a cropped frame and detection mask is forwarded for classification purposes. The classification is being processed on cropped image, but in original resolution. Detailed classification method is being part of ongoing separate research in SHREC project. Simultaneously to classification, a text analysis is being processed on vessels' labels, when they extracted from cropped frame. Information of classification and text recognition results are passed into identification layer with corresponding quality measures.

Here, the main identification process takes place. First, the collected information for a single frame is checked if it is sufficient for fast identification (a classification ratio and percentage of recognized text allows comparing it with referenced information in the traffic systems database). When it is positively identified, the information about ship and the quality of the identification with the original data frame is passed into Vessel Identification Log and later Identification History Database. If not, the recognition results are passed into AI-Based Identification module, which uses additional information to identify a vessel. Primarily, it uses a buffered, short term history of frames that were analyzed before the current candidate frame. A built-in voting system, using fuzzy logic [17], allows classifying a ship based on earlier results from n video stream frames. The output of the ship type classification algorithm for each frame is fuzzified, which means that there is a quality indicator for each class telling how good the adjustment is to each ship type. When the indicator value is firm, it outputs one ship type of high positive quality. However, sometimes the classification shows good or average matching to few types based on one frame. The fuzzy processing is used to calculate the final ship type and the voting is based on the output of this process and on a series of n previous results.

Secondly, the system can perform analysis with the use of rough sets theory [18] using systems Identification History, that stores the information on identified vessel, and the corresponding identification quality measure. When the spatial configuration of cameras in the monitoring system is known (e.g., two cameras point at the same area), then a Multi-View Analysis can be performed using recognition results from frames of two video streams from Short Term History. Rough sets are used to build decision rules needed to perform final identification. Multiple input arguments from the modules mentioned above are mapped into conditional attributes. Decisional attributes are different types of identification output: no ship, moving unknow ship, ship with known type, locally identified ship (e.g, the ship was previously seen by the system), or externally identified ship (e.g., the ship's registration number was matched with an external ships' registry). That approach helps to manage ambiguous cases that occur due to properties of coastal and inland video monitoring. The biggest influence on the proposed approach has an existence of a large amount of poor quality data.

IV. Evaluation

The proper verification of the ship identification method is a complex task and requires preparing a database with video samples that can be used in automated benchmarks. In SHREC, the database consists of video samples and corresponding files with structured description. The video samples are divided into two data sets. The first one contains around 500 samples taken from publicly available video streams from different ports in Europe. The second one consists of around 2000 video samples that were gathered on waterways around Szczecin by our team during the summer of 2018. The next step is to describe these samples using expert opinion, i.e., an expert must identify exact points in time (frames in a video sample) where she or he thinks the ship should be detected, its type recognized and identified. That later allows to compare answer given by the system with actual data that was visually confirmed by a witness/expert. The description for each sample is written to a structured file (a spreadsheet), so an automatic test can be easily executed.

The quality of the identification algorithm will be measured using two parameters. The first parameter is a False Negative Identification Ratio (FNIR). It will measure the ratio of ships that have not been identified to all ships identification events. It is worth mentioning that it does not matter if a ship that passes through camera is identified based on one frame or more frames. The positive identification event is a situation when the occurrence of a ship is properly identified in a video sample regardless of the number of frames that contain that ship. The second parameter is a False Positive Identification Ratio (FPIR). It measures the ratio of incorrect ship identification events to all ships identification events.

Before we will start testing the identification algorithm, the detection algorithm, as well as the ship type classification And the text recognition algorithms will be tested using a similar approach. Based on our video samples database and structured description, the FNIR and FPIR will be measured. Regarding the identification algorithm, we assume that positive result is when a ship is properly detected or recognized through its occurrence in front of a camera one or more times. Additionally, the algorithms will be tested on the frame basis using a parameter that will show a ratio of frames in which the ship was detected to the number of frames provided by an expert.

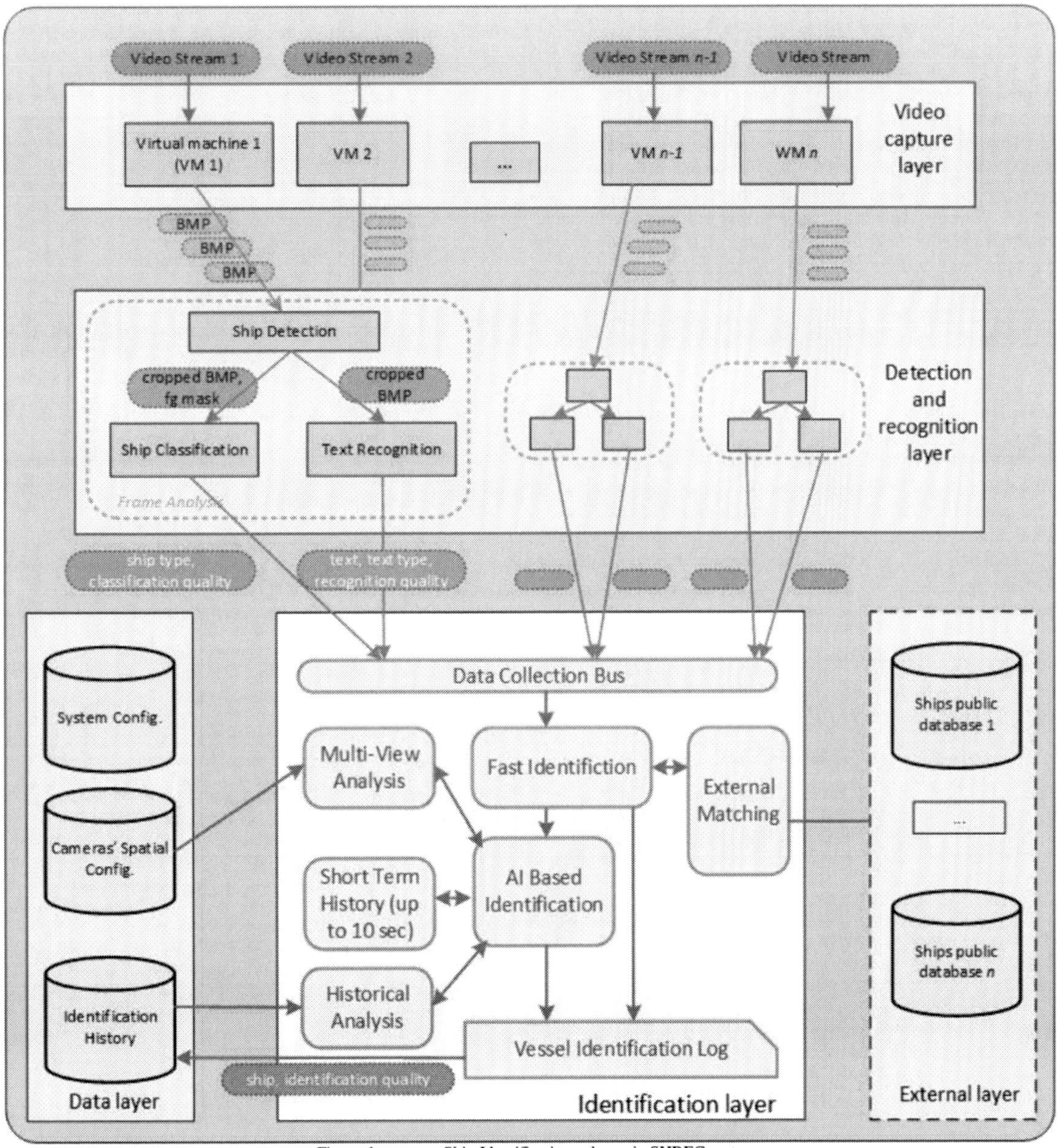

Figure 1. Ship Identification schema in SHREC system.

V. Conclusion and Future Work

We have presented a vessel identification method using video surveillance that is a part of traffic information services and is an ongoing research in SHREC project. The architecture of VTS/RIS systems allows using these systems' databases as a reference crucial for the identification process. Also, the databases can also be used when VTS/RIS has access to external systems (authorities, shipowners).

The main purpose of the research is to develop a flexible solution that identifies voyaging vessels regardless of their size and other passive identification systems. In the SHREC system, a single camera stream is analyzed separately using image processing methods for detection, classification and text recognition to properly recognize a ship. When the recognition quality is sufficient, matching with data from a traffic system database provides identification. When the quality of recognition is unsatisfactory then identification using historical data and AI methods, namely, fuzzy logic and rough sets theory, are used. Multi-view analysis is also possible, when monitoring system' configuration allows recognizing that two cameras point at the same area.

Some limitations were discovered in initial tests of each part of the proposed system. They are concerning the visual layer, such as quality of camera image, the maximum distance between ship and camera that allows for a detection/recognition, visibility of vessels plate, etc.. They were expected and will be precisely specified in further development of the system. However, the biggest challenge to overcome seems to be the performance limitations that appear due to massive computational effort, which needs to be conceived especially for better classification results. This issue can be reduced by introducing some manual interference into the systems operation, e.g., limiting the area where ships can appear in the cameras' scene.

Nevertheless, the proposed solution will automate the process of visual tracking of a camera image by the operator of the surveillance system. The system can work as an independent service and use SOAP protocol to push information of identified ships to other subsystems of vessels traffic information services.

Acknowledgment

This scientific research work was supported by National Centre for Research and Development (NCBR) of Poland under grant No. LIDER/17/0098/L-8/16/NCBR/2017).

References

[1] International Maritime Organisation, "SOLAS International Convention for the Safety of Life at Sea", 1974.

[2] A. Stateczny, D. Gronska, and W. Motyl, "Hydrodron – new step for profesional hydrography for restricted waters", Proceedings of Baltic Geodesy Congress BGC, IEEE, June 2018, pp. 226-230, DOI: 10.1109/BGC-Geomatics.2018.00049

[3] A. Stateczny, "Sensors in River Information Services of the Odra River in Poland: Current State and Planned Extension". Proc. Baltic Geodesy Congress (BGC), IEEE, June 2017, pp.301-306, DOI: 10.1109/BGC.Geomatics.2017.77

[4] N. Wawrzyniak and A. Stateczny, "Automatic watercraft recognition and identification on water areas covered by video monitoring as extension for sea and river traffic supervision systems," Polish Maritime Research, vol. 25, no. s1, June 2018, pp. 5-13, DOI:10.2478/pomr-2018-0016..

[5] S. Chaturvedi, Ch. Yang, K. Ouchi and P. Shanmugam "Ship recognition by integration of SAR and AIS". Journal of Navigation, Vol. 65(02), 2012, pp. 323-337, DOI:10.1017/S0373463311000749

[6] Ch. Corbane, L. Najman and E. Pecoul, "A complete processing chain for ship detection using optical satellite imagery", Dec. 2010 INT J REMOTE SENS. 31(22), pp. 5837–5854 DOI:10.1080/01431161.2010.512310.

[7] F. Maquera and E. Gutierrez, "Wakes-ship removal on high-resolution optical images based on histograms in hsv color space", IJACSA , vol.9 (7), 2018, pp.223-227, DOI:10.14569/IJACSA.2018.090732

[8] G. Margarit and A. Tabasco, "Ship classification in single-pol SAR images based on fuzzy logic," IEEE Trans. Geosci. Remote Sens., vol. 49, no. 8, pp. 3129-3138, 2011

[9] G . Margarit , J. J. Mallorqui, J. M. Rius, and C. Lopez-Martinez, "On the usage of GRECOSAR , an orbital polarimetric SAR simulator of complex targets, to vessel classification studies," IEEE Trans. Geosci. Remote Sens., vol. 44, no. 12, pp. 3517-3525, 2006.

[10] M. D. Sullivan and M. Shah, "Visual surveillance in maritime port facilities", Mar. 2008, SPIE Proceedings, Visual Information Processing XVII, vol. 6978, pp.8 DOI:10.1117/12.777645

[11] D. Bloisi, F. Previtali, A. Pennisi, D. Nardi, and M. Fiorini, "Enhancing Automatic Maritime Surveillance Systems With Visual Information", Aug 2016, IEEE Transactions on Intelligent Transportation Systems, vol.8(4) pp.824-833, DOI:10.1109/TITS.2016.2591321

[12] D. Bloisi, L.Iocchi, M. Fiorini, and G. Graziano „Automatic maritime surveillance with visual target detection" Proceedings of the International Defense and Homeland Security Simulation Workshop DHSS, pp. 141-145, 2011

[13] K. Prasad, D. Rajan, L. Rachmawati, E. Rajabaly, and C. Quek, "Video processing from electro-optical sensors for object detection and tracking in maritime environment: A Survey,"Intelligent Transportation Systems, IEEE Transactions on Intelligent Transportation Systems , 2017, vol. 18(7), pp. 1993-2016, DOI: 10.1109/TITS.2016.2634580

[14] R. da Silva Moreira, N. F. F. Ebecken, A. S. Alves, F. Livernet, and A. Campillo-Navetti, "A survey on video detection and tracking of maritime vessels," International Journal of Research and Reviews in Applied Sciences, vol. 20, no. 1, July 2014, pp. 37–50.

[15] Q. Zhou, L. Ma, M. Celenk, and D. Chelberg, "Object Detection and Recognition via Deformable Illumination and Deformable Shape", Nov 2006, pp. 2737 – 2740, DOI:10.1109/ICIP.2006.313113

[16] J. C. Ferreira, J. Branquinho, P. C. Ferreira, and F. Piedade, "Computer vision algorithms fishing vessel monitoring—identification of vesselplate number," Ambient Intelligence–Software and Applications – 8th International Symposium on Ambient Intelligence (ISAmI 2017), J. F. De Paz, V. Juli'an, G. Villarrubia, G. Marreiros, and P. Novais, Eds. Cham: Springer International Publishing, 2017, pp. 9–17, 10.1007/978-3-319-61118-1_2.

[17] K. Valášková, T. Kliestik, and M. Mišanková, "The Role of Fuzzy Logic in Decision Making Process", Proc. of ICMIBI 2014, Jan 2014, Lecture Notes in Management Science, vol.44 DOI: 10.5729/lnms.vol44.143

[18] N. Wawrzyniak and T.Hyla, "Managing Depth Information Uncertainty in Inland Mobile Navigation Systems". In: Kryszkiewicz et al. (eds) 2014 Joint Rough Sets Symposium, Springer LNCS (LNAI), vol. 8536 pp. 343-350,

Investigating the Feasibility to Estimate System Performance Based upon Limited Data of the Taipei Metro System

Tzu-Chia Kao and Snow H. Tseng
Department of Electrical Engineering,
National Taiwan University,
Taipei 10617, Taiwan
e-mails: {b03901004, stseng}@ntu.edu.tw

Abstract—**Data analysis may yield information regarding the system performance. In this study, we analyze the maintenance data provided by Taipei Rapid Transit Corporation (TRTC); the data consists of limited maintenance records of the Taipei metro system. However, the accuracy to ascertain the system lifetime based upon limited maintenance records of a still young metro system is yet to be determined. Furthermore, the Taipei metro system is renowned for its good maintenance and performance, which further complicates the analysis with additional variable introduced by replaced new parts. Based on limited maintenance records, the research objective is to assess the feasibility of extracting reliable information indicative of the current stage of life, and, the remaining lifetime of the metro system.**

Keywords-degradation; maintenance; metro; MRT; performance analysis; data analysis.

I. INTRODUCTION

The Mass Rapid Transit (MRT) system of Taipei Rapid Transit Corporation (TRTC) began operation on March 28, 1996; it has been operating for 22 years [1]. Most of the equipment has not yet been replaced. In this research, we investigate the feasibility of extracting information from the Taipei MRT maintenance records. The research objective is to determine whether it is possible to acquire reliable information of the system performance from the limited time-span maintenance records. If the maintenance data indeed contains such information of the current system status, our goal is to assess the current stage of life of the Taipei MRT system and determine the remaining lifetime.

The performance and degradation of metropolitan metro systems have been the focus of general public. Various studies have been reported, including technical issues of the MRT. Rail track condition monitoring is an important technical concern of the MRT system [2]. However, constant monitoring of the MRT system is not available; typically the usual maintenance is performed once a month or less. The track condition has attracted much attention since it is a potential threat to the railway system. Studies to prevent such threats have been reported [3]-[5]. To improve the reliability of a mass rapid transit system is the general goal of such research and technical modifications.

Analysis of information regarding other metropolitan mass transport systems may be helpful. As reported in [6], train model R36 of the New York City subway serviced from 1964 to 2003, a total of 39 years. R160s were used to replace 45-year-old trains. In another news report about old trains [7], the oldest trains for New York City Subway were planned to serve for 58 years. Now, this type of train is considered too old, has very high failure rate and is not appealing to passengers. The subway train lifetime is estimated to be around 40 to 50 years. For example, some lines of Singapore Mass Rapid Transit (SMRT) have been operating since 1987, 30 years from today. Thus, the actual wear-out period of a metro system, assuming they are similar, may roughly lie between 20 years (the oldest TRTC asset), and 40 years (New York City Subway). However, all of these metropolitan metro systems are different in various aspects, such as: model, company, maintenance, management culture, etc. It is natural that the characteristics of these MRT systems are not the same and may even differ dramatically. With unknown number of variables involved, the accuracy of assessment may be very limited.

Determining the current system status may be essential. The degradation curve is commonly employed for estimation of the system current status. Analysis of the reliability is based on failure rate and maintenance records [8]. To study the maintenance and performance characteristics, various approaches have been reported [9]-[17], including the popular bathtub curve analysis [18]-[23]. Typically, the bathtub-shaped curve is employed for system performance analysis [24]. Analysis based upon the bathtub curve has been extensively applied to various problems; various modifications to improve applicability have been reported [11][25][26]. It is possible that the bathtub-shaped curve could be affected by human factors; for example, if the asset retired in its early stage, the curve may not rise up during the wear-out period and may even descend. If properly maintained, the curve may not rise in the wear-out period. However, few MRT systems in reality exhibit degradation behavior similar to the bathtub-shaped curve model [27]. It is possible such bathtub curve may not be the ideal model for analyzing the metro system performance.

This paper is organized as follows. Section I consists of an introduction of the problem. The research method is discussed in Section II. Research findings are reported in Section III, and finally, a summary is presented in Section IV, followed by an acknowledgement.

II. METHOD

The bathtub-shaped curve model [24] is commonly employed to assess the system condition. It consists of a break-in trend as the system condition improves, followed by a plateau regime where the system condition is stable. After this stable regime, the system condition withers with increased malfunction rate, followed by a steep increase of malfunction rate where the malfunction rate increases with time rapidly whereas the system breaks down. Together, the bathtub-shaped curve represents the various stages of an ideal system.

However, the bathtub-shaped degradation curve is a theoretical model used in many problems. It is an idealized trend that depends on various factors. The feasibility of applying such bathtub-shaped curve may depend on the specific application and the various factors involved. Specifically, the system condition may not follow the same degradation curve, also, each equipment system may exhibit different characteristics depending on the specific application.

Furthermore, each equipment in the Taipei metro system consists of various brands and various models that may possess different intrinsic characteristics. Since each equipment is maintained by humans, the degradation curve may be influenced by human factors and fall short to follow a universal bathtub-shaped curve. By analyzing the maintenance data, our goal is to decipher the feasibility to assess the MRT current stage of life based on available data ranging over a limited time-span.

III. DATA ANALYSIS

In this study, we investigate the maintenance data of the Taipei metro system. Based on the maintenance data records provided by TRTC, we analyze the maintenance data of the escalator system, elevator system, and Electric Multiple Unit (EMU) air conditioner of the metro system. These three systems are essential components of the metro system. The elevator and escalator are used regularly by the commuting people.

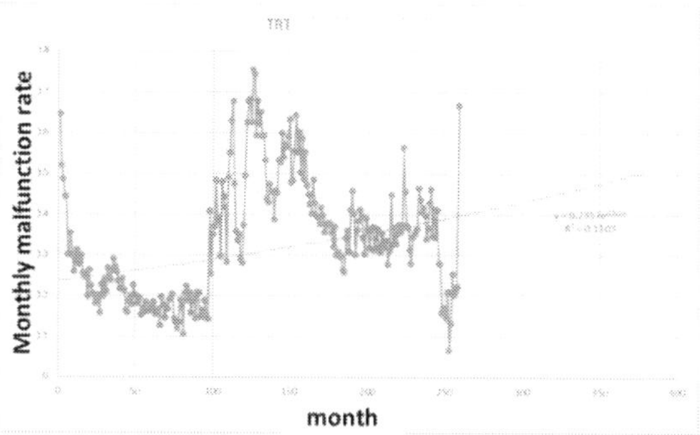

Figure 1. The reported average number of malfunctions each month of the Taipei metro station escalators.

The maintenance records of the elevator, escalator, and EMU air conditioner are analyzed. Figure 1 depicts the maintenance record of the escalator. We notice that the trend of the malfunction rate is irregular. Possibly because of the limited span of the maintenance data the specific stage of life-time is not apparent; further analysis is therefore required.

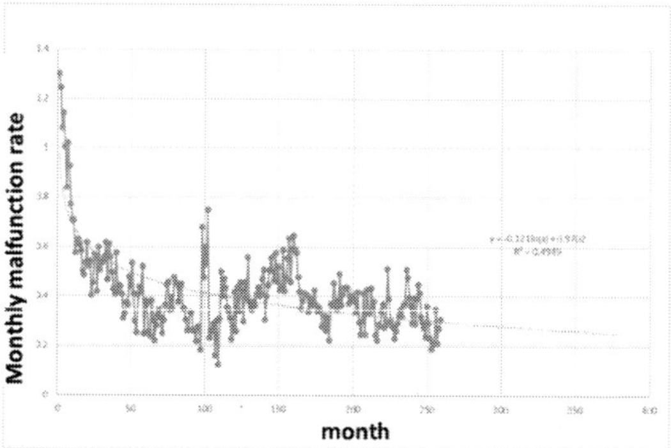

Figure 2. The reported average number of malfunctions each month of the Taipei metro station elevators.

Next, the maintenance records of the elevator system is shown in Figure 2. The maintenance records decrease with time. Trend of the maintenance records monotonically decrease with time. The monotonic decrease trend appears to be easier to match with the ideal bathtub-shaped curve.

Lastly, the maintenance records of the EMU air conditioner are shown in Figure 3, also exhibiting the malfunction rate decreasing over time. However, compared to the smooth trend of Figure 2, the EMU air conditioner maintenance data is more volatile. Though the maintenance data of the three systems differ, they all roughly decrease with time, suggesting that the system is still young whereas the performance is still improving. Or, the system is being well-maintained such that the malfunction rate does not reflect the system performance accurately.

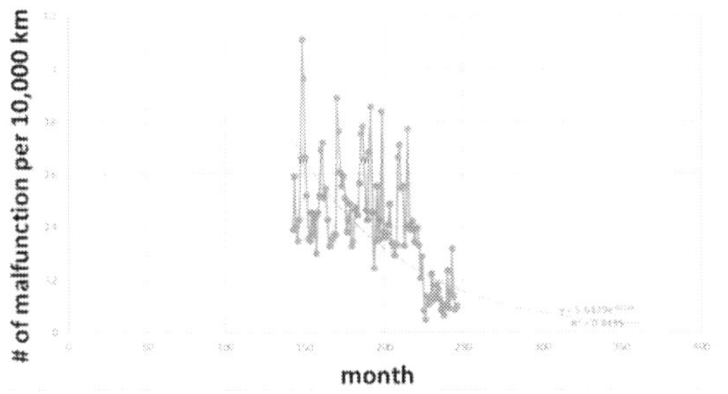

Figure 3. The reported average rate of malfunctions (per 10,000 km of operation) of the Taipei metro EMU air conditioners.

The maintenance records provided by TRTC consists of only the number of malfunctions per month. However, the severity of each malfunction may be drastically different, from as simple as the replacement of light bulb, up to power combustion resulting in system complete breakdown. Yet, in the available maintenance records, there is no information describing the severity of the malfunction event. The statistical analyses of these three systems (escalator, elevator, and EMU air conditioner) exhibit no apparent degradation of the system. Trends of the maintenance records suggest that the system condition improves with time, which is not the typical of a withering system.

IV. CONCLUSION AND FUTURE WORK

The objective of this research is to determine the current condition of the metro system, and, furthermore, if possible, to estimate the remaining lifetime. By means of data analysis, our goal is to identify characteristics indicative of the current status of the metro system, remaining lifetime, and estimate its future trend. However, the desired information may not be fully contained in the provided dataset and therefore limiting the accuracy of system lifetime assessment. Research findings show that the accuracy to assess the system lifetime based upon the provided maintenance records of a still-young metro system is limited.

Data analysis of the Taipei metro system maintenance records revealed the general trend and characteristics of the system condition and performance. Yet, information regarding the total lifespan of the system, current stage-of-life, and remaining lifetime he not been ascertained. Possible reasons include: 1) the system being still young, 2) the regular maintenance altered the natural deterioration trend, 3) the available data being far from complete to make meaningful estimations of lifetime information. Further analysis to help answer these questions are in pursuit.

Based on the available maintenance records of the Taipei metro system, the statistical analysis suggests that the maintenance of the Taipei metro system is well conducted; no signs of deterioration or withering. The data analysis falls short to yield information regarding the total lifespan, the current stage of life, and the remaining lifetime. If data with longer span and more variables is available, it is possible that such information can be ascertained.

ACKNOWLEDGMENT

We thank TRTC for providing maintenance records for analysis. This research is supported by the Taiwan National Science Council Grant MOST-106-2112-M-002-008 and MOST-107-2112-M-002-011.

REFERENCES

[1] "Taipei Metro," https://english.metro.taipei/News_Content.aspx?n=07DAD5F7351B8882&sms=2190547C60526D6B&s=FD5C094216AE77AB.

[2] X. K. Wei, F. Liu, and L. M. Jia, "Urban rail track condition monitoring based on in-service vehicle acceleration measurements," *Measurement*, vol. 80, pp. 217-228, Feb 2016.

[3] M. Molodova, M. Oregui, A. Nunez, Z. L. Li, and R. Dollevoet, "Health condition monitoring of insulated joints based on axle box acceleration measurements," *Engineering Structures*, vol. 123, pp. 225-235, Sep 2016.

[4] G. Lederman, *et al.*, "Track-monitoring from the dynamic response of an operational train," *Mechanical Systems and Signal Processing*, vol. 87, pp. 1-16, Mar 2017.

[5] R. Jiang *et al.*, "Network operation reliability in a Manhattan-like urban system with adaptive traffic lights," *Transportation Research Part C-Emerging Technologies*, vol. 69, pp. 527-547, Aug 2016.

[6] Metropolitan Transportation Authority. (2017). *New York City Transit - History and Chronology*. http://web.mta.info/nyct/facts/ffhist.htm

[7] D. Rivoli. (2015). *Ancient subway trains on C and J/Z lines won't be replaced until 2022, documents say*. http://www.nydailynews.com/new-york/ancient-subway-trains-won-replaced-2022-article-1.2323289

[8] H. Yin, K. Wang, Y. Qin, Q. Hua, and Q. Jiang, "Reliability analysis of subway vehicles based on the data of operational failures," *EURASIP Journal on Wireless Communications and Networking*, journal article vol. 2017, no. 1, p. 212, Dec. 2017.

[9] Z. G. Li, J. G. Zhou, and B. Y. Liu, "System Reliability Analysis Method Based on Fuzzy Probability," *International Journal of Fuzzy Systems*, vol. 19, no. 6, pp. 1759-1767, Dec. 2017.

[10] A. Z. Afify, G. M. Cordeiro, N. S. Butt, E. M. M. Ortega, and A. K. Suzuki, "A new lifetime model with variable shapes for the hazard rate," *Brazilian Journal of Probability and Statistics*, vol. 31, no. 3, pp. 516-541, Aug 2017.

[11] T. Kamel, A. Limam, and C. Silvani, "Modeling the degradation of old subway galleries using a continuum approach," *Tunnelling and Underground Space Technology*, vol. 48, pp. 77-93, Apr. 2015.

[12] D. Brancherie and A. Ibrahimbegovic, "Novel anisotropic continuum-discrete damage model capable of representing localized failure of massive structures: Part I: theoretical formulation and numerical implementation," *Engineering Computations*, vol. 26, no. 1-2, pp. 100-127, 2009.

[13] R. Tahmasbi and S. Rezaei, "A two-parameter lifetime distribution with decreasing failure rate," *Computational Statistics & Data Analysis*, vol. 52, no. 8, pp. 3889-3901, Apr. 2008.

[14] C. F. Daganzo and N. Geroliminis, "An analytical approximation for the macroscopic fundamental diagram of urban traffic," *Transportation Research Part B-Methodological*, vol. 42, no. 9, pp. 771-781, Nov 2008.
[15] C. Kus, "A new lifetime distribution," *Computational Statistics & Data Analysis*, vol. 51, no. 9, pp. 4497-4509, May 15 2007.
[16] C. D. Lai, M. Xie, and D. N. P. Murthy, "A modified Weibull distribution," *IEEE Transactions on Reliability*, vol. 52, no. 1, pp. 33-37, Mar 2003.
[17] O. O. Aalen and H. K. Gjessing, "Understanding the shape of the hazard rate: A process point of view," *Statistical Science*, vol. 16, no. 1, pp. 1-14, Feb 2001.
[18] S. K. Maurya, A. Kaushik, S. K. Singh, and U. Singh, "A new class of distribution having decreasing, increasing, and bathtub-shaped failure rate," *Communications in Statistics-Theory and Methods*, vol. 46, no. 20, pp. 10359-10372, 2017.
[19] Q. H. Duan and J. R. Liu, "Modelling a Bathtub-Shaped Failure Rate by a Coxian Distribution," *IEEE Transactions on Reliability*, vol. 65, no. 2, pp. 878-885, Jun 2016.
[20] W. J. Roesch, "Using a new bathtub curve to correlate quality and reliability," *Microelectronics Reliability*, vol. 52, no. 12, pp. 2864-2869, Dec 2012.
[21] J. Navarro and P. J. Hernandez, "How to obtain bathtub-shaped failure rate models from normal mixtures," *Probability in the Engineering and Informational Sciences*, vol. 18, no. 4, pp. 511-531, 2004 2004.
[22] S. Rajarshi and M. B. Rajarshi, "Bathtub distributions - a review," *Communications in Statistics-Theory and Methods*, vol. 17, no. 8, pp. 2597-2621, 11988.
[23] M. V. Aarset, "How to identify an bathtub hazard rate," *IEEE Transactions on Reliability*, vol. 36, no. 1, pp. 106-108, Apr. 1987.
[24] K. L. Wong, "The bathtub does not hold water any more," *Quality and Reliability Engineering International*, vol. 4, no. 3, pp. 279-282, 1988.
[25] H. T. Zeng, T. Lan, and Q. M. Chen, "Five and four-parameter lifetime distributions for bathtub-shaped failure rate using Perks mortality equation," *Reliability Engineering & System Safety*, vol. 152, pp. 307-315, Aug 2016.
[26] D. N. P. Murthy and R. Jiang, "Parametric study of sectional models involving two Weibull distributions," *Reliability Engineering & System Safety*, vol. 56, no. 2, pp. 151-159, May 1997.
[27] G. A. Klutke, P. C. Kiessler, and M. A. Wortman, "A critical look at the bathtub curve," *IEEE Transactions on Reliability*, vol. 52, no. 1, pp. 125-129, 2003.

A Low-Cost Virtual Coach for Diagnosis and Guidance in Baseball/Softball Batting Training

Hou-Chin Liu

Department of Computer Science
National Tsing Hua University
Hsinchu, Taiwan
Email: johnnyliu505@gmail.com

Chung-Ta King

Department of Computer Science
National Tsing Hua University
Hsinchu, Taiwan
Email: king@cs.nthu.edu.tw

Abstract—**Baseball and softball are popular sports worldwide. In baseball/softball, batting is a fundamental action, but it is also one of the most difficult skills to master. Batting requires constant practice and proper guidance. Experienced coaches can provide instant diagnoses and feedbacks tailored for individual players. In the absence of such coaches, tools such as motion tracking systems or sports bracelets may help to assist the players. Unfortunately, they are either too expensive and awkward to use, or too limited in providing useful diagnosis and guidance. In this paper, we introduce a low-cost diagnosis and guidance tool for batting training in baseball/softball. The tool requires only one wearable device and one camera, such as the one on the smartphone, to capture the player's motion. The collected data are summarized and analyzed to derive the distinct features of the player's actions in different swing stages. The tool then pinpoints the mistakes and discrepancies in player's batting actions by comparing with expert actions, which in turn guides the player to perfect the action. Evaluations on real users show the effectiveness of our tool in comparison with experienced coaches.**

Keywords–Motion evaluation; Motion segmentation; Sport training; Wearable device; Semantic guidance.

I. INTRODUCTION

Baseball and softball are popular sports in the world. People not only watch the games but also play the games, from professionals to amateurs. In baseball/softball, batting is commonly accepted as one of the most difficult skills to master. Batting is not only swinging the bat. It requires the coordination of the whole body, from wrists, arms, waist, knees, to ankles, to concentrate the force on the bat to hit at the ball. It also involves the use of the muscle strengths at the right time.

To learn the skill, players need to practice constantly. During practice, an experienced coach or expert by the side can evaluate the batting actions and provide instant diagnoses and feedback tailored to the individual players, thereby shortening the learning curve. Unfortunately, such guidance is not always available. Many coaching tools are thus developed to assist the players. At one end, there are sophisticated motion tracking systems that use multiple surrounding cameras to capture detailed motions of a player for experts to analyze [1]–[4]. However, these tools are very expensive, mostly used in indoor and specially controlled environments and requiring specialists to operate and analyze. At the other end, wearable devices or smartphones are used for tracking players' physical and physiological status [5]–[7]. However, they are mainly purposed for data collection and can only give very crude information about the player's postures, not to mention to provide useful guidance to improve the skill.

In this paper, we introduce a low-cost coaching tool for baseball/softball batting training that can be used by amateur and novice players in the field and provide useful and immediate suggestions on improving the batting action, down to each stage of the action. Our tool not only evaluates the posture of the player but also the strength exercised by the player. To do so, the tool requires only one wearable device on the wrist to measure the strength and one low-cost camera, such as the one on the smartphones, by the side to capture the player's motion. Note that the proposed tool serves different purposes from those more expensive systems, which aim for professional player training.

Our tool has to perform two main tasks: (1) segmenting the recorded data to correspond to different stages of a batting action, and (2) identifying discrepancies of the player's action in each stage and providing suggestions to improve. There are challenging issues in each task. First, novice players may not perform the batting action right, making it very difficult to partition their motions into stages. The problem is aggravated by the low-cost cameras and very short duration of the batting action. For example, a batting action takes only a second or less, and a camera recording at 30 FPS (Frames Per Second) will have only a handful of frames per batting stage, increasing the difficulty in segmenting the video. Worse yet, low-cost cameras often drop frames. For the second task, the challenge lies in the fact that action evaluation is very subjective and the professional judgments of coaches are very difficult to quantize. How to extract coaches' experiences and program the tool to make similar judgment remains an issue.

To address the above challenges, we make several key observations. First, the impact point when the bat hits the ball has a very distinct feature that can easily be detected by a wearable device worn on the dominant wrist. The impact point can be leveraged to segment the batting action into stages. The second observation is that the batting motions of expert players are very similar and consistent. Therefore, we can develop a reference out of their batting actions. The reference is then used to assist segmenting the motions of novice players into stages and to evaluate the mistakes in the batting action of a player. The third observation is that sport coaches can often tell whether the player performs an action right or wrong, but they only provide imprecise suggestions such as harder, wider, or higher. To translate these experiences and judgments into numbers that our tool can use to evaluate a batting action, we build a statistic model based on the evaluation results of real baseball coaches and set appropriate thresholds for common mistakes of players in batting.

The main contributions of this paper are as follows.

- We introduce a novel tool to diagnose bat swing motions and provide useful guidance for amateur baseball/softball players down to each stage of the action. The tool is low-cost and can be operated by ordinary users in the field for immediate feedback.
- The tool can properly segment the whole batting sequence into batting stages and extract corresponding motion features, even for novice players whose motions may be prone to errors and from low-quality videos taken by the low-cost camera.
- A statistic evaluation model is developed that reflects the judgment experiences of human coaches for evaluating the batting actions and providing improvement suggestions.
- Experiments by real players and coaches are conducted to show that the proposed tool can effectively detect motion mistakes and provide useful guidance to players comparable to the guidance provided by experienced coaches.

The remainder of the paper is organized as follows. In Section II, we discuss related works on motion assessment and bat swing motion analysis. Section III introduces the design and implementation of the system and the different phases in analyzing a batting action. Section IV presents the experimental setup and results. Section V concludes the paper and gives directions for future works.

II. Related Works

In motion assessment, people usually evaluate physiological and physical motion performances of the subjects. An intuitive approach is to analyzing their motion videos. Leightley et al. [8] propose a framework to automatically recognize and evaluate human motions using a depth camera. Patrona et al. [9] present a real-time framework for action detection, recognition and evaluation based on captured motion data. The outputs of the framework are semantic feedback generated by fuzzy logic. Parmar et al. [10] present multiple frameworks that use visual information for action quality assessment in evaluating and scoring Olympic sports. Qiao et al. [11] use the principle of gesture distance to develop a real-time 2D human gesture evaluation system.

The systems constructed by visual sensors are limited in sensing and evaluating detailed movements, which can be critical in practical motion training. Wearable sensors, on the other hand, are able to collect high-quality and fine physical and physiological data of specific parts of the body. In fact, for sports training, many motion assessment systems prefer wearable sensors. In [12], an ambulatory motion analysis framework is introduced that uses wearable inertial sensors to accurately assess an athlete's activities in an outdoor training environment. Sharma et al. [13] use a smart watch to capture and store inertial sensor data and develop a phase-based analytic system for tennis serving. The system can provide feedback for players to improve their serving performances. A wearable platform is presented in [14], which collects dominant body parts of the bat swing motion to provide baseball players with corrective feedback.

Hybrid approaches that combine wearable sensors and visual sensors to provide postural correction guidance and physical motion assessments have also been introduced. Kwon et al. [15] introduce a framework that combines wearable sensors and visual sensors for real-time motion training. They found out that the visual sensors are less effective for assessment feedback. Hirayama et al. [3] qualitatively compare batting motions using a motion capture system. Unfortunately, such motion capture systems are typically expensive and can only be used in the laboratory environments.

In the specific application domain of baseball batting, most motion assessment systems use wearable sensors to provide physical and physiological information [5]–[7]. In [14], baseball swing motions are evaluated using the motion transcripts to measure line segments and joints of the body. The swing motion quality is then assessed by comparing the intersegment coordination of a test swing to that of the template swing. In [16], Nakata et al. present detailed analyses of physiological status data for each phase in the swing motion between skilled and unskilled players. Other similar works, such as [17] and [18], propose different methods for segmenting bat swing motion and analyzing the stages to assess the motions.

Our work is different from previous studies. Our tool requires only one wearable device and one camera, such as the one on the smartphones, to provide not only assessments but also improvement suggestions for baseball/softball batting practice. The tool is low cost and can be operated by ordinary players in the field, unlike the expensive motion capture system.

III. System Design and Implementation

In this section, we describe the design and implementation of the proposed system. The wearable device is worn on the player's dominant hand to record the motions of the bat and the wrists. Any wearable device that contains an accelerometer and a gyroscope and provides a proper API to retrieve the collected data can be used. The camera is positioned in front of the player to record the full swing motion of the whole body in video. The height of the camera and its distance to the player can be normalized by preprocessing steps and thus may be flexible. However, the angle between the camera and the player may affect the evaluation accuracy and hence should be placed more carefully.

The clocks on the wearable device and the camera should be synchronized so that their recorded data can be timestamped and aligned along time. There is a host to synchronize the clocks and collect the recorded data for further processing. The host can be the smartphone that installs the camera and connects to the wearable device through Bluetooth. After the player performs the batting actions and the recorded data are collected, our system starts to analyze the data and provide suggestions to improve the actions.

Our system consists of three phases. The first phase is preprocessing, which transforms and normalizes collected raw data to make them consistent across different plays. In the second phase, the collected video and sensor data are processed to segment the batting motion into five stages in order to provide a stage-based analysis. Finally, in the third phase, features from the segmented data are extracted and a statistic evaluation model is applied to find out common mistakes in

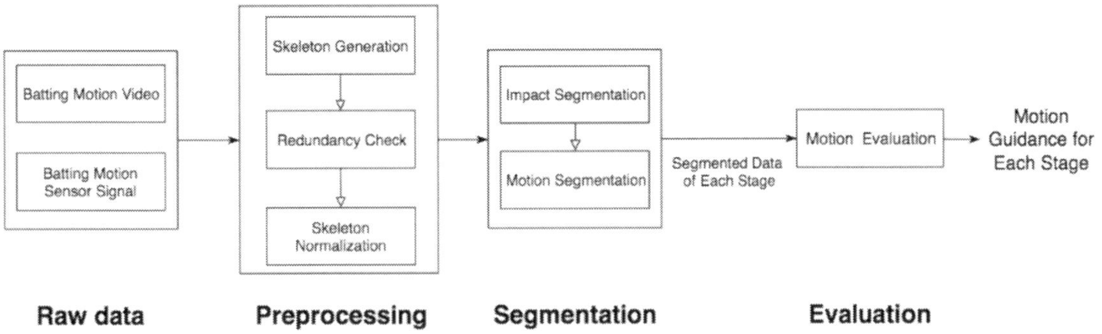

Figure 1. Overview of the proposed system.

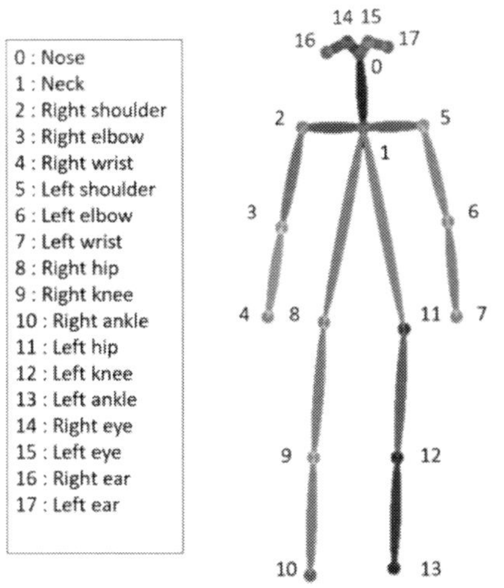

Figure 2. The 18 body joints generated from OpenPose.

the batting motion. Appropriate guidance and suggestions for improving the batting action in each stage are then provided according to the detected mistakes. The overview of the system is shown in Figure Figure 1 and the details of each phase are described next.

A. Preprocessing

The collected raw data need to be processed before they can be analyzed to segment the batting motion into stages. To extract postural information from the video, we first utilize the OpenPose library to generate body skeletons in each frame [19]–[21]. The library takes a color image as input and produces two-dimensional body, hand and facial keypoints for all the people in the image. From our single batting motion video, the OpenPose library can provide the positions of 18 body joints in each frame, including 2D skeleton joint coordinates and their corresponding confidence scores. Figure 2 shows the 18 body joints generated from OpenPose.

However, because the camera used to record the bating motion is low-cost and readily available on devices such as smartphones, some frames in the video may be dropped and adjacent frames are repeated to fill in the gap. To detect redundant frames, we compute the Mean Square Error (MSE) value of each frame and its previous one. If the MSE is lower than a threshold, we mark the frames as repetition and replace the redundant frame by the one that is interpolated based on the 18 body joints from the adjacent frames. The redundancy threshold is empirically set. A video containing four consecutive repeating frames is considered broken and will not be processed further.

Finally, we need to handle the case in which the players have different heights and widths, and the camera may be positioned inconsistently across plays, e.g., the distance to the player. Our solution is to normalize the raw data. The original 2D positions of the 18 body joints are provided in a camera coordinate system. We first transform the camera coordinate system to body coordinate system with the origin at the neck joint. Next, we measure the distance from the neck joint to the line across the right ankle joint and left ankle joint. That distance is then used to scale all the body joints to obtain normalized body joint positions.

B. Segmentation

A baseball/softball batting action can generally be divided into several stages [16]–[18]: *waiting*, *shifting body weight*, *stepping*, *landing*, *swing*, *impact* and *follow through*. Since the waiting stage has very little effect on the batting action and different players have very different poses at the waiting stage, we thus do not consider this stage in our system.

As mentioned earlier, there are two challenges to meet in segmenting a batting action. First, the batting action lasts for a second or less, but we need to segment the action into six stages. On average, a stage contains only a few frames using a low-cost camera recording at 30 FPS. If we segment the video sequentially starting from the shifting-body-weight stage, errors can easily accumulate towards the last stage. Second, novice players may not perform the batting action right. Thus, their actions may lack of distinguishable stages and lead to incorrect segmentation and wrong analyses.

To address the first challenge, we leverage the obvious characteristic of the impact of the bat on the ball [22] to identify the impact stage. From there, we can divide the segmentation problem of the batting motion into segmentations before and after the impact stage. This dramatically improves the accuracy of motion segmentation. The second challenge is addressed by using the batting actions of expert players as reference. For expert players, their batting motions are very similar and consistent, which can be segmented by applying Hidden Markov Models (HMMs) on sensor readings [22]–[25]. The result then serves as a reference, by which the motions of

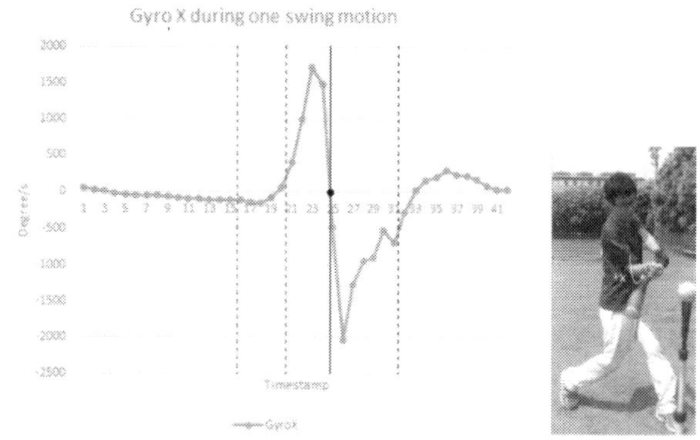

(a) (b)

Figure 3. (a) Variations of the GyroX value, (b) wrist rotation before the impact stage.

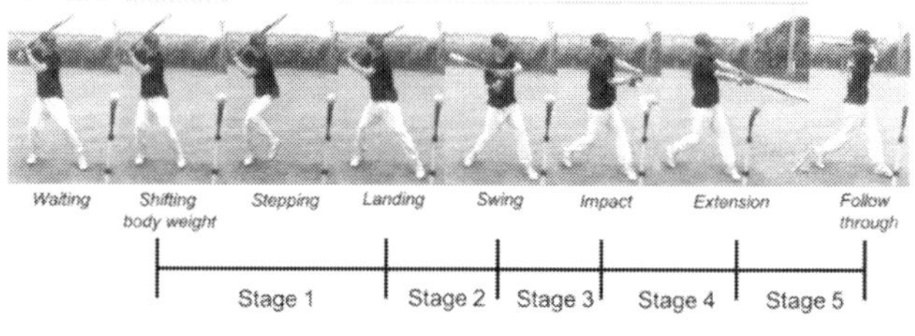

Figure 4. The five-stage batting motion based on HMM.

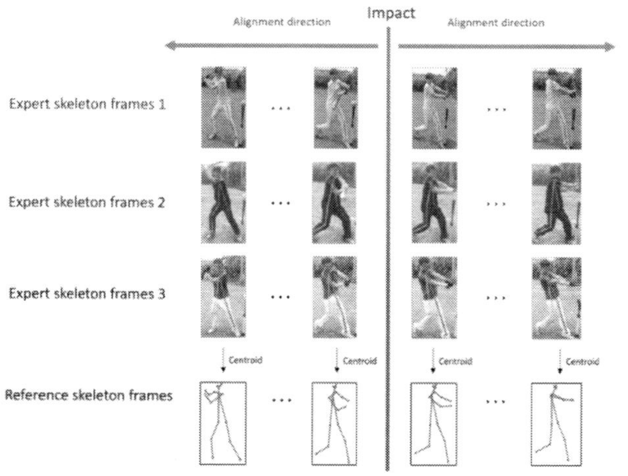

Figure 5. Reference skeleton frames generated from the videos of all expert players.

the novice players can be segmented through matching their characteristic features with those in the reference. Details are given in the following subsections.

1) Impact Stage Detection: The impact stage detection is based on the observation that when the bat hits the ball, there is a very fast twist of the wrist, which causes a drop in the angular acceleration of the X-axis (GyroX) towards zero on the wearable sensor. Figure 3(a) shows the variations of the X-axis values of the gyroscope around the impact point. The dot indicates the impact point. Figure 3(b) shows the rotational twist of the wrist just before the impact stage. With such a distinct feature, the sensor data and the corresponding skeletons of a batting action can thus be segmented by the impact stage.

2) Reference Segmentation from Expert Players: The batting motions of expert players are very similar and can serve to build a reference for segmenting the batting actions. Based on [22] for tennis serving, we first derive HMMs for the batting action from the wearable sensor readings. In fact, two HMMs are obtained, one before and another after the impact point. For the example gyroscope readings in Figure 3(a), the five stages identified by the HMMs are marked by vertical lines. The solid line indicates the impact point.

From the HMMs and timestamps of the wearable sensor data, we next partition the skeleton frames from the video also into five stages. Since the bat swing speeds of different expert players may be different, causing a small variation in the bat swing postures, the skeleton frames of expert motions need to be temporally aligned. To do it, we observe that the skeleton frames of expert players just before the impact point have almost the same postures. Thus, we align the skeleton frames before the impact point in a reverse order, starting with the last skeleton frame just before the impact point and working towards the beginning of the video.

The resulting segmentation of the video identified by the HMMs of the wearable sensor is shown in Figure 4. To compare with the five stages marked by a human, which are shown in the top half of the figure, we can see that Stage 1 in the first HMM covers the shifting-body-weight, stepping, and landing stages. Stage 2 overlaps with landing and swing, while Stage 3 covers swing and impact. The second HMM that uses sensor data after the impact point segments the video frames into two stages. Stage 4 extends from impact to extension stages and Stage 5 covers extension and follow through. Note that even though the batting stages identified by our tool are different from those identified by a human, what matters is a consistent reference segmentation that can be used to partition the motions of novice players and to detect their mistakes, which is discussed next.

To build reference segmentation using data from expert players, we first extract two features from the sensor readings of expert players: (1) the average time spent in each stage, and (2) the maximum strength value before and after the impact stage. It is found that these two features have very distinct values for expert and novice players. The time spent on each stage indicates the bat swing speed, and the maximum strength value indicates the effectiveness in concentrating the muscle forces. The strength value is determined by the X-axis acceleration, which is dominated by the bat swing strength.

Next, we build the *reference skeleton frames* of the five stages. The skeleton frames of all expert players with the same aligned timestamp are examined to calculate, for each skeleton joint, the centroid point of that joint in all those skeleton frames. The central points of all the 18 skeleton joints then produce a reference skeleton frame corresponding to that timestamp. Figure 5 shows the generated reference skeleton frames.

3) Novice Player Motion Segmentation: Novice players may not perform the batting action right. It is thus difficult to partition their batting motions using HMM due to the irregular sensor readings. Our solution is to find the most similar posture to match the expert reference skeleton frames.

Then, the corresponding frame is classified into the batting stage indicated by the reference skeleton frame. To match the skeleton postures, we reference the work in [26], which proposes trainable skeleton pose detectors to automatically learn a representation of skeleton poses by modeling the spatial arrangement of skeleton joints with respect to a reference point. The pose detectors are trained to learn actions formed by skeleton frames and are able to classify an action.

Given a prototype skeleton frame from our reference skeleton frames, the pose detector learns a model S to determine the position (x_i, y_i) of its skeleton joints, $j_i, i = 0...17$. Note that OpenPose outputs 18 body joints. The skeleton joints in the prototype frame can be described by (j_i, w_i), where w_i is the weight of that joint. Generally, the more a joint position varies, the more important it is. Therefore, the weight of a skeleton joint is determined by the variations of the joint position in the prototype skeletons.

Given a skeleton frame of a novice player, we want to find out the most similar frame from our reference skeleton frames. The measurement of skeleton similarity is a summary of the *similarity scores* of all the joints, which are calculated from the distance between the joint in the reference frame and that in the novice skeleton. The distance is weighted with a Gaussian function, which allows for spatial deformations. The score $r(t_i, j_i)$ is computed as:

$$r(t_i, j_i) = e^{-\frac{D(t_i, j_i)}{2\sigma_i^2}}, \quad (1)$$

where t_i is a joint in the novice skeleton, j_i is its corresponding joint in the reference skeleton, and $D(t_i, j_i)$ is computed by the Euclidean distance between positions of t_i and j_i. The σ_i is the standard deviation of the Gaussian weighting function for i-th joint. This value regulates the tolerance to the position of the i-th joint with respect to the position of its homologous. It is determined by the skeletal distance $\hat{d}(j_i, j_b)$ between the position of the reference point j_b and that of the reference skeleton joint j_i, where

$$\sigma_i = \sigma_0 + \alpha \cdot \hat{d}(j_i, j_b). \quad (2)$$

The value of σ_i increases with the skeletal distance of the i-th point from the reference point. The reference point j_b is denoted by the barycenter, which is determined by three joints, including neck, right hip and left hip. The principle of σ_i is that terminal joints have more mobility than those joints close to the body, and the value σ_i shows various tolerances in those joint positions. The distance $\hat{d}$ is the sum of line segments that connect the joints j_i and j_b. Notice that σ_0 and α regulate the tolerance values for deformation and are both tunable in the application phase. The weighting function shows the tolerance range in the position of skeleton joints and contributes robust deformations of the prototype skeleton.

After the similarity score of each joint is calculated, they can then be combined to determine the total skeleton similarity R as:

$$R(T, S) = (\prod_{i=1}^{|S|} r(t_i, j_i)^{w_i})^{1/\sum_{i=1}^{|S|} w_i}, \quad (3)$$

where T denotes the novice skeleton and S denotes the reference skeleton.

Once the pose detectors are developed, they can then be applied to match similar frames in each stage. The pose detectors are computed with the reverse direction before the impact stage and the in-order direction after the impact stage. We have set the similarity threshold of skeleton detection to ensure the detection precision. The starting and ending frames are determined by the previous stage. After we identify proper skeleton frames for each stage for novice players, the sensor data for each stage can then be segmented by the identified frames. Figure 6 shows an example of frame matching on stage 3. The upper row shows the reference skeleton frames, and the lower row shows the skeleton frames of a novice player. The frames with the dotted line are the frames that are the most similar to the reference ones.

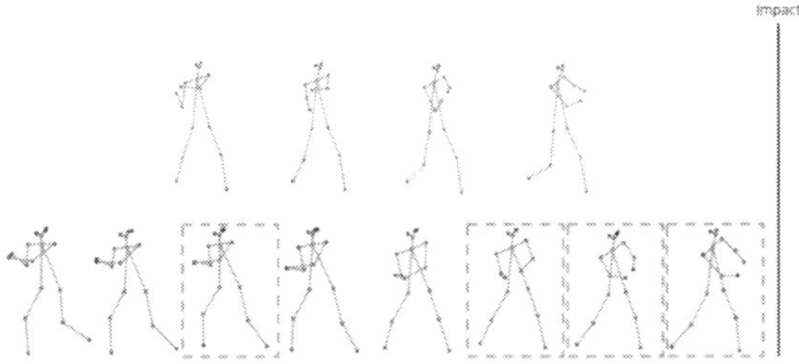

Figure 6. Frame matching result of stage 3.

TABLE I. COMMON MISTAKES OF BATTING ACTIONS AND CORRESPONDING FEATURES

Common mistakes	Features
Center of body weight moved	Center of body weight
Right arm turned straight too early	Right arm angle
Left arm turned straight too early	Left arm angle
Right leg not bent	Right leg angle
Left leg not straight	Left leg angle
Swing too slow	Time spent on stages 2 and 3
Not enough swing strength	AccX of stage 3
Not enough extension strength	AccX of stage 4

C. Batting Action Evaluation

After the batting motion of the player is segmented into stages, we need to evaluate the actions in each stage for possible mistakes and for providing suggestions for improving the actions. As mentioned earlier, the problem is challenging because the judgments of human coaches are very subjective and hard to quantized. Our solution is to collect statistics of the judgments of human coaches to establish thresholds for tolerating the deviations of the player's actions from the reference skeletons. Since stage 1 has more personalized features and stage 5 is the finishing motion after the extension, both are less helpful when assessing a batting motion. Therefore, we focus on the remaining three stages.

By consulting experienced baseball/softball coaches, we first establish a list of common mistakes in batting action, as shown in Table I. The table also shows the features that can be used for detecting the mistakes. The mistakes are stated from the perspective of a coach and are thus descriptive and lacking precise quantitative definitions.

To derive meaningful measures for detecting mistakes in batting actions, we propose to use assistance from human coaches and the reference segmentation introduced above. The idea is to ask coaches to view the videos of batting actions and label the parts that the players perform incorrectly according to Table I. The skeleton features of the labeled frames are then extracted to be compared with those from the reference

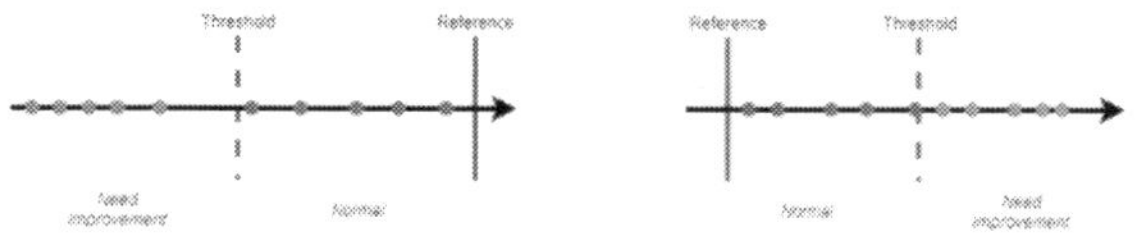

Threshold type	Threshold value < Reference value	Threshold value > Reference value
Feature	Left leg angle, Center of body weight, AccX of Stage 3, AccX of Stage 4	Right/Left arm angle, Right leg angle, Center of body weight, Time spent on stage 2 and stage 3

Figure 7. Types of threshold values illustrated.

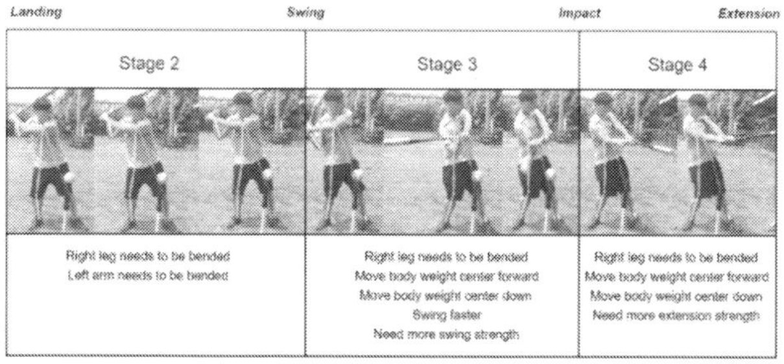

Figure 8. Evaluation results of a batting action.

skeleton frames. Distribution of the differences for each feature is then examined to determine a threshold value for tolerance. The resultant threshold values for all the features in Table I constitute a *statistic evaluation model* in our tool.

The threshold values can be classified into two types: one defines the upper bounds and the other defines the lower bounds, as shown in Figure 7. For example, according to Table I, the left leg should be as straight as possible. Hence, its value should not exceed that of the reference feature, and the threshold value should bound that feature value from above.

The features extracted from the player's motion data are compared with the reference values based on the thresholds to give a correct/incorrect mark. The sensor data of the player are also compared with the reference sensor data in terms of two features: time spent on each stage and the maximum strength value before and after the impact stage. Next, frame-level marks of the same stage are combined by majority voting to form mistake vectors at the stage level. These vectors are then used to determine the motion correction guidance to provide at each stage.

Correction guidance is actually the opposite side of motion mistakes. Once a motion mistake is identified, the corresponding correction guidance can be fed back immediately. Figure 8 shows an example of a batting action and the correction guidance provided by our system.

IV. EXPERIMENT

A. Experimental Setup

One wrist-worn device and one camera on a mobile phone (HTC A9) are used to record a player's batting action. The wearable device, NuMaker TRIO, is a low-cost wireless device that consists of a 32-bit low-power microcontroller, a 6-axis Microelectromechanical sensor, a wifi and a Bluetooth module (BT3.0 and BLE). To measure the physical status of a batting motion, the 6-axis Microelectromechanical sensor is used to collect sensor readings of 3-axis acceleration and angular velocity. The data are then sent back to a computer through Bluetooth. The sampling rate of the wearable device is 30Hz, and its measuring ranges are ± 16g for the accelerometer and ± 2500 degree/s for the gyroscope. The camera on the HTC A9 is used to record the whole batting action in video with a frame rate of 30 FPS, which is the same as the sampling rate of the wearable device. We also put timestamps in the video for time synchronization with the wearable device later.

Figure 9. Experimental setup for motion data collection.

We have collected a set of batting motion data for training and evaluating the proposed system (see Figure 9). Twelve players were invited in the data collection. They were asked to wear the wearable device and perform batting motion in front of the camera. Four of them were experienced players, who were on the softball team of our department. They had played softball for about 4 to 6 years and were all sluggers on the team. The other three of the twelve players had baseball or softball experiences, but they seldom played the sport. The remaining five players had no prior experience. We had collected 1139 batting actions, including 673 from experienced players and 466 from the other players. After removing broken files, the remaining data count was about 950.

B. Experimental Results

The four experienced players are considered expert, and their batting motions are used to generate the reference motion and build the statistic evaluation model. The hitting coach, who served on the softball team, was asked to label the videos of the other eight players for possible mistakes according to Table I. The labeling results are denoted as the ground truth, which can be compared against the results from our tool. The *recall, precision*, and *F-measure* (F1 score) metrics are used for comparison, where:

$$Recall = \frac{TruePositive}{TruePositive + FalseNegative} \tag{4}$$

$$Precision = \frac{TruePositive}{TruePositive + FalsePositive} \tag{5}$$

$$F_1 = 2 \cdot \frac{Precision \cdot Recall}{Precision + Recall} \tag{6}$$

The recall metric calculates the proportion of actual positives that are identified correctly, and the precision metric calculates the proportion of positive identifications that are actually correct. To combine these two metrics, we apply the F1 score to compute the harmonic average of the recall and precision. These metrics are very useful in verifying the ability of model classification.

TABLE II. COMMON MISTAKES OF BATTING ACTIONS AND CORRESPONDING INDICES

Index	Common Mistakes
m1	Left leg not straight
m2	Right leg not bended
m3	Center of body weight moved backward
m4	Center of body weight too high
m5	Right arm turned straight too early
m6	Left arm turned straight too early
m7	Swing speed too slow
m8	Not enough swing strength
m9	Not enough extension strength

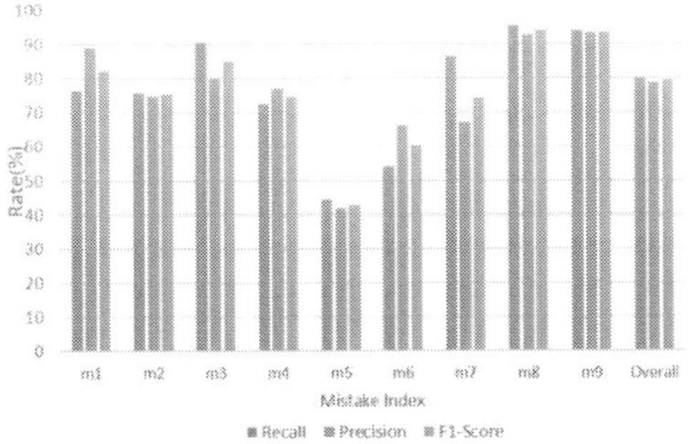

Figure 10. Detection rate for each common motion mistake.

The collected batting actions are separated into two parts, 80% for training and 20% for testing. To train the proposed system, we use 5-fold cross-validation to have optimal effects. The system results are used to tune the threshold parameters of the statistic evaluation model. We use majority voting for combining stage-level judgments from our system into a final mark for the whole batting action in order to compare with the ground truth for error detection accuracy.

For evaluate purposes, we consider the common mistakes listed in Table II and assign an index to each. We removed two mistakes in Table I due to insufficient samples (less than 10).

The detection rate for each common motion mistake is shown in Figure 10. This experiment shows the detection abilities of our system for all common mistakes. We can see that most of the detection rates are higher than 70%. However, for m5 and m6, the detection accuracy is lower than the others. The F1 score of m5 is 42.86%, while the F1 score of m6 is 60.38%. The features of m5 and m6 seem to be the key factor. Without depth information from images, the arm angle is hard to measure correctly. Even if the arm keeps the same angle during the batting motion, the angle measurement might still change because of different facing directions in a 2D video. This makes angle measurement imprecise. Although the detection rates of m5 and m6 are lower, the overall F1 score is still 79.25%, which suffices to show the effectiveness of our proposed system in detecting common mistakes.

Next, we evaluate motion mistake detection results of each player (see Figure 11). Players p1, p2, and p3 have played baseball/softball but without much experience. They are classified as mid-level players. The other players are new to the sport and are classified as novice players. The experiment is to verify how well the proposed system works for different types of players.

From Figure 11, we can see that the proposed system is

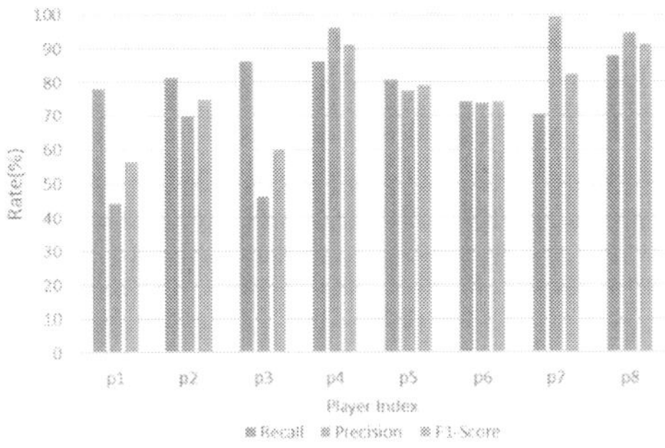

Figure 11. Detection rate of motion mistakes for each player.

TABLE III. DETECTION RATE OF MOTION MISTAKES FOR DIFFERENT TYPES OF PLAYERS

Player Type	Recall(%)	Precision(%)	F1-Score(%)
Mid-level	85.07	52.67	65.02
Novice	77.96	85.94	81.74

able to detect motion mistakes of various players. However, the F1 score of mid-level players seems to be lower than the others. By closely examining the detection rate of common mistakes for each type of players, shown in Table III, we can see that the precision rate of mid-level players is only 52.67%, which is lower than the novice players. The F1 score of novice players is also higher. It seems that our proposed system works better on the novice players rather than mid-level ones. This is expected, because mid-level players have already had some experiences and their motions should be more like experts'. Novice players usually perform more obvious mistakes in a bat swing motion.

Next, we evaluate the effects of using the impact point to divide a batting action into stages. Recall that our tool first detects the impact point with the wearable sensor, based on which the whole sequence of batting motions is divided into stages (see Figure 3). Table IV shows the overall performance results with and without impact point detection. We can see that the overall F1 score increases from 71.43% to 79.25% with impact point detection. This clearly shows its effectiveness in segmenting the batting motions.

Finally, we evaluate the effectiveness of reverse alignment of sensor data with video frames before the impact point. The intuitive way for alignment is sequential. Our tool reverses the alignment direction before the impact stage. From Table V, we can see that the overall F1 score increases from 73.20% to 79.25% using reverse alignment. Other metrics also show improvements, which suffice to demonstrate the effectiveness of reverse alignment on system performance.

To summarize these experiments, we can see that our proposed system can effectively detect common mistakes in baseball/softball batting actions and provide proper guidance for the players to improve. The system is especially suitable for novice players. Note that we did not compare our tool with

TABLE IV. EVALATION EXPERIMENTS FOR IMPACT POINT DETECTION

Method	Recall(%)	Precision(%)	F1-Score(%)
w/o impact segmentation	75.64	67.69	71.43
w/ impact segmentation	79.97	78.60	79.25

TABLE V. EVALUATION EXPERIMENTS FOR REVERSE ALIGNMENT

Method	Recall(%)	Precision(%)	F1-Score(%)
w/o reverse alignment	74.45	72.05	73.20
w/ reverse alignment	79.97	78.60	79.25

professional systems because they serve different purposes as ours and thus have different requirements in terms of error detection and guidance provided. Due to time and budget limitation, we could not experiment with more subjects in this paper and we only had one coach to label the batting videos. In the future, we hope that this discrepancy can be remedied. Generalization of the proposed tool requires further studies. After all, baseball/softball batting is a very specific motion that the player is fixed in location. It is thus easy to capture the motion with one camera.

V. CONCLUSION

In this paper, we introduce a diagnosis and guidance system for baseball and softball batting motions. Our tool extracts skeletal information from player's motion video and segments the motion data of sensor and skeleton into five swing stages. The segmented data is evaluated by a statistic evaluation model. By evaluating the results of each stage, we then detect common mistakes in batting and provide proper guidance to the player. The experiments show that our proposed system has about 80% accuracy in detecting common batting mistakes and can provide proper guidance to players. In the future, we would like to cooperate with multiple coaches and use majority voting in labeling the batting videos to provide a more robust motion judgment. Batting action evaluation based on machine learning techniques may be exploited to see whether they can provide judgments and guidance that are comparable to those provided by professional coaches. To overcome the problem of angle measurement, two or three cameras might be needed to provide the depth information for measuring the motions with a 3D view. To provide a more robust guidance for players of various types, more advanced algorithms of computer vision would be very helpful. Furthermore, generalization of the proposed tool could be explored.

ACKNOWLEDGMENT

This work was supported in part by the Ministry of Science and Technology, Taiwan, under Grant MOST 107-2218-E-007-035 and by Information and Communications Research Laboratories of Industrial Technology Research Institute, Taiwan.

REFERENCES

[1] D. Dharmayanti, M. Iqbal, A. Suhendra, and A. B. Mutiara, "Velocity and acceleration analysis from kinematics linear punch using optical motion capture," in Proc. Second International Conf. on Informatics and Computing (ICIC), Nov. 2017, pp. 1–6.

[2] B. Dowling and G. S. Fleisig, "Kinematic comparison of baseball batting off of a tee among various competition levels," Sports Biomechanics, vol. 15, no. 3, Sept. 2016, pp. 255–269.

[3] D. Hirayama, K. Yoshizawa, H. Sogo, and T. Henmi, "Quantitative comparison of technical differences in baseball batting motion by motion analysis," in Proc. International Conf. on Advanced Mechatronic Systems (ICAMechS), Nov. 2016, pp. 115–120.

[4] K. Kolykhalova, A. Camurri, G. Volpe, M. Sanguineti, E. Puppo, and R. Niewiadomski, "A multimodal dataset for the analysis of movement qualities in karate martial art," in Proc. 7th International Conf. on Intelligent Technologies for Interactive Entertainment (INTETAIN), June 2015, pp. 74–78.

[5] http://www.zepp.com/en-us/baseball/. [Last retrieved: Jan. 2019].

[6] https://buy.garmin.com/en-US/US/p/579018. [Last retrieved: Jan. 2019].

[7] https://smashprosports.com/. [Last retrieved: Jan. 2019].

[8] D. Leightley, J. S. McPhee, and M. H. Yap, "Automated analysis and quantification of human mobility using a depth sensor," IEEE Journal of Biomedical and Health Informatics, vol. 21, no. 4, July 2017, pp. 939–948.

[9] F. Patrona, A. Chatzitofis, D. Zarpalas, and P. Daras, "Motion analysis: Action detection, recognition and evaluation based on motion capture data," Pattern Recognition, vol. 76, April 2018, pp. 612–622.

[10] P. Parmar and B. T. Morris, "Learning to score olympic events," in Proc. IEEE Conf. on Computer Vision and Pattern Recognition Workshops (CVPRW), July 2017, pp. 76–84.

[11] S. Qiao, Y. Wang, and J. Li, "Real-time human gesture grading based on openpose," in Proc. 10th International Congress on Image and Signal Processing, BioMedical Engineering and Informatics (CISP-BMEI), Oct. 2017, pp. 1–6.

[12] A. Ahmadi, E. Mitchell, F. Destelle, M. Gowing, N. O'Connor, C. Richter, and K. Moran, "Automatic activity classification and movement assessment during a sports training session using wearable inertial sensors," in Proc. 11th International Conf. on Wearable and Implantable Body Sensor Networks, June 2014, pp. 98–103.

[13] M. Sharma, R. Srivastava, A. Anand, D. Prakash, and L. Kaligounder, "Wearable motion sensor based phasic analysis of tennis serve for performance feedback," in Proc. IEEE International Conf. on Acoustics, Speech and Signal Processing (ICASSP), March 2017, pp. 5945–5949.

[14] H. Ghasemzadeh and R. Jafari, "Coordination analysis of human movements with body sensor networks: A signal processing model to evaluate baseball swings," IEEE Sensors Journal, vol. 11, no. 3, March 2011, pp. 603–610.

[15] D. Y. Kwon and M. Gross, "Combining body sensors and visual sensors for motion training," in Proc. of ACM SIGCHI International Conf. on Advances in Computer Entertainment Technology (ACE), 2005, pp. 94–101.

[16] H. Nakata, A. Miura, M. Yoshie, and K. Kudo, "Electromyographic activity of lower limbs to stop baseball batting," Journal of strength and conditioning research, vol. 26, no. 6, 2012, pp. 1461–1468.

[17] R. Gray, "A model of motor inhibition for a complex skill: Baseball batting," Journal of experimental psychology: Applied, vol. 15, no. 2, 2009, pp. 91–105.

[18] E. S. Chang, M. E. Bishop, D. K. Baker, and R. V. West, "Interval throwing and hitting programs in baseball: Biomechanics and rehabilitation," American journal of orthopedics, vol. 45, no. 3, 2016, pp. 157–162.

[19] Z. Cao, T. Simon, S.-E. Wei, and Y. Sheikh, "Realtime multi-person 2d pose estimation using part affinity fields," in Proc. IEEE Conf. on Computer Vision and Pattern Recognition (CVPR), 2017, pp. 1302–1310.

[20] T. Simon, H. Joo, I. Matthews, and Y. Sheikh, "Hand keypoint detection in single images using multiview bootstrapping," in Proc. IEEE Conf. on Computer Vision and Pattern Recognition (CVPR), 2017, pp. 4645–4653.

[21] S.-E. Wei, V. Ramakrishna, T. Kanade, and Y. Sheikh, "Convolutional pose machines," in Proc. IEEE Conf. on Computer Vision and Pattern Recognition (CVPR), 2016, pp. 4724–4732.

[22] D. Yang, J. Tang, Y. Huang, C. Xu, J. Li, L. Hu, J. Zhang, G. Shen, M. Liang, and H. Liu, "Tennismaster: An imu-based online serve performance evaluation system," in Proc. of 8th ACM International Conf. on Augmented Human (AH), 2017, pp. 1–8.

[23] L. R. Rabiner, "A tutorial on hidden markov models and selected applications in speech recognition," Proceedings of the IEEE, vol. 77, no. 2, Feb. 1989, pp. 257–286.

[24] L. R. Rabiner and B. H. Juang, "An introduction to hidden markov models," IEEE ASSP Magazine, vol. 3, 1986, pp. 4–16.

[25] K. Liu, C. Chen, R. Jafari, and N. Kehtarnavaz, "Fusion of inertial and depth sensor data for robust hand gesture recognition," IEEE Sensors Journal, vol. 14, no. 6, June 2014, pp. 1898–1903.

[26] A. Saggese, N. Strisciuglio, M. Vento, and N. Petkov, "Action recognition by learning pose representations," in Workshop of Recognition and Action for Scene Understanding (CAIP Conf. 2017), 2017.

Octopus Algorithm as a New Support in Solving TSP

Marek Sosnicki, Iwona Pozniak-Koszalka, Leszek Koszalka, Andrzej Kasprzak
Dept. of Systems and Computer Networks
Wroclaw University of Science and Technology
Wroclaw, Poland
e-mail: {marek.sosnicki, iwona.pozniak-koszalka, leszek.koszalka, andrzej.kasprzak}@pwr.edu.pl

***Abstract*—In this paper, a designed and implemented algorithm, named Octopus is applied for solving the Travelling Salesman Problem (TSP). In general, the Octopus algorithm can be used as both a method of finding good solutions of the optimization problem and a way to get starting points for other meta-heuristic algorithms used in problem solving, for instance Tabu Search (TS). Octopus takes into account multiple solutions gathered by the meta-heuristic algorithms and combines them to obtain new ones. The results of simulation experiments show that Octopus may be considered as very promising.**

Keywords-algorithm; TSP; Tabu Search; experimentation system; simulation.

I. INTRODUCTION

TSP is one of the most popular optimization problems. The problem consists in finding a path between points (e.g., cities on the map) with known location. The path (route) has to allow for visiting all points as fast as possible or using the shortest possible route. In practice, when the best route between dozens or hundreds of points should be found then one can realize that it is a real NP-hard problem (nondeterministic polynomial) [1].

Many authors have tried to solve this problem using different approaches, e.g., Branch and Bound [2], but such methods can provide solution in reasonable time only to small instances of the problem, namely, a few locations, only. Another way to find the solution is using heuristic algorithms. These algorithms can provide solutions, which are close to optimal ones but the process of finding them is much quicker than for exact methods. There are many types of heuristics which can be used. It is worth to mention such algorithms as Parallel Evolutionary [3], Artificial Bee Colony (ABC) [4], Ant Colony Optimization (ACO) [5][6], Tabu Search (TS) [7]-[9].

We are interested in algorithms which have some starting solutions and then they try to construct improved solutions by slightly changing them and checking, i.e. optimizing them. Such a process is then repeated multiple times until getting the best or satisfying solution. Local search algorithms are great in finding good solutions in very short time, but they have one disadvantage. They tend to get stuck in local minimum. It usually happens when we cannot find any way to change our current solution so that it gets better in next iterations.

The Octopus algorithm proposed in this paper deals with the problem of getting stuck in local minimum areas with local search algorithms. The proposed approach allows combining multiple different algorithms, anticipating that they can give better results when used together while working in parallel environments [10]. The algorithm requires activities on three stages: (*i*) taking many good solutions from local search algorithms (starting from different random solutions); (*ii*) combining these solutions and generating new starting points, which keep some information about good solutions; (*iii*) running algorithms again from the new starting points.

The rest of the paper is organized as follows. In Section II, the mathematical model of the considered TSP problem is formulated, and we provide the justification why TSP was chosen for investigation concerning the proposed Octopus algorithm. In Section III, the implementation of Tabu Search which was taken as meta-heuristic algorithm for testing a new algorithm is briefly described, as well as the core of the paper – the Octopus algorithm is presented in detail. The presentation of research has been contained in Section IV. Investigation concentrates on properties of the proposed algorithm, and its advantages in comparison with known algorithms to solving the considered TSP problem. The conclusion and plans for the future work to improving Octopus algorithm appear in the last Section V.

II. PROBLEM FORMULATION

The considered TSP problem can be formulated as follows.

Given:

- A graph G = (V; E), where V = {1, 2, …, n} is a vertex set of points and E = {{i, j}: $i \neq j$, i, j ϵ V} is an edges set (e.g., paths between cities).
- A nonnegative cost (distance) matrix $C = [c_{i,\ j}]$ defined on E.

To find

- A route $\pi = (\pi(1), \pi(2),\ldots,\pi(n)) \ \epsilon \ \Pi$, which is represented as permutation of vertices [3] that passes through each point exactly once, and returns to the starting point on a G.

Such that

- The optimal solution (π*) minimizes the cost (fitness) of the route defined as the arithmetic sum of all paths between points, which belong to π.

In this paper, only the symmetric version of TSP is considered as it is a more common usage, but the proposed algorithm can also work for the asymmetric version.

There are three main reasons why the above problem was selected for testing the performance of Octopus algorithm.

- Every permutation of nodes in this problem is a feasible solution. That allows us to mix solutions easier. In many optimization problems it is hard to even find a random permutation, as most of possible permutations are not feasible.
- The local search algorithms work very well and fast in this problem. It is due to the fact that it is easy to find a value of a fitness function for neighbor solutions.
- There are many local search metaheuristic algorithms invented for solving TSP, so the new algorithm may become helpful to combine them.

The proposed algorithm should also work for any other problem, which fulfills the first reason.

III. OCTOPUS ALGORITHM

In the first subsection, the collaborating algorithm Tabu Search (TS) is briefly presented. The next subsections describe three stages of the performance of the Octopus algorithm.

A. *Tabu Search for Testing*

For testing the Octopus algorithm, the implemented version of TS algorithm was taken. The pseudocode for TS [11] is presented in Figure 1.

```
⌂ produce an initial solution π;
π* ← π;
initiate tabu list T;
while termination criterion is not satisfied do
        get all neighbors N(s) according to π and T;
        find the best solution π^b in N(s);
        π* ← π^b;
        update T;
          if fit(π) ≤ fit(π*) then
          π* ← π;
          end if
end while
return π*
```

Figure 1. Pseudocode of the implemented Tabu Search.

The neighborhood is generated as all possible swaps of two elements of permutation. The tabu list is saving two indices of permutation, which were swapped in the previous iteration. Tabu list size is fixed, e.g., could be set to 100. The termination criterion is taken as the number of iterations, which is a parameter of the algorithm. The initial solution is treated as another TS parameter.

B. *The First Stage – Local Search*

The first stage of the algorithm is gathering solutions. The exemplary metaheuristic TS algorithm is running N times starting from random permutations, with the same number of iterations in each run. Several performances of TS could run in separate threads as they do not need to exchange information between each other. To obtain satisfying results, the minimum of N is fixed as N=50, thus different solutions must be collected. It can be noticed that the obtained permutations are similar to each other in a way the distances to each other [12], are smaller than distances to permutations chosen at random.

C. *The Second Stage – Combining Solutions*

After Octopus gathered permutations $P=\{\pi_1, \pi_2,\ldots, \pi_N\}$, by performing in the previous stage, it makes changes in the introduced matrix called Order Matrix (OM). The matrix OM is created taking into account all permutations. An element of OM denoted as $a_{i,j}$ is equal to 1 if $\pi^{-1}(i) < \pi^{-1}(j)$, and is equal to 0, otherwise. Then, all matrices are combined together by summing them and creating the matrix S expressed by (1).

$$S = A_1 + A_2 + \ldots + A_N \quad (1)$$

D. *The Third Stage – New Starting Points*

To get the new start points, the procedure shown in Figure 2 is proposed.

```
⌂ produce an initial permutation
π ← {1};
while π ≠ n d
        ⌂ Repeated until permutation has all elements
        i* ← 0;
        v* ← -∞;
        for all i ∈ {2, 3,..., n} do
          if i ∈ π then
          continue;
          end if
          for all Possible insert positions p do
                  ⌂ p = 0 is inserted between all elements,
                        ⌂ p = 1 is after first, etc.
              Calculate v = V (π, i, p);
              if v > v* then
                  v* ← v;
                  p* ← p;
                  i* ← i;
              end if
          end for
        end for
        insert i* into π at p* position;
end while
return π
```

Figure 2. Pseudocode of the implemented Tabu Search.

The introduced formula to calculate the inserted value is expressed by (2).

$$V(\pi, i, p) = \Sigma\eta_{p,k}\ (S_{i,\eta(k)} - S_{\eta(k),i}) \quad (2)$$

where:

- The summation in (2) goes from $k=0$ to the absolute value of p;
- The coefficient $\eta_{p,k}$ introduced in (2) is equal to -1 if $p < k$ or is equal to +1, otherwise.

This formula is proposed to select such inserts which are most common among the permutations calculated in the first stage. That means, e. g., if node 6 is always after 5 in the obtained solutions, then putting 6 after 5 in permutation would have very high insert value.

After such new solution π is obtained, the OM of this solution is subtracted from S and the procedure is repeated to find the next solution (based on the new matrix S).

Unfortunately, the proposed approach allows us to obtain about M=0.2$\cdot$N reasonable solutions. When we try to generate more permutations than M, the produced permutations become more and more random, and do not have the desirable features that can be observed in the first permutations. After we obtain M new permutations, we run our local search algorithms on them to obtain new, better solutions. We can repeat these stages all over, but we must remember that the number of processed permutations may decrease by 80% with each third stage of Octopus.

IV. RESEARCH

The main goal of the research was to check whether the Octopus algorithm can give good solutions to the considered TSP, and to observe if the features of good solutions are remembered in the new permutations when using the proposed approach.

The simulation experiments have been made taking into account five instances from TSPLib., namely kroA100, kroB100, kroC100, kroA200, kroB200 [13]. The first three instances concern TSP with 100 nodes (points), and the next two instances concern TSP with 200 nodes (points).

A. *Testing TS*

Firstly, Tabu Search algorithm was tested for random permutations generated as start points, to show that the implementation can give promising results. TS was run with different number of iterations.

The results obtained for kro100A test instance are presented in Figure 3. It may be observed that the implemented TS algorithm produced good solutions for not a big number of iterations and that the first 200 iterations were crucial.

Table 1 shows the results obtained by TS with 1000 iterations in comparison to the best known solutions for the considered instances. Also, it can be seen that the solutions found by TS are worse only approximately 10 % in average than the best solutions listed in TSPLib. This can justify the fact that the algorithm works properly and can give satisfactory results.

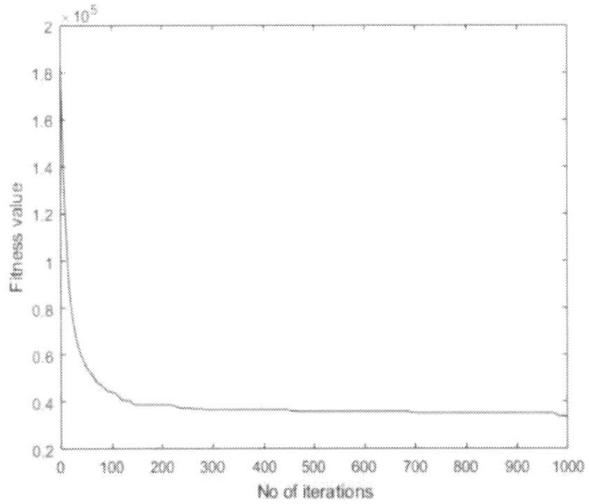

Figure 3. TS algorithm for kroA100 instance.

TABLE I. COST FUNCTION FOR SOLUTIONS OF TSP

Test instance	TS result	Best known
kroA100	23405	21282
kroB100	24240	22141
kroC100	22733	29749
kroA200	35456	29368
kroB200	35311	29437

B. *Testing Octopus*

Next, we checked if the new start points obtained when Octopus is utilized can ensure better solutions than these obtained when random start points are taken into account. A single simulation experiment consisted of six steps. Each experiment was conducted using following the procedure:

***Step* 1**. The number of 100 permutations was chosen at random.

***Step* 2.** TS was applied for each of them for 5000 iterations (in case of problems with 200 nodes) or 1000 iterations (in case of problems with 100 nodes).

***Step* 3**. Octopus algorithm was run the first time on the obtained solutions by TS and 20 new start points were created.

***Step* 4.** TS was run again using these 20 solutions (start points) for the same number of iterations.

***Step* 5**. The second run of Octopus algorithm was performed and finally four solutions were taken.

***Step* 6**. TS algorithm was performed once more using these four solutions.

In Figure 4, the exemplary results of solving TSP for instance kroB200 with two runs of Octopus are shown.

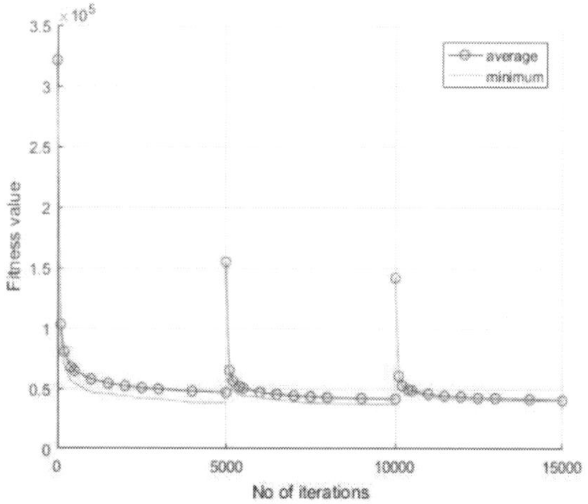

Figure 4. Octopus – runs with 5000 iterations for kroB200.

In Figure 5, the results for the same case are presented but with the first 100 iterations of TS removed in order to increase readability.

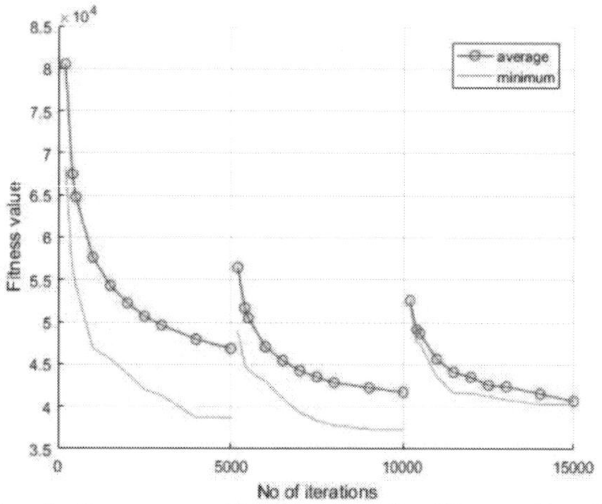

Figure 5. Octopus – runs with 5000 iterations (first 100 removed in each run) for kroB200.

C. *Testing TS with Octopus*

The aim of this complex experiment was the comparison of results obtained in solving TSP for the considered instances with a sequence of 3 runs:

Run 0: Using the standard version of TS with start points generated randomly.

Run I. Using TS with the first run of Octopus (with new start points).

Run II. Using TS with the second run of Octopus (with additional start points).

Table II presents the results obtained for five instances. In columns show the average values of the fitness function (denoted as Avg) for the start points in successive runs.

TABLE II. AVERAGED FITNESS VALUES OF START POINTS

Test instance	Avg (0)	Avg (I)	Avg (II)
kroA100	170657	101347	86391
kroB100	170696	89900	78432
kroC100	169766	104592	89334
kroA200	340429	205334	178054
kroB200	334684	198752	171779

We can see that the first run of Octopus gave much better start points than random ones for all considered instances. We define Profit as the percentage decrease in the fitness function, as expressed by (3).

$$\text{Profit}\ (x+1) = \{[\text{Avg}\ (x) - \text{Avg}\ (x+1)]\ /\ \text{Avg}\ (x)\} * 100\ \%. \quad (3)$$

where x = 0, 1. In Table III, the values of the obtained Profit are specified. The Profit from the first run of Octopus was of more than 40 % and may be considered relatively large. It indicates that Octopus can be used to find new starting points based on some already known solutions. The second run of Octopus was not so effective, giving a modest increase in quality of 13.7 %, which is almost three times less than the first run of Octopus.

TABLE III. PROFIT GIVEN BY OCTOPUS

Test instance	Profit (I)	Profit (II)
kroA100	40.6 %	14.8 %
kroB100	47.1 %	12.8 %
kroC100	38.2 %	14.4 %
kroA200	39.7 %	13.1 %
kroB200	40.7 %	13.6 %
mean	41.3 %	13.7 %

Table IV presents the results obtained for all instances after Run (0) and Run (I) with Octopus. The notation Min (x) represents the best solution of TSP.

TABLE IV. SOLUTIONS MADE WITH OCTOPUS RUNS

Test Instance	Min (0)	Avg (0)	Min (I)	Avg (I)
kroA100	25690	31177	24538	28517
kroB100	26617	31780	26090	28724
kroC100	26829	30659	25472	30378
kroA200	38882	44300	37508	42185
kroB200	38499	43888	38232	41199

The analysis of the results presented in Table IV confirms that using Octopus can improve the process of finding the solution to TSP with the implemented TS.

V. CONCLUSION AND FUTURE WORK

Based on the results of experiments, we can say that the proposed Octopus algorithm seems to be promising. The basic idea of this algorithm is to combine solutions in order to create new ones, by keeping the good features of the old ones. The new start points that are created by Octopus possess some features of the old permutations. Using Octopus gives a chance to avoid being stuck in local minimum areas.

However, the proposed approach is not perfect. The drawback is that, with each step of the algorithm, we reduce the number of processed solutions by 80%. Moreover, we are starting from random points, and we cannot be sure if after using Octopus algorithm we would not try to check some permutations multiple times, which would be a waste of processing power.

In our further work, we plan:

- To apply Octopus algorithm for solving optimization problems other than TSP.
- To use Octopus in collaboration with other local search algorithms.
- To improve getting more reasonable start points from a single run.
- To consider possibility of implementing Octopus on GPU (Graphics Processing Unit) threads, as well as using MPI (Message Passing Library).
- To implement an experimentation system along with the rules described in [14].

ACKNOWLEDGMENT

This work was supported by the statutory funds of the Department of Systems and Computer Networks under grant no. 0401/0132/18, Faculty of Electronics, Wroclaw University of Science and Technology, Wroclaw, Poland.

REFERENCES

[1] K. Ilavarasi and J. K. Suresh, " Variants of Traveling Salesman Problem: A Survey," Proc. of International Conference on Information, Communication and Embedded Systems (ICICES), February 2014, pp. 1-7, IEEE, doi:10.1109/ICICES 2014.70338550.

[2] R. Grymin and S. Jagiello, "Fast Branch and Bound Algorithm for the Traveling Salesman Problem," Proc. of IFIP conference on Computer Information Systems and Industrial Management, 2016, pp. 206-217.

[3] W. Bozejko and M. Wodecki, "Parallel Evolutionary Algorithm for the Traveling Salesman Problem", Journal of Numerical Analysis, Industrial and Applied Mathematics, 2 (3-4), 2007, pp. 129-137.

[4] N. Pathak and S. P. Tiwasi, "Traveling Salesman Problem Using Bee Colony with SPV," International Journal of Soft Computing and Engineering (IJSCE), vol. 2, July 2012, pp. 410-414.

[5] K. Baranowski, L. Koszalka, I. Pozniak-Koszalka, and A. Kasprzak, "Ant Colony Optimization Algorithm for Solving the Provider – Modified Travelling Salesman Problem" Proc. of ACIIDS conference, April 2014, Springer, Lectures Notes in Computer Science, pp. 493-502.

[6] P. Jarecki, P. Kopec, I. Pozniak-Koszalka, L. Koszalka, and A. Kasprzak, "Comparison of Algorithms for Finding Best Route in An Area With Obstacles," Proc. of International Conference on Systems Engineering (ICSEng), Las Vegas, USA, August 2017, pp. 163-168.

[7] Y. He, Y. Qiu, G. Liu, and K. Lei, "A Parallel Adaptive Tabu Search Approach for Traveling Salesman Problem," Proc. of IEEE Internat. Conference on Natural Language Processing and Knowledge Engineering, November 2005, pp. 796-801.

[8] Y-F. Lim, P-Y. Hong, R. Raml, and R. Khalid, "An Improved Tabu Search for Solving Symmetric Traveling Salesman Problems," Proc. of IEEE Colloquium on Humanistic Science and Engineering (CHUSER), December 2011, pp. 851-854.

[9] E. Osaba and F. Daz, " Comparison of Memetic Algorithm and Tabu Search Algorithm for the Traveling Salesman Problem," Proc. of Federated Conference on Computer Science and Information Systems. (FedCSIS), September 2012, pp. 131-136.

[10] W. Yen and D. McLean, "Combining Heuristics for Optimizing A Neural Net Solution to The Traveling Salesman Problem," Proc. of International Joint Conference on Neural Networks (IJCNN), June 1990, pp. 259-264.

[11] Y-W. Zhong, C. Wu, L-S. Li, and Z. Y. Ning, "The Study of Neighborhood Structures of Tabu Search Algorithm for Traveling Salesman Problem," Proc. to 4th International Conference on Natural Computation (ICNC), October 2008, p. 491.

[12] A. B. Rathod, "A Comparative Study on Distance Measuring Approaches for Permutation Representations," Proc. of IEEE International Conference on Advances in Electronics Communication and Computer Technology (ICAECCT), December 2016, pp. 251-256.

[13] TSPLibrary [Online]. Available from: http://comopt.ifi.uni-heidelberg.de/software/TSPLIB95 [retrieved: December 2018].

[14] M. Hudziak, I. Pozniak-Koszalka, L Koszalka, and A. Kasprzak, "Multiagent Pathfinding in the Crowded Environment with Obstacles," Journal of Intelligent and Fuzzy Systems 32(2), 2017, pp. 1561-1573.